Rosie Goodwin is the four-million-copy bestselling author of more than thirty-five novels. She is the first author in the world to be allowed to follow three of Catherine Cookson's trilogies with her own sequels. Having worked in the social services sector for many years, then fostered a number of children, she is now a full-time novelist. She is one of the top 50 most borrowed authors from UK libraries. Rosie lives in Nuneaton, the setting for many of her books, with her husband and their beloved dogs.

Rosie
GOODWIN
A Season
for Hope

ZAFFRE

First published in the UK in 2022
This paperback edition first published in 2023 by
ZAFFRE
An imprint of Bonnier Books UK
4th Floor, Victoria House, Bloomsbury Square, London, England, WC1B 4DA
Owned by Bonnier Books
Sveavägen 56, Stockholm, Sweden

This is a work of fiction. Names, places, events and
incidents are either the products of the author's
imagination or used fictitiously. Any resemblance to
actual persons, living or dead, or actual
events is purely coincidental.

A CIP catalogue record for this book is
available from the British Library.

ISBN: 978–1–83877–360–1

Also available as an ebook and an audiobook

1 3 5 7 9 10 8 6 4 2

Typeset by IDSUK (Data Connection) Ltd
Printed and bound in Great Britain by Clays Ltd, Elcograf S.p.A.

Zaffre is an imprint of Bonnier Books UK
www.bonnierbooks.co.uk

This book is for all the lovely readers who have supported me since publication. You are all very special, thank you xxx

Chapter One

The laundry room was suddenly plunged into gloom as a figure blocked the doorway. The young woman pounding the washing in the deep tub with a wooden dolly stick stilled and glanced hopefully towards it. Her stomach swooped with nerves and happiness at the sight of the master standing there, looking resplendent in his riding gear, his fair hair tousled from the ride.

He quickly glanced over his shoulder to make sure they couldn't be overheard before telling her softly, 'The large barn, ten o'clock tonight.' Then he turned on his smart leather heel and was gone, leaving the girl leaning heavily against the wooden tub, her heart pounding. She normally never minded being summoned – in fact she looked forward to it – but tonight would be different.

Barnaby Greenwood was her master and as well as employing her as a laundry maid at his enormous house, he also employed her father and brothers. He was one of the richest and most powerful men in Whitby. He owned a large fleet of fishing trawlers and a shipyard, as well as most of the dwellings that the fishermen lived in. Her father and two of her brothers worked on one of the trawlers, while her other two brothers were employed at his shipyard. And tonight

1

she had something to tell him and she had no idea how he would react to it. With a shuddering sigh, she bent to the task at hand and got on with her work.

The day passed interminably slowly but at last, at seven o'clock, she put the next day's washing in to soak, and after drying her rough hands on her pinafore, wearily made her way to the kitchen for her supper.

The noise of the staff chattering and the warmth from the range met her when she entered the room. Seeing her, the cook nodded towards the table saying, 'About time too. I were about to send a search party out for you. Sit yourself down and get something on your plate afore it's all gone.'

Jimmy, the young groom, immediately shuffled along to make room next to him on the long oak bench that stretched down one side of the table, and not wanting to hurt his feelings, the girl sat down beside him, causing a few giggles from the female staff and some chuckles from the males. Jimmy made no secret of the fact that he was sweet on Amber, although she had never given him any encouragement.

'Here you go, Amber.' Without being asked, Jimmy began to load a generous portion of meat and potato pie onto her plate along with a selection of vegetables and she managed a wavering smile. Usually she was ravenously hungry by the time she finished work but tonight the food seemed to stick in her throat and she had to keep taking sips of water to wash it down.

The higher-up servants – the mistress's lady's maid, the butler, the parlourmaids and the housekeeper – had eaten their meal some time ago after the family had been served

2

theirs. Now the lowly staff were the last to eat and whereas Amber usually enjoyed their banter, tonight she just longed for the privacy of the little room she shared with her good friend Nancy, the scullery maid, up in the attic in the servants' quarters.

There was a large bread and butter pudding and a jug of creamy yellow custard to follow the main meal but Amber excused herself when it was served and without giving anyone time to ask any questions, she scuttled away up the steep wooden staircase, leaving Jimmy with a disappointed frown on his face.

'I wonder what's wrong with her?' the cook said thoughtfully when Amber had gone. 'It ain't like her to let good food go to waste.' She looked pointedly at Nancy but the girl merely shrugged and turned her attention to the food in front of her.

It was part of Nancy's job to help the kitchen maid tackle the enormous pile of dirty dishes after each meal, and it was going on for nine o'clock that evening before they were all washed and dried and put away in their rightful places. Only then did Nancy manage to get away to join Amber upstairs.

When Nancy entered their room, Amber was brushing her hair. Although she couldn't be termed as classically beautiful – she was rather tall for a girl and although she was seventeen, her figure was boyish – but her deep tawny-coloured eyes and her glorious mass of rich strawberry-blonde curls more than made up for that. It hung down her back like a glorious silk cloak and reminded Nancy of the setting sun. Nancy's hair was, as her mother termed it, as straight as pump water and a mousy colour, and she was slim to the point of being skinny. Her eyes were a dull grey and although she had always envied Amber her looks, it didn't stop her caring for her.

'So you've had the royal summons again, 'ave yer?' Nancy said disapprovingly as she quickly closed the bedroom door behind her. Outside, the gardens were slowly coming back to life after a long cold winter but it was still cold up in the attics.

Amber nodded miserably.

'And are you goin' to tell 'im tonight?'

'I don't have much choice, do I?' Amber sighed. 'This ain't somethin' that I'll be able to hide for much longer.' As she spoke, she absent-mindedly stroked her still flat stomach as Nancy chewed on her lip.

'An' what do yer think he'll say?'

Amber shrugged. 'I won't know till I tell him, will I?'

Hearing the wobble in her friend's voice, angry colour flowed into Nancy's thin cheeks and she hurried across to squeeze Amber's slim shoulders.

'He's a bloody disgrace, that one is,' she said. 'Didn't I tell you from day one that nothin' good'd come o' these meetins? Why, for two pins I'd go an' tell t'mistress what he's been up to.'

Amber shook her head hurriedly. 'No, you mustn't do that, Nancy,' she told her sharply. 'For a start, the mistress would never believe you, an' don't forget, me whole family rely on the work he gives 'em. We'd all end up in t'poor house if he were to turn 'em out o' the cottage. Not that he ever would – he loves me!' she said quickly.

'Huh! So you say, but we'll see now, won't we? An' what are you goin' to do if he don't stand by you? What'll your da say when you turn up back at home wi' your belly full?'

Amber blinked back tears. She had wondered the same thing herself. In fact, she'd thought of nothing else for days. But then she was sure it wouldn't come to that. Barnaby would stand by her, he had to. He'd told her often enough that he loved her, hadn't he? And this might be just the push he needed to make him leave his wife, as he'd promised he would when the time was right. But what if he doesn't? a niggly little voice in the back of her mind asked. Her da was a kind, gentle man and he loved his family but were he ever to discover who had fathered this baby she dreaded to think what he might do to the master if he didn't stand by her.

'I shan't tell him who it were,' she told Nancy and the girl looked horrified.

'But you'll *have* to!'

'I've told you, everything is gonna be all right.'

Amber glanced at the little tin clock on the small table by the window. 'Anyway, I'd best be off now an' ger it over wi'.' And with that she left the room as Nancy stared worriedly after her.

Once downstairs, Amber took the door that led into the yard rather than the one to the kitchen, pausing to look around to ensure no one was about. It was as quiet as the grave, so lifting her drab grey skirt she took a deep breath and picked her way across the cobbles to the barn. It had been early in November when her affair with the master had begun. It had started with smiles and the odd word and then, late one evening when Amber had gone out into the yard to get some air, she had met him coming out of the stables. They had just talked on that first evening and she found that she felt at ease with him. He was an incredibly handsome man and Amber had been flattered when he showed an interest in her and confided that he wasn't happy in his marriage. The staff were aware that he and his wife Louisa had separate rooms, and Amber had felt sorry for him. From then on, they had started to meet and eventually she had given herself to him up in the hayloft as he whispered words of endearment in her ear.

'One day when the time is right, I shall tell Louisa that I love you,' he had promised. 'And then we'll be together for always.'

And she had believed every word he said. She could still remember the first time she had given herself to him as if it was yesterday. She had no regrets because she loved him with all her heart but now she wondered how he would take the news that he was about to become a father. Hopefully, this would be the spur he needed for them to be together. And so, taking a deep breath, she lifted her chin and moved on; there could be no more delaying.

After entering the barn, she stood for some minutes allowing her eyes to adjust to the gloom, then jumped back in alarm as a large tabby cat in pursuit of a rat almost as big as itself narrowly avoided racing across her foot. Her heart had been beating wildly before but now it was racing so much that she was worried it would leap out of her chest. And it was then that she heard the creak of the enormous barn door behind her and spinning about she saw the master striding towards her.

'Hello, Amber,' he said with a worried frown, holding his arms out towards her. 'Come here, there's something I need to speak to you about.' Barnaby wasn't looking forward to this conversation because he knew it was going to hurt her.

'An' I need to tell you sommat an' all,' Amber said nervously as she licked her dry lips. 'The thing is . . . I think I'm in the family way . . .'

He looked shocked. 'And you're telling me that the child is mine? Is that it?'

Hurt showed in her eyes before she nodded and said quietly, 'Of course it is. I ain't never laid wi' no one else, you know that.'

She was disappointed at his reaction but then she supposed she should have known that it would come as a terrible shock.

He moaned deep in his throat and began to pace up and down, kicking up the loose straw that lay about the floor, causing a storm of dust to rise into the air.

Hurrying to him she took his large hands in her rough, calloused ones. 'Look, this won't be so bad,' she told him urgently. 'You allus said we'd be together one day. Happen this can just make things come about sooner than we'd thought.'

Something about his stiff stance disturbed her and she felt the first stirrings of panic. Surely he wouldn't turn his back on her when they meant so much to each other, especially now he knew that she was carrying his child?

Barnaby, meanwhile, was shaking his head as he struggled to come to terms with what she had told him. He turned away, running his hand distractedly through his thick thatch of hair, and when he turned back to her the look on his face made her heart skip a beat.

'I-I know what I promised,' he said. 'But the thing is . . . something has happened and I can't leave Louisa.'

Amber recoiled as if she had been slapped in the face. 'What do you mean? Of course you can, we're going to have a baby . . .'

He shook his head regretfully and she watched him fumble in the pocket of his smart trousers before handing her a shining gold sovereign. It seemed to burn into her skin as she stared down at it.

'I'm so sorry, Amber,' he told her in a choked voice. 'But I think it might be better if you got rid of it. There's a woman on the outskirts of the town, I believe, who helps women in your position.'

In that moment all her hopes and dreams turned to ashes and tears sprang to her eyes. She knew immediately who he was speaking of: Lil Bentley was an old lady who the townsfolk said was a witch. She had helped many young women out of the plight Amber found herself in but some of them had ended up in an early grave because of it, and Amber knew that she would never do as he asked, although she wasn't quite brave enough to tell him so.

'So you never meant *any* of what you said?' she whispered dully as she felt her heart break. 'You just used me!'

'No, no, I *do* care about you, *really* I do but . . .' He spread his hands. How could he make her understand what he had to lose?

She backed away from him as if she was suddenly seeing him for the first time.

'Perhaps when you've got rid of the baby you could come back,' he suggested. The thought of never seeing her again was painful. But she shook her head. How could she ever trust him or believe a word he said ever again?

'I'll tell Mrs Boswell that I have given you a few days off because your mother is ill or something,' he said desperately.

'Yes, *sir*.' Amber bobbed her knee and walked away leaving Barnaby Greenwood to stare after her, his shoulders sagging as shame swept through him. He knew what he was doing to Amber was wrong but he was so confused and miserable that he had convinced himself it was right – or at least he had tried to.

It was ironic, he thought, that all he and his wife Louisa had ever wanted was a child of their own and now that he had the chance to be a father he had ordered the girl to get rid of it!

Amber knew that Mrs Boswell, the housekeeper, wouldn't be at all pleased when she told her that the master had given her permission to be away from her post, but that was the least of Amber's troubles for now. First, she would have to face her mother and she quaked at the thought.

'So how did he take the news?' Nancy was sitting up in her bed when Amber crept back into their room. In response, Amber opened her palm to reveal the gold sovereign lying there.

'Lordy . . . has he give you the sack?' Nancy asked.

Amber shook her head. 'No . . . he gave me this an' told me to get rid o' the bairn,' she answered in a wobbly voice.

Nancy gasped as her hand flew to her mouth. 'But you ain't goin' to go along that road, surely?' she said fearfully. 'There's so many things can go wrong.'

'I know.' Amber sank onto the end of her bed dejectedly. 'He says I can come back once I've got rid of it but I don't think I can; I ain't brave enough.'

'The lousy bastard! Didn't I allus tell you this would end in tears?' Nancy ranted. 'What'll you do now?'

Amber shrugged. 'I ain't give it much thought yet but I'll leave first thing in t'mornin' an' go and see me mam, though Lord knows what she'll say when I tell 'er. I won't dare let on to me dad who the bairn's father is, cos if he finds out he'll be so angry I don't know what he'd be capable of.'

Nancy gave a deep sigh as she reached out to stroke Amber's arm sympathetically. 'Well, all I can say is, rather you than me, lass!'

Chapter Two

The day looked set to be bright and clear when Amber left early the next morning, although there was still a distinct chill in the air. Tugging her shawl tightly about her shoulders and clutching her small bundle of belongings, she set off for Whitby.

Greenacres, the Greenwoods' home where Amber worked, was about two miles out of town, perched high on the headland with a view of the sea to one side and the beautiful rolling Yorkshire moors on the other. Amber had loved working there, but now she wondered if she would ever return. In the distance she could see the ruins of Whitby Abbey overlooking the town, and her footsteps slowed as she began to tremble with fear. Hopefully her father would be out at sea fishing when she reached her home so she would be able to have a private talk with her mother. But that would only delay the inevitable. Her father would have to be told eventually and she quaked as she wondered how he would react.

She moved on and soon she could see the fishing trawlers bobbing in the harbour, which as usual was crawling with fishermen who looked like little ants from this distance as they scurried about either preparing to set sail or unloading the fish they had caught into the warehouse lining the quay. Many of the townswomen would be there, ready to start gutting the fish and packing them into salted barrels for transporting, but Amber knew her mother wouldn't be amongst them. For the last few years she had suffered from ill health, which had restricted what she could do, so now when she wasn't cleaning the little house they all lived in, or cooking, she spent her time repairing fishing nets or knitting the thick woollen ganseys her brothers and father wore when they were at sea. Any spare ones were sold and the little money this brought in made Alice Ainsley feel that she was still contributing to the family's income. However, Amber and her family were better off than most of the folk there abouts. Unlike some, they had never known what it was to be hungry even if at times their diet had consisted mainly of fish, and now that Amber and her brothers were working there was really no need for their mother to, although they all understood her need to feel useful.

Amber had been so busy thinking about what she might say to her mother that it was almost a shock when she reached the brow of the hill that led down to her home in Argument's Yard. The majority of the community lived in such yards, each of them sloping steeply down to the sea. Each yard consisted of flights of steps with small two-up, two-down houses that were crammed together so tightly on either side that the sunshine rarely reached the steps between them. The houses were far from salubrious but to Amber, who had never known any other, it was home and usually when she reached this point on her day off, she would be smiling. But not today. Beyond the boats anchored in the harbour the weak morning sunshine was reflecting off the sea making the crests of the white waves look as if they had been scattered with crushed diamonds, but she could see no joy in anything as she plodded on, a feeling of dread settling about her like a heavy cloak.

'Mornin', Amber, lass,' a neighbour who was outside on the steps beating a carpet shouted when Amber turned into her yard, and although her heart was heavy Amber forced a smile.

'Mornin', Mrs Preston. Me mam in, is she?'

'Oh arr, she's in all reet, lass, I saw her not half an hour since.'

Much as Amber liked the woman, she was painfully aware that Mrs Preston was the worst gossip in the yard and now she had no doubt word would spread like wild-fire that she was home in working hours. Still, there was nothing she could do about it so she moved on and when she reached the door of her home, she took a deep breath and entered.

It was dark in the kitchen-cum-sitting room and her mother was at the scrubbed pine table rolling pastry for a fish pie. She was like an older version of Amber with the same orange-brown eyes and strawberry-blonde hair and she smiled with pleasure as she caught sight of her daughter. It was rare that she got to see her since she'd gone into service, apart from on a Sunday.

'Why lass, whatever are you doin' here?' Alice Ainsley quickly clapped the flour from her hands before rubbing them down the coarse huckaback apron that enveloped her from the waist down. 'Shouldn't you be at work?'

'Aye, I should, Mam . . . but the thing is . . . I have somethin' to tell you.' Amber shuffled from foot to foot as shame coloured her cheeks.

Her mother advanced on her and gave her an affection-ate squeeze before holding her at arm's length and saying tightly, 'Then you'd best spit it out. But first I'll put t'kettle on. There ain't nowt seems so bad when you've a good strong brew to hand.'

Amber flopped down onto one of the hard-backed chairs pushed against the kitchen table as she watched her mother fill the kettle from the bucket of water she had standing on the long wooden draining board. Once that was done Alice hung the kettle on the hook that was suspended above the fireplace and swung it into the fire to boil and only then did she join her daughter at the table to ask, 'Well?'

Amber hung her head as tears slid down her cheeks. 'The thing is, Mam . . .' she began hesitantly but the words seemed to be sticking in her throat. 'Th-the thing is . . . I'm goin' to have a bairn!'

'Oh, dear Lord!' The colour drained from her mother's cheeks like water from a dam as her hand rose to her mouth and different emotions flitted across her face. There was shock and denial but most of all disappointment, for she would never have believed in a million years that her girl would be loose with her favours before she had a ring on her finger. There was more than one lad had already tried to put one there to be fair, and one in particular, but Amber had never shown a vestige of interest in any of them. She'd always insisted that she was too young to be wed, unlike some of her schoolfriends who already had a bairn or two clinging to their skirts. And so for her mother to discover this news now was even more shocking.

'And are you goin' to tell me who the daddy is?' Alice asked, her face as straight as a poker. 'Cos as sure as eggs is eggs your daddy is goin' to want to know.'

'It would be better if I didn't tell you,' Amber muttered and raising her head she saw her mother frown.

'Well, I wouldn't mind bettin' it was Bertie Preston, although I never thought you were that keen on him. Or is it that Jimmy that's sweet on you from up at the house?'

'It . . . it isn't either of them.' Amber's shoulders were hunched and she looked so miserable that her mother couldn't help but feel sorry for her even if she did want to clout her round the ear.

'But who else could it be?' Her mother knew that the only day off Amber had was on a Sunday and she spent much of that at home with her family. She tutted and stared off into space for a moment before saying, 'So if it ain't them, is the father in a position to marry you?'

When Amber shook her head and began to cry, she sighed. 'Then there's only one thing for it. Bertie is as keen as mustard so even if the bairn ain't his you'll have to let him court you an' think it is. How many courses have you missed?'

'I've missed two, an' even if I wanted to marry Bertie, which I don't, what would I tell him when the baby appears two or three months ahead of its time?' Amber retorted bitterly. 'He ain't soft in the head you know, Mam.'

'Aw, lass, whatever were you thinkin' of after all the warnin's I gave you?'

'He . . . he told me he loved me.' Amber sniffed and her mother sighed.

'Aye well, you ain't the first an' you won't be the last, I dare say, but now what are we to do about it? There'll be all hell let loose if your dad finds out about it.'

Her mother got up and began to pace up and down the floor as she tried to think. Her husband was a kind man but fiercely protective of his only daughter and she dreaded to think what his reaction would be when he heard the news.

'The only other option I can think of is for you to go an' stay wi' your uncle in Scarborough till it's over,' she said.

Amber's head snapped up. '*What?* Stay with Uncle Jeremiah?' She looked horrified at the very idea of it. Her uncle was her mother's older brother by some ten years and was very set in his ways. He had never been married nor shown any inclination to be since being jilted at the altar some long time ago, according to the letters that he wrote to Alice from time to time. Soon after, heartbroken and humiliated, he had started to sell buckets and bowls from a handcart in the market and he had worked hard to make something of himself. Now he had his own thriving hardware shop in the town and lived a stone's throw away from it in a grand house overlooking the sea with his housekeeper and a little maid who kept it running like clockwork, and although he had never been unkind to her, Amber knew that she wouldn't be happy there. It had been some years since she had visited with her mother and even though his house made their small cottage look like a hovel, she had no wish to have to stay there.

'That would never work,' Amber said sharply. 'And Uncle Jeremiah wouldn't want me there once he knew that I was going to have a child.'

'He would if we were to tell a few white lies.' Alice stopped her pacing and stared at her daughter with a serious expression on her face. 'We could tell him that you'd been widowed – that your husband had been a fisherman and lost at sea and you needed somewhere to stay just until the baby arrives. Then when it comes you can leave it on the steps of the poorhouse and come home. They'll take care of it. I'm presuming you don't want the bairn?'

'O' course I don't . . . but the *poorhouse*!' It seemed too cruel to do such a thing to a helpless baby, but then how could she keep it, even if she wanted to, with no job and no husband to support her?

'Think of it, if we did that you could come home and no one but your uncle would ever be any the wiser. You could start again with no blemish to your name an' it would save breakin' your dad's heart.'

'But what would we tell dad and the boys about why I'm going?' Amber fretted.

'Hm' – her mother tapped her lip thoughtfully – 'I'll think o' somethin'. So lass, there's your choice from where I'm standin'. Which is it to be?'

Amber chewed on her lip. Neither of the options were very attractive to her. As her mother had said, Bertie Preston would wed her tomorrow if she gave him half a chance; they'd grown up together in Argument's Yard and he'd chased after her since she'd been in pigtails, but could she see her herself tied to him forever? No, she couldn't.

Admittedly he was one of the handsomest chaps in the town, but he well knew it and half the lasses round about were always chasing after him – a fact he took full advantage of. Bertie was well-known for being a bit of a rogue with his fingers into all sorts of pies and he only worked on a trawler at sea with his father and brothers when he was down on his luck. The trouble was he then spent almost everything he had earned in one inn or another, drinking his wages away and Amber could just imagine the sort of life she would have with him, living hand to mouth and breeding a baby a year. *No thank you,* she thought, *that's not for me.* So that only left her with her mother's second suggestion to consider and much as she hated the thought of it, she supposed it made more sense to go with that one. It wasn't as if she wanted this baby, after all, and surely the people who ran the poorhouse would take good care of it. They might even find it a home with parents who really wanted a child. The thought made her feel slightly better and turning her teary face to her mother she told her, 'All right. I'll go to Uncle Jeremiah's, if he'll have me, that is.'

'Reet, in that case we need to get things organised.' Her mother went to her dresser and took her ink, a quill pen and a sheet of paper from a drawer, saying, 'The sooner we can get you there the better. I'm goin' to write to Jeremiah reet now then I'm goin' to the pawnshop to get you a weddin' ring. There'd be no point tellin' Jeremiah you're a widow if you've no ring on your finger. I'll tell Sid in the shop I've lost mine so he don't ask questions. An' then while I'm in town, I'll enquire when the next coach to Scarborough is leavin'. The sooner we get you away from here the better. Your dad an' two o' the lads is due home tomorrow night so it'll be best if you've gone afore then.'

Alice took a seat at the table and while she thought about what to write she fiddled with the tiny amber stone set in a silver band that sat next to her wedding ring. Her husband had bought it for her on the day their only daughter had been born and she had been so thrilled with the stone that she had decided to name her daughter after it. Once she'd decided what to say, she quickly scrawled a note to Jeremiah. This done she folded it carefully and handed it to Amber before collecting her shawl from a nail on the back of the door and telling her, 'I'll not be gone long. You can finish the pie off for me an' pop it in the oven then peel some tatties to go wi' it.'

After she'd left, Amber sighed, fingering the gold sovereign in her pocket. She would have liked to have given it to her mother to pay for the ring, but she didn't want to spend it. One day she would return it to Barnaby and then she would owe him nothing. Everything was happening so fast she hardly knew if she was on her head or her heels and all because she had been stupid enough to fall for the master's sweet talking, damn him. But, she consoled herself, she must be at least two months gone now and that only left seven to go and then she could perhaps return to some sort of normality, although she had no idea what she might do. One thing was for sure, she wouldn't be going back to work at Greenacres again. Barnaby Greenwood had broken her heart and she hoped she would never have to see him again.

An hour later her mother returned and after fumbling in her pocket, she handed Amber a paper-thin gold band, saying, 'Best I could get for the money but it'll do the job, lass. Now slip it on. And the good thing is there's a coach bound for Scarborough leavin' from the town hall tomorrow mornin' at ten. When Ted an' Will come home tonight we'll just tell 'em you're here because you've been unwell.'

'But what will you tell 'em when I don't come home of a Sunday?'

Her mother scowled and shook her head. 'One thing at a time, eh, lass? I ain't thought that far ahead yet but I'll think o' somethin', never you fear.'

Like their mother, her brothers were surprised to see her when they got home from the shipyard that night and they greeted her warmly as they washed in the hot water their mother had ready before drying themselves on a piece of huckaback.

'Sorry to hear you ain't been too well, sis,' Will said once they all sat down to dinner and their mother explained why Amber was there.

William, was twenty and the brother next to Amber in age. He was the spitting image of their mother, whilst at twenty-two, Edward, or Ted, took after their father with blue eyes and dark hair. Her two older brothers, Reuben and Amos, were twenty-three and twenty-four and were fishermen like their father.

'The gaffer called to the shipyard in a reet good mood this afternoon,' Will said through a mouthful of fish pie and Amber's ears pricked up.

'Oh, an' why would that be?' Alice asked.

'Happen he found out today that the mistress is expectin' another bairn.'

'Then let's hope it goes reet fer her this time,' she answered. 'How many has she lost now? Three durin' her term an' two born sleepin', ain't it?'

'Aye, five in all,' Will agreed as he loaded his fork. 'An' I don't reckon the master'll let her rest till she's produced a live bairn, poor woman. Everyone knows it's the grandaddy, his missus's father, who wants the gaffer to have an heir.'

Amber lowered her head, feeling as if someone had punched her in the stomach. So *that* was why Barnaby had turned his back on her – that must have been what he had been about to tell her when she had given him *her* news. Because of the legitimate heir that his wife was carrying he had decided that their baby was worthless and told her to get rid of it. Her heart broke afresh as she choked back tears and she knew in that moment that she would never trust another man for as long as she lived.

Chapter Three

'Oh Ruffy, I'm *so* bored!' From her seat by her bed-room window overlooking the rolling green lawns of Greenacres, Louisa Greenwood pouted as her maid placed a cup of hot chocolate on the small table to the side of her.

'Bored or not you're to drink this. You have the two of you to think of now,' Ruffy scolded, and yet she was smiling as she looked at this young woman who she had loved and cared for for as long as she could remember. Louisa was the only child of wealthy, indulgent parents and Ruffy had started out as her nanny when Louisa had been less than a month old some twenty-eight years ago. When she had been of an age when she no longer needed a nanny, Maude Ruffin, or Ruffy as Louisa had affectionately named her, found that she was unable to leave the girl and she had become her maid. Even Louisa's marriage to Barnaby Greenwood some ten years before had not separated them and Ruffy had followed her young mistress from her par-ent's estate in Pickering to Greenacres – the house Louisa's parents had given her as a wedding present.

Ruffy was now well past middle age: her dark hair pep-pered with grey and her figure matronly, and she no longer thought of the life she might have had if she hadn't been so devoted to her young mistress. Her own husband had died before they'd had a chance to have a family, and Louisa had become the daughter she had never been blessed with, and she was totally devoted to her.

Louisa sighed as she lifted the cup and sipped at the chocolate before grimacing. 'Ugh, you've put lots of sugar in it again, Ruffy, you would have me be as fat as a pig if I let you,' she said miserably. 'And I don't need you to remind me that I'm with child again. I feel like a breeding mare! I really can't understand Barnaby and my father's obsession with having an heir, I really can't. But then, I suppose being in this delicate condition does have *some* compensations. At least now Barnaby might leave me alone for a few months and hopefully sleep in his dressing room again.'

Laying the cup aside she absently stroked the ears of the little Cavalier King Charles spaniel curled up on her lap as Ruffy began to tidy the pile of magazines that Louisa had carelessly dropped onto the floor after glancing through them. She always dressed in the very latest fashions and every week magazines were delivered to Greenacres regardless of the expense.

Louisa always reminded Ruffy of a fragile little doll. She had long fair hair that Ruffy teased into ringlets each morning before tying them with ribbons that would match the gown she was wearing that day. Her eyes were a rich, deep brown colour and she was so delicate that there was an almost ethereal quality about her. She had never been short of suitors but Barnaby Greenwood had attended a ball at her parents' home and had literally swept her off her feet. He had been somewhat older than her and after the empty-headed young men she had been used to she had soon fallen head over heels in love with him.

Their wedding had been a sumptuous affair attended by over three hundred people, and Louisa had floated down the aisle in a froth of silk and lace on her proud father's arm. The reception following the church service took place in a huge marquee within the grounds of her parents' stately home and was so grand that it was still talked about in the area to that day. Top chefs had been drafted in from London to do the catering and people had whispered that they had never in their lives seen a spread like it. There had been whole suckling pigs, huge gammons, enormous joints of beef and every type of meat and pie available, as well as a huge selection of cakes and pastries made by a famous pastry chef. Louisa was sure it had been the happiest day of her life, and later that evening as she and Barnaby had boarded a ship bound for the South of France for their honeymoon the feeling had remained.

It was only then that she realised that some aspects of marriage weren't as pleasant as she had expected them to be and she had spent most of her wedding night curled up in a chair sobbing broken-heartedly as Barnaby tried to comfort her. She had found the physical side of things painful and dirty and nothing like the tender, adoring kisses she was used to, despite the fact that Barnaby had tried to be gentle with her.

'But darling, this is what married people do. It's how we make babies,' he had told her gently after she had fought him like a wildcat. 'It only hurts the first time. I promise you, you will enjoy it the next time if you'll only relax.'

But Louisa hadn't enjoyed it the next time, or the time after that and after that and she had lain as stiff as a plank every time he claimed his marital rights and simply endured it as she prayed for it to end.

The first time she had found she was with child she had been mortified. 'But Ruffy, I shall get fat and ugly. Lace my stays up a little tighter, please do,' she had begged.

'You might get fat but you'll never be ugly,' Ruffy had admonished her. 'And just think how lovely it will be when you hold your first baby in your arms.'

Louisa had scowled. 'When it's born, I shall hand it straight over to a wet nurse,' she'd declared petulantly. 'Babies are such *noisy*, dirty little things. A friend of Mama's called on us for afternoon coffee with her new baby and its nanny once, and it didn't stop crying the whole time she was there. *And* her nanny had to take it away to change its bindings.' She had shuddered with disgust as Ruffy grinned.

'Hm, let's just wait and see how you feel once the bairn is here,' Ruffy had replied with a secret smile as if she knew something that Louisa didn't. But that day had never dawned, for three months into the pregnancy Louisa started to bleed and lost the child. The same thing happened twice more over the next two years and then she had managed to carry two babies to full term but they were both born dead. Barnaby had been heartbroken, whilst she herself was indifferent. And now here she was in the same position yet again and clearly none too happy about it.

'I think I shall take Tumble for a little wander around the lawns,' Louisa said as she planted an affectionate kiss on the dog's head. Like his mistress, he was very spoilt. He had been a wedding gift from Barnaby along with an amethyst necklace that Louisa favoured above all her other much more expensive jewellery. Ruffy nodded indulgently as her mistress placed the little dog on the floor and headed for the door, collecting her sun parasol on the way.

Minutes later as she watched them from the bedroom window Ruffy frowned. Would her young mistress be lucky this time and finally give the master the child he so longed for? she wondered. There could be no way of knowing, it was all in the lap of the Gods now, so with a sigh she turned to tackle the piles of clothes that Louisa had strewn about the place when she had been trying to decide what to wear.

As Louisa strolled around the lush green lawns with Tumble scampering at her heels, Barnaby rode up the tree-lined drive on his stallion. As always of late, he had pushed the poor horse too hard and it was sweating and foaming at the mouth. Spotting his wife, he drew to a stop beside her, smiling down at her and she simpered at him in return. There were times when her childlike behaviour almost drove him to distraction. And yet he could remember a time not so long ago when he had been besotted with her. When he had first met her he had been sure that he had never seen a more beautiful young woman. But once they had married he had quickly discovered that her nature didn't quite match her looks. The sexual side of their relationship wasn't good for a start off, for she would gaze at him with a look of dread on her face the minute he entered her bedroom. And her tantrums if she didn't get her own way! He shuddered to think of them, but he kept his smile in place as he said, 'Good morning, my love. You're not overdoing things, I hope? We don't want anything to go wrong this time, do we?'

Her smile disappeared and she pouted, aware that he was talking about her condition again. Surely having her as his wife should have been enough for him.

'I am only taking a gentle stroll,' she pointed out with a scowl. 'Or would you have me stay indoors and waste away for the next seven months?'

'Of course not, my little dove. I accept that you need some fresh air.'

Tumble was scampering about the horse's hooves, barking and making the stallion skittish. 'Could you pick Tumble up, please,' Barnaby asked. 'He's going to get hurt if Star rears up.'

'Tumble, come here, my darling.' She leant down in a flurry of yellow silken skirts and scooped the little dog into her arms, frowning after her husband as he turned away without another word and rode towards the stables.

He, meanwhile, was frowning too. His wife could be so damn annoying at times and it was her lack of enjoyment in the marital bed that had made him turn to other women for release – Amber Ainsley being the latest. He was still bitterly ashamed of the way he had ordered her to get rid of the child they had made together. Amber might not have been quite as beautiful as Louisa, nor had she had the advantages that Louisa had had and yet she didn't make constant demands either, and Barnaby had found he could talk to her and feel easy in her company. This was why he hadn't dismissed her and now he hoped that it wouldn't be too long before she came back and they could pick up where they left off. Because strangely, even though she'd only just left, he found he was missing her.

As he rode into the stable yard the head groom came out to meet him and he saw the man scowl as he looked at the state of the horse.

'Now don't glare at me like that, Jed.' He laughed as he leapt nimbly down from the saddle and threw the reins to him. 'Star enjoys working up a sweat and a good gallop.'

'Hm, I wonder if you'll say the same when the poor beast drops down dead wi' a heart attack, sir,' Jed answered boldly as he stroked the horse's nose. He had known Barnaby since he was a young boy and as a youth when he was struggling to build up his business.

'He'll be right as rain once you've given him a good rub down.' Barnaby turned on his heel and headed round to the other side of the house to enter by the front door as Jed – shaking his head – led the horse into the cool stables. He really didn't know what had got into the young master lately; not so long ago he would never have pushed the poor horse so hard.

Barnaby had only just entered the enormous hallway when Ruffy appeared.

'Ah, Mr Greenwood,' she greeted him. 'I hear congratulations are in order . . . again,' she said drily and Barnaby flushed.

'Yes . . . yes, they are, Mrs Ruffin.'

'Then let's just hope your wife doesn't suffer too much this time, eh?' Mrs Ruffin said worriedly. 'Though I wouldn't hold my breath on it. Didn't I warn you some time ago that she wasn't built for bearing children? Why, she's so delicate and fragile one good puff of wind would blow her away and all these pregnancies can't be doing her health any good at all.'

'I'm well aware of that, Mrs Ruffin,' he answered coldly. 'Now, would you excuse me?' And with that he strode away, leaving her in no doubt that she had upset him.

An hour later, Louisa and Barnaby sat in the formal dining room having lunch at a highly polished mahogany table that could quite easily seat twenty people – and frequently had in the past.

'I had a look at the account books today,' Barnaby informed his wife proudly as he sipped at the tasty lobster soup starter. 'And it appears that the boats and the shipyard are doing well. The new trawler that was ordered should be finished in a week or two.'

Trying her best to hide her boredom, Louisa kept her eyes downcast, wondering why, whenever she and her husband got together, they always ended up discussing business. She would much rather have discussed the latest fashions and hairstyles.

'That's good isn't it, my love?'

Louisa glanced up as she realised that Barnaby was expecting a reply. 'Yes, yes, you are very clever,' she replied a little sarcastically.

Realising that she wasn't in the least interested he changed the subject. 'With regards to the baby, I was thinking perhaps this time we ought to send for a doctor from London to keep an eye on you? We don't want anything to go wrong with this one, do we?' he said gently.

When colour burnt into her cheeks, Barnaby rushed on, 'You mustn't get worrying, I have a good feeling that all will be well this time. And you must promise to take extra care of yourself, my darling.'

Louisa nodded numbly. Barnaby could always have this effect on her. Sometimes, she rued the day she had agreed to marry him and although she knew it was wicked to have such thoughts, she often wished he would just die.

As soon as the meal was over and she could excuse herself, Louisa left Barnaby and hurried up to her room where she found Ruffy waiting for her with her new afternoon gown laid out ready on the four-poster bed.

'Barnaby is already talking about fetching a doctor from London,' she said bitterly as she stamped her small satin-slipper-clad foot on the floor.

'Calm down, my love.' Ruffy hurried over to her and planted a gentle kiss on her forehead before helping her to undress. 'At least he's showing his concern for you.'

Louisa pouted and once she had taken off her gown, she slipped on a silk robe and lay down for a short nap. The bed was draped with thick, pink velvet curtains to match the ones that hung at the window, and a deep pile carpet of a slightly paler colour covered the floor. The walls had been decorated in a soft dove-grey silk wallpaper which she had ordered from London, and the furniture was all highly polished rosewood. Everything had been chosen by Louisa before her marriage, and the room was beautiful and luxurious and never failed to make her smile. She just wished she didn't have to share it with Barnaby whenever he came to demand his marital rights.

'After dinner this evening you may tell Barnaby that I have a headache,' she told Mrs Ruffin pettily as Tumble bounced onto the bed and snuggled down beside her. 'And that I am requesting that he doesn't disturb me and stays in his dressing room.' With that she burrowed down the bed and pulled the silken sheets over her head.

Mrs Ruffin sighed. As much as she loved her young mistress, there were times when she tried her patience sorely and she almost felt sorry for the young master. Oh, she'd heard the rumours about the shenanigans he'd got up to with the young laundry maid but, she asked herself, in truth could she really blame him when his young wife was so indifferent to him? Louisa loved to be kissed and petted admittedly, but anything beyond that clearly filled her with dismay so was it any wonder that the poor soul wandered? It was very rarely that Louisa allowed him into her bedchamber now. It was a shame, she thought, that Louisa hadn't found the same joy that Ruffy herself had found so briefly with her own husband. But seeing as she hadn't, then what else was Barnaby to do? With another sigh she dimmed the lamp that stood on the bedside table and quietly left the room hoping that her young mistress would be in a happier frame of mind when she woke up.

Chapter Four

'Now are you quite sure you have the letter for your uncle, lass?'

Amber smiled weakly as she tapped the carpetbag she was holding. 'You've asked me that at least ten times already, Mam, and the answer is still the same. Yes, it's tucked safe here in me bag.'

Her mother glanced at the tin clock ticking away on the mantelshelf. 'Reet, in that case you'd best be off, lass.' She hastily swiped away the stray tear that trickled down her face with the back of her hand as she turned her daughter towards the door. She was painfully aware that this might be the last time she would see her until after the baby had been born and her heart broke at the thought. Alice would have her very first grandchild, one she would never see. But even though the thought was painful she knew it was for the best, and pulling herself together with an effort she looked her daughter up and down.

Today Amber was wearing her Sunday-best skirt made from black alpaca and her white frilled blouse. She also wore her new straw bonnet and Alice's best shawl about her shoulders, and with her long blonde hair hanging down her back in thick gleaming curls she looked reet bonny!

'You'll do,' she said with a wobble in her voice as she leant forward to kiss Amber one last time. 'Be off with you. An' . . . stay safe, lass.'

Amber nodded as she opened the door and stepped out into the yard where she almost bumped into Mrs Preston who was making a great show of cleaning her windows for the first time that either Amber or her mother could ever remember.

'Off on a little 'oliday are you, lass?' she asked as her eyes rested on the bag Amber was carrying.

'Actually, Molly, Amber is away to look after me poor brother in Scarborough,' Alice told her before Amber could answer. 'He's been reet poorly so she'll stay there till he's back on his feet again.'

'Oh ar!' Molly sniffed. 'An' what's up wi' him then?'

Amber gave her mother a hasty peck on the cheek and hurried away, well aware that Alice was more than capable of handling Molly Preston, and soon she turned out of the yard and headed for the town hall. It was a grand building, paid for by the lord of the manor, Nathaniel Cholmley, and built by Jonathan Pickernell, and normally Amber would always take time to admire it but today she had other things on her mind.

The coach was already parked there and the four black horses that would pull it were pawing the ground restlessly as the driver fastened the passenger's luggage to the roof. Amber quickened her steps, afraid it would leave without her.

'Is there room for one more?' she asked breathlessly.

The tall man paused and nodded. 'Aye lass, just one seat left. You're lucky, another two minutes an' we'd have been gone.'

When he had taken her luggage and fastened it to the roof of the carriage, Amber quickly paid him and climbed aboard. There were three other people inside the coach: a stout, finely dressed gentleman who looked quite well-to-do and an elderly couple who gave her warm smiles.

Amber settled back against the grubby leather squabs and watched miserably from the window as the horses pulled away and began their journey.

The first part went slowly as the horses plodded up the 199 steps, the steep hill that led out of town, and Amber swallowed deeply to try and prevent the tears that had sprung to her eyes from falling. How changed her life would be the next time she returned. By then she would have given birth to her baby and parted with it. It was a sobering thought and as the horses picked up speed and hurried past Whitby Abbey, perched high on the hill, her mood was sombre.

'Off to visit someone are you, lass? Or perhaps it's a day out?'

Amber started as she realised that the elderly lady was talking to her. In truth, she just wanted to be quiet but not wishing to be rude she answered, 'I'm, er . . . going to work there for a time . . . for my uncle.'

'Ah, that's nice. We're off to see our daughter, Miriam, aren't we, Fred?' She flashed a smile at the old man seated next to her who was now happily puffing on a pipe, filling the carriage with smoke that stung Amber's eyes. 'Just had a baby she has.' The old woman smiled proudly. 'Her fifth it is, another boy an' all, an' her were so desperate for a little lass.' She chuckled. 'Still, like I told her, so long as the little soul is healthy, eh? She'll have her own football team at this rate!'

Amber managed a weak smile before returning her attention to the window and thankfully soon after, when she peeped at the woman from the corner of her eye, she saw that she had fallen into a doze.

Her mother had told her that it was approximately twenty miles from Whitby to Scarborough and would probably take about two to three hours by carriage so for the next hour Amber sat back quietly and when the old woman roused, she closed her own eyes and pretended to be asleep. It was a shock when, in what seemed like no time at all, she felt someone gently shaking her arm and she realised that she really had dropped off.

'Come on, lass. We're here,' the old lady told her cheerily. 'I hope the job wi' your uncle goes well. Ta-ra for now!'

Amber knuckled the sleep from her eyes and lifting her carpetbag she scrambled out of the carriage and looked around before fumbling in the top of it for her uncle's address as the coach driver lifted her suitcase from the roof.

Marine View, Royal Albert Road, she read and after asking directions she set off to find it. As far as she could recollect, she had only every visited her uncle once with her mother when she was a little girl, so the streets were unfamiliar to her, but at last she found herself walking along Marine Parade, and she stared at the grand houses that looked out across the sea in amazement. They were so high they seemed to reach the sky and were far grander than she'd expected. But then she recalled her mother telling her that her uncle owned his own shop so he could probably well afford to live in such a house.

Eventually she came to one with a sign that announced this was 'Marine View' and she gawped at its frontage in awe. It was three storeys high and the many windows winked in the sunshine. There was a low railing all along the front that led up to a smart red door with a shiny brass knocker on it and to the left further steps went downwards to what she guessed would be a kitchen. *But which way should I go?* she mused.

Making a hasty decision she raised her chin and self-consciously smoothed her skirt. She would enter by the front door – if she was admitted, that was – she was family after all. Taking a deep breath, she climbed the steps and raised the brass knocker and seconds later she heard footsteps beyond the door and it inched open. She found herself staring into the face of a woman who looked to be in her late forties to early fifties and she supposed that this must be the house-keeper that her mother had told her worked for her uncle.

'Good afternoon.' Amber gave the woman a polite smile. 'I am here to see my uncle, Mr Jeremiah Harding.'

The woman looked her up and down, seeming mildly surprised. She noted the girl was shabbily dressed but spotlessly clean. 'I'm afraid Mr Harding is at work. I am his house-keeper, Mrs Carter.' She was tall and slim and although she was no longer young, Amber thought she was still attractive, or at least she could have been if her clothes and her hair-style weren't quite so severe. She was dressed in a black alpaca gown with no trimmings whatsoever and her dark hair was peppered lightly with grey at the temples and pulled tightly into an unbecoming knot in the nape of her neck, but even so her eyes were a striking shade of blue and her skin was smooth.

'Oh!' Amber gulped. 'Could you tell me what time he'll be home?'

'The shop shuts at five thirty and he'll be home at six o'clock on the dot. Mr Harding is a creature of habit.' Seeing the look of disappointment on Amber's face she opened the door a little wider and invited, 'Won't you come in for a moment.'

'Ta very much, missus.' Amber stepped into a large hallway and gratefully placed her bags on the floor. She was sure they were now twice as heavy as they had been when she started out and her arms were aching from carrying them.

Mrs Carter eyed the young woman curiously. It had been some years since Jeremiah's sister had visited him and Amber had been little more than a child then, but now she saw that she had turned into an attractive young woman with the most glorious head of hair she had ever seen. 'Do you wish to see your uncle urgently?'

'Well, er . . . yes, I suppose I do,' Amber answered nervously. More than ever, now that she was finally here, she was convinced that this had been a bad idea.

'Then in that case, why don't you leave your bags here and go and see him at the shop?' Mrs Carter suggested not unkindly.

'But I-I don't know the way.'

'Oh, don't worry about that. His shop is in Hope Street and I can draw you a little map. I assume you can read?'

Colour flared into Amber's cheeks. 'O' course I can read,' she answered indignantly. 'Me mam allus made sure that we all went to school.'

'Very well, wait there a moment then.' Mrs Carter hurried away, returning minutes later with a roughly drawn street map. 'Now, keep going left until you come to Albert

37

Road, turn there and walk on . . .' She quickly talked her way through the route and Amber smiled gratefully.

'Thank you. I won't be long, I hope.'

'I assume that you'll be staying for dinner?'

'Er . . . hopefully,' Amber mumbled as she bent to take the letter her mother had written from the bag.

'Very well, I shall make sure that we lay an extra place for you at the table.'

Amber inclined her head and stepped back outside, carefully following the map that Mrs Carter had drawn for her. When she reached Hope Street, she continued along it until she came to a shopfront with a brightly coloured sign hanging above it declaring that it was Harding's Hardware Store.

Amber was quite amazed at the size of it. It took up at least two of the average shopfronts and judging by the number of people going in and out it was doing a roaring trade. Outside on hooks in the wall were a number of buckets and bowls, and brooms of all shapes and sizes stood against the wall in a huge bin. Next to that was another bin containing every garden tool a gardener could possibly need as well as tubs full of screws and nails.

Suddenly she was nervous and as she stood there dithering, a young man, who looked to be slightly older than her, came out with a lady and helped her to choose a broom. Once the woman had chosen and gone back into the shop to pay for it, he turned to Amber and asked cheerfully, 'Can I help you, Miss?'

He was very tall with dark hair and grey eyes and Amber liked him immediately. He was so friendly it would have been hard not to.

'Er . . . no, you can't. I'm here to see my uncle actually . . . Mr Harding.'

'Oh!' He looked surprised. 'Well, you'll find him inside, Miss.'

'Thank you.' Amber inclined her head and after taking a deep breath she entered the shop.

She saw her uncle immediately. He was standing behind the counter serving a customer so she stood back until he'd finished. He looked older than she remembered, but then it had been some years since she'd seen him. His hair was streaked with grey now but his eyes were still exactly the same colour as her mother's and she could tell straightaway that they were related. She approached the counter cautiously and when he looked up, she said, 'Hello, Uncle Jeremiah, I'm Amber. Your sister Alice's daughter.'

He stared at her for a moment before nodding. 'Yes, I can see you are now. But my, how you've grown. You were just a child the last time I saw you. How is your mother and what brings you here?'

Amber blushed as she noticed that some of the customers who were browsing in the shop were staring at her. Jeremiah noticed too and lifting the lid on the counter he beckoned to her. 'Come on through to the back. Young Archie here can mind the shop for a while.'

Archie proved to be the young man she had met outside and he gave her a smile as her uncle ushered her into a small room at the back of the shop. There was a little stove in the corner where they obviously boiled water for their tea breaks and two mismatched wing chairs that had certainly seen better days. The rest of the room was stacked with surplus stock.

'So,' he said as lifted the kettle onto the small stove to boil. 'I hope you're not the bearer of bad news?'

Without a word, Amber handed him the letter from her mother and wrung her hands as he placed a pair of spectacles on the end of his nose and proceeded to read it. Once he was done, he narrowed his eyes and stared at her as Amber shifted uncomfortably from foot to foot.

'So why can't you stay at home with your mother until the child is born?' he asked curiously and Amber gulped.

'I, er . . . that is, me husband and me had our own place an' I've had to give it up,' she mumbled. She had never been very good at lying. 'An' me mam ain't got room for me there wi' all me brothers an' all. But just as soon as the baby is born, I can go back,' she hurried on. 'An' me mam will have found a place fer me by then an' . . .' Her words trailed off as she saw the look on her uncle's face. He clearly didn't believe a word her mother had written and certainly nothing she'd said.

Her shoulders sagged as she slowly turned to leave, but before she had reached the door her uncle's voice stayed her as he said gently, 'So why don't we start again and we'll have the truth this time.'

She turned back and stared at him for a moment and then stumblingly she began to tell him what had happened. Of her affair with her master and the gold sovereign he had given her to get rid of the child, and once she was done, tears were raining down her cheeks.

'I . . . I thought he loved me,' she choked. 'But I was a fool, he was just using me.'

Jeremiah frowned. 'Hm, well it seems to me that what has happened to you isn't all your fault. You were led astray by someone who should have known better and I can see why you couldn't stay at home,' he said cautiously. 'But what are you planning to do with the child once it's born?'

'I, er . . . was goin' to leave it on the steps o' the poorhouse,' Amber admitted in a small voice.

'I see.' He stroked his chin as the kettle began to sing. 'Look, I'm going to need to think about this. Go back to the house. Mrs Carter will take care of you and we'll talk more tonight when I get home.'

Amber nodded and on feet that felt like lead she slowly left the shop to retrace her steps. Once she had reached the house again, she took a deep breath and this time when she knocked on the door it was opened by the maid. Mrs Carter had obviously told her about Amber's visit and she ushered her into the hallway just as Mrs Carter came bustling along towards her.

'Ah, you're back then. Did you manage to see your uncle?'

'Yes, thank you, he told me to wait here till he got home from work.'

'Then we must get you something to eat to tide you over till dinner time. You must be hungry,' Mrs Carter said, not unkindly, and turning to the maid she asked her, 'Bring some bread and cheese and a pot of tea into the drawing room, would you please, Biddy?'

Biddy nodded as she stared at Amber curiously. She was a short, plump woman who Amber judged to be in her mid- to late-thirties. She was neatly clad in a plain grey gown over which she wore a white apron, and her mousy-coloured hair was covered by a white mob cap, which sat askew on her head.

'Yes, ma'am,' she answered as she turned away and Amber noted that she had a severe limp that made her waddle from side to side as she set off in the direction of the kitchen.

'Right, my dear, this is the drawing room,' Mrs Carter told Amber ushering her into a large room with a deep bay window that had a glorious view across the road towards the sea. It was plainly but comfortably furnished and very much a man's room. There were no flowers or feminine touches about the place and as Mrs Carter saw Amber taking it all in she lifted a cushion from a leather wing chair to one side of the empty fireplace and plumping it up she grinned. 'Your uncle has very simple tastes,' she told her as if she could read her mind. 'He's never been one for frills and furbelows. Oh, and I should warn you, Biddy is a little, er . . .' She tried to think of a kindly way to explain the woman. 'Slow,' she said eventually. 'But she's a good worker and totally devoted to Mr Harding. She's worked here for almost as long as I have. He took her from the poorhouse when she was fourteen years old. They were going to turn her out on to the streets but Mr Harding took her in for a trial and she's been here ever since. Biddy and I keep the house running between us. I do the cooking and manage the accounts and Biddy does the laundry and the majority of the cleaning.'

At mention of the poorhouse Amber's stomach sank. Would her child be tipped on to the streets when it reached fourteen? she wondered. But then she pushed the thought away. There was no point in going soft now; she had chosen the path she must go down and there could be no going back.

Biddy hobbled back in shortly after with a tray of sandwiches and a pot of tea which she placed on a small table in the bay window and now Amber saw what Mrs Carter had meant about her. There was a childlike manner in the way she spoke and she seemed to be constantly looking at Mrs Carter for instructions.

'You may go now, Biddy. Perhaps you could go out to the yard to see if the washing is dry?' Mrs Carter suggested, and with a lopsided smile the woman shuffled away and Mrs Carter turned back to Amber. 'I'll leave you to enjoy your snack for now then, Miss Ainsley.'

'Oh please . . . just call me Amber.'

'Very well, Amber,' the woman answered with a kindly smile before she swept from the room in a rustle of stiff skirts and petticoats.

The rest of the afternoon passed slowly for Amber as she sat watching the world go by from the window, until at six o'clock sharp, just as Mrs Carter had predicted, she saw her uncle heading along the road. She took a deep breath. All she could do now was pray that he would allow her to stay here until after the baby's birth. If he didn't, she had no idea what she was going to do, but one thing was for sure, there could be no going back home. If she did she dreaded to think of what her father might do when he learnt she was with child, or worse still, what Barnaby might do when he discovered that she hadn't got rid of it as he'd ordered!

Chapter Five

Sitting across the dining room table from her uncle, Amber pushed the food about her plate. Apart from acknowledging her when he had returned home and requesting that she join him for dinner, he had said not a word and now she was nervous as she wondered if he would allow her to stay.

The meal – pork chops served with boiled potatoes and vegetables – was simple, although nicely cooked and presented, but Amber found that she couldn't swallow a mouthful of it and so she was thankful when her uncle finished and dabbed at his lips with a napkin.

Only then did he look at her and say, 'So, what's to be done regarding your situation, eh?'

'Well . . . as my mother said in her letter, we were hoping you'd let me stay here, just till after the baby's born, sir,' she added hastily. She didn't want him to think that she was hoping to foist herself on him forever. 'I can work,' she hurried on. 'An' I don't mind what I do, I'm used to hard work. I could help out in the shop, or per'aps help Mrs Carter here?'

'Hm.' Her uncle stroked his chin as he stared at her thoughtfully. 'I suppose you could help out in the shop, at least until your condition becomes evident,' he mused. 'I'm a great believer that idle hands make work for the devil. But what about what we discussed earlier – about your leaving the child at the poorhouse once it's born? What will happen if you can't go through with parting with it and you decide you want to keep it?'

'But I *won't* want to keep it!' Amber answered vehemently. 'How could I? I know I could *never* take to it knowin' how its father has treated me!'

'Very well then, in that case you may stay here until after the birth, which will be when?'

'I reckon about early September,' Amber answered in a small voice and he nodded.

'In that case be ready to leave for the shop with me at seven thirty sharp in the morning. Mrs Carter will show you to your room and for the time you are here you will eat with me in here.'

'But I don't mind eatin' wi' Mrs Carter an' Biddy in the kitchen.'

He shook his head. 'No, you are my niece and it wouldn't be seemly, so if you want breakfast before we leave in the morning be in here for seven o'clock. Goodnight, Amber.'

She watched him leave the room closing the door gently behind him and let out a breath of relief. All she had to do was get through the next six to seven months and then hopefully she would be able to put this all behind her. It couldn't come quickly enough.

Within a week she was actually enjoying working in the shop thanks to Archie Moorcroft who almost fell over himself trying to assist her in any way he could. He was a lovely young man and Amber enjoyed his company. It was soon clear that he was her uncle's right-hand man and knew almost as much about running the shop as her uncle did. Archie had happily told her that he lived with his widowed mother and two young sisters in Scarborough but whenever he asked her anything about her own personal life, she changed the subject feeling that the least he knew about her past the better. Her only concern with Archie, though, was that she had a horrible feeling he might be forming romantic feelings for her and she didn't want that. She didn't want any man now and doubted that she ever would again after the way Barnaby Greenwood had treated her. In any case, in a few months' time she would be gone and it would be highly doubtful she would ever see Archie again. She knew that her uncle had informed him that she was a widow but she wasn't even sure if Archie was aware she was carrying a child as yet and she felt it was best left that way.

It had also quickly become clear to her that Mrs Carter had fond feelings for her employer. Uncle Jeremiah appeared to be completely oblivious to it and Amber thought it was a shame because she was sure they could have made each other happy. Even so, she was just grateful to her uncle for allowing her to stay and so she kept her thoughts to herself.

Two weeks after she had started working at the shop, however, her stomach sank when Archie asked her one Saturday, 'I were wonderin' if you'd like to come to my house for tea to meet me mam an' me little sisters tomorrow?'

They both worked each weekday from eight till five in the afternoon and on Saturday they worked from nine till four, so Sunday was the only day off they had. Her uncle had already told her that he would expect her to attend the chapel with him on Sunday morning and now Amber was in a tizzy. She didn't want to hurt Archie's feelings but the last thing she needed was to get romantically involved with anyone and she knew that if he was thinking along those lines and she accepted the invitation, it might give him false hope. And so with a cheery smile she told him, 'Thanks, Archie, that's really kind of you but, well . . . it's not so long since I lost my husband and . . .'

When her voice trailed away poor Archie blushed to the colour of a beetroot. 'Oh . . . I'm sorry . . . I weren't thinkin'.'

Amber grinned. 'But if you're after a bit of company why don't you ask that young Daisy, the little maid from the big house up the road that comes into the shop every chance she gets? I'm sure she's taken with you. I couldn't help but notice how her eyes follow you everywhere whenever you're about.'

'Daisy Saunders!' Archie looked shocked. He had known Daisy for years; they'd practically grown up together but he'd never looked at her in that way before and he'd certainly had no idea that she liked him. She was a very pretty girl though, now he came to think about it, and he looked thoughtful as he got on with what he'd been doing.

It was mid-afternoon when Amber's uncle drew her to one side and pressed some money into her hand saying brusquely, 'Slip out and get yourself some lengths of material from the ladies' dress shop up the road. And while you're at it go into the bootmaker's and order yourself some new shoes. Those boots you're wearing will be far too big and cumbersome with the spring upon us.'

'Oh, but Uncle you really don't need to do this,' Amber protested, even though she knew that although they were spotlessly clean, the clothes she was wearing were very shabby indeed.

'I want you looking smart in the shop,' he said as he busied himself tidying the counter. 'Spend it on whatever you need.'

Amber was tempted to kiss his cheek for his kindness but thought better of it. Her uncle wasn't a demonstrative man and she didn't think he'd appreciate it, so, needing no more persuasion, she thanked him and scurried away. She couldn't remember ever having a brand-new gown in her whole life. Her mother had usually bought their clothes from the second-hand stall in the market and altered them to fit and even the uniform dress she had worn at Greenacres had been worn before. In addition, once she had the material, the making of the gowns would give her something to do of an evening. Her uncle always retired quite early after dinner and she'd found the hours before she herself went to bed passed slowly, giving her too much time to think and fret about what lay ahead.

There was a spring in her step for the first time in some while as she entered the dressmaker's and the portly woman who owned the shop immediately confused her as she produced bolt after bolt of material. Amber was completely spoilt for choice!

'This might be nice for the spring and summer,' the kindly shopkeeper suggested as she unrolled a pretty cotton print. It had a white background sprigged with tiny yellow rosebuds and Amber fell in love with it instantly.

'It's perfect.' She smiled. 'But perhaps something a little more sober for working in my uncle's shop?'

'How about this one?' The woman reached for a bolt of slightly thicker material in a warm russet colour. 'It would look beautiful with your blonde hair and eyes. You could perhaps trim it with this dark brown braid around the neck and the cuffs?'

Amber beamed at her and nodded, and once the material had been cut and she was told the price she fingered a warm shawl with a thick fringe. It was all autumn colours and she knew that it would go with the russet dress beautifully on cold mornings.

'Seein' as you've bought enough material for two gowns, I could do that a bit cheaper fer you if you were interested?' the shopkeeper offered, and after hesitating, Amber nodded and waited again while that too was wrapped in brown paper and tied with string.

The next stop was the bootmaker's and once he had measured her feet, he produced a book full of designs.

'I don't want anything too fancy,' she said worriedly, although some of the designs were so beautiful they made her heart race. 'These will be just right,' she said eventually, pointing to a pair of shoes with a small heel, a round toe and a strap across the arch.

'Good choice, lass. Pretty but practical.' The cobbler nodded approvingly. 'An' what colour leather would yer like 'em made in? I've got a nice bit o' soft brown here that would work a treat wi' that style an' I can have 'em ready fer you a week from today.'

Amber almost skipped back to work and that evening, instead of dreading the empty hours ahead, she could hardly wait to get started on her new gowns.

Mrs Carter kindly helped her cut them out. 'I think we should go for a really full skirt and pretty short sleeves on this one,' she suggested as she fingered the sprigged cotton. 'It will be your Sunday best after all. And perhaps something a little more restrained for the russet one?'

Amber nodded. 'And can we please allow for me letting them out as the baby grows? And perhaps I should make the russet one first so that I have a smart dress to wear in the shop?' she said in a small voice.

Mrs Carter nodded in agreement and began to snip.

When she and her uncle returned from work on the following Monday, Amber found a letter from her mother waiting for her. She longed to open but first she had to have dinner with her uncle. He was pedantic with his habits and Mrs Carter always served their meal at six fifteen on the dot. As usual the meal was plain but wholesome. Tonight they were served lamb chops with freshly chopped mint sauce, creamed potatoes and vegetables followed by one of Mrs Carter's delicious apple pies with creamy custard. The pudding was one of her uncle's favourites and he helped himself to seconds before finally excusing himself and retiring to his study where he would enjoy a glass of port and a cigar with his newspaper as he did every night after his evening meal.

At last Amber could open the letter from her mother so she hurried up to her room where she would not be disturbed. Like all the other rooms in the house, it was plainly furnished but even so it was far grander and larger than any other room she had ever slept in and Amber never tired of the panoramic view across the sea from the window.

Dear Amber,

You could 'ave knocked me down with a feather today when I opened the door to find yer old gaffer, Mr Greenwood, standing there on the doorstep an' you can just imagine how the curtains were twitchin' in the yard. Old Mrs Preston almost fell out of the winder tryin' to see who it was. Of course I asked him in and he then asked me why you hadn't returned to your job. I told him what we'd agreed – that your uncle had been taken ill and you'd gone to look after him for a while till he were on the mend. He looked perplexed and asked when you would be home but I just said it all depended on how quickly your uncle recovered. I hope this means he is keeping your job open for you. Everyone here has been told the same story so I hope you're sticking to it there too. It will make it so much easier for you when you come home.

I do miss you so, my lass, an so does yer dad an yer brothers and we hope that you are keeping well. I wish I could be there with you to see you through this difficult time but I know that Jeremiah will keep you safe. Do give him my love and take good care of yerself. I will do my very best to come and see yer when the time for the birth draws a little nearer.

Until then I send you all my love,

Mam xxx

Amber took a deep breath and chewed on her lip as she tried to digest what her mother had told her. Why would Barnaby Greenwood care if she went back to work or not after the way he had treated her? she wondered. As far as she knew, he didn't usually bother to check on any of the other staff who had left his employ. But then, they weren't carrying his baby and she was. Her hand dropped to her stomach. It was still flat as a pancake and it was hard to believe that there really was a tiny little being in there. As yet the only change in herself she had noticed was a tenderness in her breasts and a feeling of nausea first thing in the morning.

Unbidden, a picture of Barnaby flashed before her eyes and the tears came again as she thought of how he had so heartlessly used her. Now for the first time she was glad she had come here. At least here there was little chance of bumping into him. With a deep sigh she laid the letter aside and lifted the gown she was working on, soon becoming absorbed in the stitches and temporarily forgetting about anything else.

From then on Mrs Carter helped her each evening and within a week, between them, the first dress was finished and Amber could hardly wait to wear it. All in all, life at her uncle's was proving to be far more pleasant than she had thought it would be, and sometimes she forgot that this was just a temporary home – because as soon as the baby was born, her time here would end. She had already decided that she didn't want to go back to working at Greenacres. Every time she laid eyes on the master it would only remind her of the pain he had put her through, and worse still, what if he wanted to resume their relationship? She knew she wouldn't be able to bear it and so soon she would have to think very hard about what she planned to do with her future.

Chapter Six

On a fine sunny morning early in June, as Mrs Ruffin was helping her young mistress to dress, Louisa stamped her foot and pouted. 'Pull the stays *tighter*, Ruffy,' she grumbled as she looked down at her thickening waistline.

'If I pull them any tighter, you'll not be able to breathe!' her faithful servant retorted. 'And any road, you're going to do damage to the baby if you keep insisting on binding your stomach so tight!'

Louisa was in danger of flying into a full-blown tantrum and threw herself down onto her silk chaise longue with tears smudging her pale cheeks.

'Oh, I feel so *fat* and *ugly*!' she declared as she mopped her face with a scrap of a lace handkerchief. 'And I just feel so sick and ill all the time. I *swear* once this is over, I shall ban Barnaby from my bedroom *forever*! I simply refuse to go through this ever again.'

At that moment there was a tap at the door and Barnaby strolled in carrying a large box of sweetmeats he had ordered from London especially for her.

'Here you are, my darling. They just arrived.' He smiled at her as she pouted back at him. He had always spoilt her but since discovering that she was with child again, her every wish had been his command and Ruffy almost felt sorry for him.

'How are you feeling? Isn't Dr Flynn calling in to see you today?'

Louisa sniffed and took the sweetmeats from him before throwing them carelessly onto the other end of the chaise longue.

'Yes he is . . . *again*.' She gave a martyred sigh. 'And I'm so tired of being poked and prodded about. He's concerned that my ankles are starting to swell! Says it could be a sign of trouble to come.' Pulling up her petticoat she displayed them to him. She had always been very proud of her shapely legs but now she was ashamed of them.

'They still look very pretty to me,' he soothed but she tossed her head.

'That's because you don't have to go through this! It's all right for you men. It's we *women* that have to suffer.'

'I understand that, but just think . . . it will all be worth it when we have a fine healthy baby,' he said encouragingly. He glanced at the corset Ruffy was holding and asked tentatively, 'Should you still be wearing those, my love?'

'No, she shouldn't!' Ruffy answered bluntly. 'I just told her she'd be doing the baby no good squashing into that thing. That's why she's in a mood. She's got to forget about having an eighteen-inch waist till the little one is here! And even then, it'll take her some time to get back into shape.'

Barnaby stood there not quite knowing how to answer. Mrs Ruffin could get away with speaking her mind far more than he could and he didn't want Louisa's bad mood to turn into a full-blown screaming fit!

'Perhaps you could ask Dr Flynn's opinion on that,' he said quietly and Louisa turned on him, her eyes blazing.

'Huh! This whole thing is past a joke now,' she spat furiously. 'I feel like I've been carrying a child forever since I married you. All you seem to care about is having a baby but what about *me*?' She burst into noisy sobs as Barnaby backed towards the door spreading his hands helplessly.

'You'd best go, sir,' Mrs Ruffin suggested as she crossed to her mistress, and only too happy to oblige Barnaby hastily escaped out of the door.

On the landing he took a crisp white handkerchief from his pocket and quickly mopped his brow, as unbidden he again thought of Amber and the heartless way he had paid her to get rid of the child she had been carrying. It had occurred to him that had she continued with the pregnancy, she and Louisa would have been due to give birth at about the same time. But he had no time to dwell on the fact because at that moment Dr Flynn, a portly old gentleman, came huffing up the stairs toting his black leather bag.

'Good morning, Barnaby. I've just come to check how that pretty little wife of yours is doing,' he told him jovially.

Barnaby sighed and shook his head. 'Well, I can't say how she's doing physically,' he answered glumly. 'But she certainly doesn't seem to be enjoying the experience.'

The doctor chuckled. 'Never mind, in another two or three months it should all be over and happen you'll be back in favour again. Now, if you'll excuse me.' And with that he tapped on Louisa's bedroom door and left Barnaby standing there.

Barnaby was crossing the hall to his study when the doctor came downstairs shortly after and when he saw the frown on the old doctor's face his heart began to race. Surely things couldn't be going wrong again? he asked himself.

'Is everything all right, Doctor?'

'Hm, well as far as I can see, but to be honest I'd be happier if the child were moving about a bit more.' He could have added that he would have liked its heartbeat to be a little stronger too but he didn't want to overly concern the expectant father. He knew how much he was looking forward to the birth of the child.

'Oh no!' Barnaby's face fell and the doctor quickly forced a smile.

'Now let's not get thinking the worst! We'll cross each bridge as we come to it, eh?' he suggested soothingly. 'It's probably just me being over-cautious because of what's happened in the past. I've suggested she stay in bed for a few days and have a good rest, which didn't go down too well, I have to admit. Apparently she had planned to go visiting this afternoon, but it can't be helped. I've told her to do away with those damned stays as well. Young women nowadays are far too vain, if you ask me.' He tapped Barnaby's arm and left.

Staring after him, Barnaby felt the first seeds of fear begin to grow in his stomach. Through the open door he could see one of the gardener's dead-heading the roses in the rose garden and hurrying out to him he ordered, 'Cut a large bunch of roses for the mistress and have one of the maids take them up to her room immediately.'

'Yes, sir. Reet away.' The gardener touched his cap as Barnaby strode towards the stables. He'd take his horse for a good gallop, he decided. It was time he visited the shipyard to see how close to completion the latest trawler his men were building was anyway.

Less than an hour later he tethered his horse and as he approached the almost-finished vessel he saw young William, Amber's brother, busily varnishing the hull.

When he stopped to speak to him, Will looked mildly surprised. It wasn't often the gaffer spoke directly to any of the workers.

'Almost finished?'

'Aye it is, sir,' Will answered respectfully. 'Another couple o' days or so should see 'er ready fer launchin'.'

'Good, good.' Barnaby tapped the side of his jodhpurs with his riding crop. 'And how is your uncle now? The one that lives in Scarborough. I saw your mother some weeks ago and she told me that your sister had gone to take care of him.'

Will shrugged as he swiped a strand of thick hair, exactly the same fiery colour as Amber's, from his brow. 'I wouldn't know, sir. Me mam keeps in touch be letter but I ain't seen hide nor hair of her since her went.'

'Oh well, I hope he recovers soon.' Barnaby inclined his head and moved on towards the office as a thought began to form in his mind. Amber had left very abruptly and had already been away for some months. What if she hadn't got rid of the child as he had ordered her to? His stomach started to churn and as he entered the office there was a thoughtful expression on his face. Perhaps it was time he paid Mrs Ainsley a visit, but first he would have to come up with an excuse to warrant it.

The visit occurred the very next day, shortly after he had been to see Louisa in her room. She was fractious and difficult because she had been confined to bed so he had made a hasty exit and soon found himself standing at the Ainsleys' door, aware of the curious glances he was getting from everyone who passed. He had no doubt that in this poor area, in his fine clothes, he must look like a rose on a dung heap.

Mrs Ainsley admitted him with an anxious frown on her face. 'Is owt wrong, sir?' As she stood before him wringing her hands he flashed her a charming smile.

'Not at all, Mrs Ainsley,' he assured her. 'It's just that whilst I was doing my accounts yesterday, I realised that I still owed your daughter some wages so I thought I would drop them in to you.'

'That's reet kind o' you, sir.' She eyed the coins he placed on the table suspiciously. 'I'll see as she gets it.' She expected him to leave now that he'd done what he'd come to do but instead he looked about the humble abode and smiled.

'You keep a very good home, Mrs Ainsley. Very comfortable.'

'Thank you, sir.' Again, he made no move to leave so she felt forced to ask, 'Would you like a cup o' tea. I was just about to have one meself.'

'That would be most acceptable. Thank you, Mrs Ainsley.' He removed his hat and, flicking the tails of his fine coat aside, he sat down at the table. She hurried to push the soot-blackened kettle over the fire and while she was preparing the cups he asked casually, 'And how is your brother now, Mrs Ainsley? Improving, I hope?'

'Er . . . yes, as far as I know,' she answered cagily. 'I ain't had a letter off our Amber fer a couple o' weeks or so now.'

'Oh, so you have no idea when she might be returning to work?'

She shook her head a little too quickly and Barnaby detected a tremor in her voice when she answered, 'Oh, I shouldn't think it'll be any time soon. Probably another two or three months at least, I should say.'

He nodded. 'Then this money might come in handy for her if her uncle is unable to work.'

'Oh, our Jeremiah ain't short of a bob or two,' she boasted proudly. 'He's got a thrivin' hardware shop in the town an' staff to run it if he ain't there, so they'll not go short.'

'That's good to hear.' They lapsed into silence while she made the tea and as soon as it was poured, he drank it hastily and departed, leaving Alice to ponder on why he should have come. The excuse that he owed Amber money didn't quite ring true somehow. But there were nets waiting to be mended and as soon as she became absorbed in her task, she forgot all about him.

Barnaby, meanwhile, was galloping homewards, content that at least now Amber's uncle should not be too hard to find. After all, he thought, how many hardware shops could there be in Scarborough? And once he found the uncle, he would find Amber.

Chapter Seven

'I was thinking,' Jeremiah said hesitantly to Amber one evening as they sat at dinner. 'Perhaps it's time you stopped working in the shop now.'

When she raised an eyebrow, he flushed and nodded towards her stomach. 'Your, er . . . condition is becoming more noticeable and I wouldn't like my customers to think that I was taking advantage of you.'

Amber sighed. She knew her uncle was right. Only the night before she had sat up until the early hours of the morning letting the waist of her dress out yet again, but the thought of the long days ahead with nothing to do filled her with dread. At least when she was working in the shop, she didn't have time to think about the way Barnaby had betrayed her.

'Very well, Uncle. If you think that is for the best.'

'I do,' he said, looking very uncomfortable. 'And I hope you don't mind me asking, but have you thought of what you might do once the baby has arrived.'

Her hand dropped to her stomach where the child was kicking lustily. It was funny, since she had started to feel it moving inside her, her feelings towards it had changed. She still had no intention whatsoever of keeping it, that was quite out of the question, but she knew now that she could no longer bear to just leave it on the steps of the poorhouse. Instead, she and Mrs Carter had come to an agreement. Once the baby was born it was Mrs Carter who would take it there saying that she had found the babe abandoned. At least that way Amber would know that the child had been passed into safe hands.

'I was planning on going back to Whitby to my old job, but I've had second thoughts about that and have no idea where I might go or what I might do yet.' She crossed her fingers behind her back as she said it knowing that she would never return to Greenacres now. It would be too painful to see Barnaby every day.

Eager to change the subject her uncle asked, 'And have you heard from your mother lately?'

Amber nodded. 'Yes, I had a letter from her only the day before yesterday. She says that it's becoming very busy in Whitby now that they've started on the trainline. It's going to run into Pickering and will make it much easier for the fishermen to get their catches transported inland. And she says that both Ted and Will are actually thinking of leaving the shipyard and going to work on the tracks.'

'Hm, but what happens when the track is finished?' he queried sensibly.

'Well, they've already looked into that, apparently. Once that train is running there are new lines springing up all across the country, so it seems the boys wouldn't be short of work for years to come. The only trouble is they would live where they were working and I don't think our mam is too keen on that idea. Still, as I told her when I replied to her letter, they're young men now and quite capable of choosing what they want to do.'

'Quite.' He dabbed at his lips with his napkin and poured himself another glass of wine. He and Amber had slipped into a routine now and he found her surprisingly good company for a young woman. She was very intelligent and loved to read the newspaper each day when he had finished with it so was able to converse on most anything. They'd discussed politics, travel and all manner of things and already he had realised that he would miss their chats when she left. In fact, her company had suddenly made him realise what a lonely existence he led. But that was life, he supposed.

'Uncle,' she said then, bringing his thoughts back to the present. 'I know it's not my place to tell you this because it's really none of my business, but as you know, Mrs Carter and I have taken to having a stroll together some evenings after dinner and I couldn't help but notice that . . .' She paused, wondering if she should go on. She shrugged inwardly, in for a penny in for a pound, she decided, before continuing, 'Well, the thing is I've noticed how she stops to stroke almost every dog we meet and when I mentioned it, she confessed it had always been a desire of hers to have her own little dog.'

Jeremiah's eyebrows almost got lost in his hairline and Amber gulped, wondering if she had overstepped the mark.

'*A dog*?' he looked incredulous.

'Yes, but only a little 'un and then she could keep it in the kitchen and the yard. You wouldn't even have to see it if you didn't want to,' Amber said cajolingly. 'And she'd be so delighted. She's such a nice woman and I think it would do her good.'

'I'd never even thought of owning a pet, let alone having one in the house,' he admitted.

Amber smiled at him. 'So what do you think of the idea?' she persisted. 'A lady we meet often on the beach was telling us that a friend of hers has the most adorable litter of miniature dachshunds.'

When he looked at her uncomprehending she rushed on, 'Some people call 'em sausage dogs. They're quite low to the ground with long bodies.'

'Hm, then I suppose I'd better give it some thought,' he answered, not wishing to commit himself to anything.

'In that case you should have this,' Amber said with a cheeky grin as she fumbled in the pocket of her gown to take out a scrap of paper. 'This is the address of the lady who has the puppies. She only lives over in Queen Street just off the north bay and I thought if you'd even entertain the idea you might want to go an' have a look at 'em.'

'Humph!' Her uncle ignored the piece of paper and when she asked to be excused from the table, Amber wondered if her request had perhaps upset him. But then, she reasoned, he didn't have to do anything he didn't want to.

She went up to her room then to give Biddy time to clear the pots from the dining-room table and shortly after, she met Mrs Carter in the hall and they set off for their walk along the front. There was a Punch and Judy kiosk on the beach and they paused to watch the children's faces as they giggled and clapped at Mr Punch with glee whist their parents looked fondly on. Others were busily building sandcastles with brightly painted tin buckets and spades while a few more daring children were paddling in the sea. The town was becoming busy with holidaymakers now and Amber couldn't help but think how nice it must be to be able to afford to stay in a hotel and be waited on – not that she begrudged them their break. It was nice to see so many happy, smiling faces.

'My uncle informed me tonight that he don't think I should work in the shop anymore,' Amber told Mrs Carter as they leant on the iron railings overlooking the beach that ran all along the sea front.

'Oh, and how do you feel about that?'

Amber shrugged. 'I suppose he's right. The least people that know about this the better an' I am showin' well now.'

'In that case we shall have to find you something to do,' Mrs Carter told her. 'I've got some nice soft linen, perhaps you could make some little nightdresses for when the baby comes.'

Amber's face became solemn as she shook her head. 'What would be the point, seein' as I ain't goin' to keep it? I dare say they supply the clothes for the babies at the poorhouse.'

'Even if they do, you'll need to keep it just for a few days or so and we'll need to make sure it has something to wear,' Mrs Carter pointed out sensibly.

Suddenly the pleasure had gone from the evening for Amber and saying that she was rather tired she turned back towards her uncle's house. Once there she went to her room where she lay on the bed, crying broken-heartedly. Suddenly everything seemed such a mess and she wondered if her life would ever be the same again. And all because she'd believed Barnaby Greenwood when he had told her that he loved her and that they would be together one day. She had fallen in love with him and gone into his arms like a lamb to slaughter, but she had meant nothing to him and now she must pay the price.

Two nights later, after a boring day sitting at her bedroom window watching the world go by, Amber tidied herself and went downstairs to wait for her uncle to return from work so that they could have dinner together. He was usually so punctual that you could have set the clocks by him, but tonight six fifteen came and went and there was still no sign of him. By the time it got to seven o'clock Mrs Carter was clearly very disturbed.

'Oh dear, I do hope he hasn't had an accident. This is most unlike him,' Martha Carter fretted as she stared along the road from the window for at least the tenth time in as many minutes. 'I'd better go and get Biddy to put his dinner on a pan of water on the stove or it will be stone cold and ruined. Would you like yours now?'

Amber shook her head, feeling sorry for the woman. She obviously cared a great deal for her uncle and she just wished he wasn't so blind that he couldn't see it. 'No, thank you, I'll wait for Uncle Jeremiah,' she told her.

'Then I'll get Biddy to keep yours warm too,' Mrs Carter said, bustling away to try and save their meal.

Deep down Amber was getting a little concerned too. Her uncle was a creature of habit, and in the time she'd been living there she'd never known him to be late for his meal once.

At last, at almost half past seven, she heard a key in the lock of the front door and she hurried from the dining room at the same time as Mrs Carter appeared from the kitchen. Suddenly, they both stopped dead in their tracks as they stared towards Jeremiah who was standing there with a large bag in one hand and a squirming puppy in the other, his face red with embarrassment.

'Wh-what's this?' Martha Carter surged forward with a look of wonder on her face and he thrust the puppy into her arms.

'Er . . . Amber mentioned that she thought you'd like a dog,' he said gruffly. 'So I, er . . . got you this one . . . It's a bitch.'

'Oh Jeremiah, she's just *perfect*,' Mrs Carter breathed in delight, her eyes shining.

Suddenly Jeremiah noticed how attractive she looked when she blushed, which made him blush all the more. It was the first time she had ever addressed him by his Christian name and he found that he quite liked it.

'So, er . . . is dinner spoilt?' he asked for want of something to say. Amber had crossed to pet the little dog too and he almost felt as if he mightn't have been there. Both women were clearly very taken with her.

'Oh yes . . . yes, of course, your meal.' Mrs Carter was so thrilled with her gift that she'd completely forgotten about his dinner but now she turned and rushed back to the kitchen.

Amber looked on with a broad smile on her face as her uncle said awkwardly, 'I got some dog food, dog dishes and a collar and lead for her. I wasn't sure what else a dog might need but I'm sure you two will be able to see to anything else.'

Amber took the bag from him, resisting the urge to stand on tiptoe and kiss his cheek. Although she had told him how much Mrs Carter would love a pet, she really hadn't expected him to act on it and it just went to show that he was wasn't as hard as he liked to make out.

'That was a lovely thing for you to do, Uncle,' she told him softly. 'I'll just take these through to the kitchen and then we can have our dinner.'

'Hmm!' He quickly strode away to wash his hands, and when Amber entered the kitchen she found Mrs Carter and Biddy both down on their knees fussing over the new member of the household as she furiously licked every part of them she could reach.

'She's just adorable,' Mrs Carter declared. 'And I can't believe that Mr Harding would do such a kind thing.' Then, suddenly remembering the meals, she went to rise.

Amber held her hand up. 'No, you settle her in,' she urged. 'I'll take our dinners through on a tray. Oh, and you might like to think what you're going to call her. She'll have to have a name, won't she?'

Mrs Carter grinned as the little dog rolled on her back for a tummy rub. 'I think I shall call her Fancy,' she declared and both Biddy and Amber nodded their approval. It suited her somehow.

By the time Amber had placed the meals on the table her uncle was seated and she smiled. 'I believe the new addition to the family is going to be called Fancy,' she informed him and again he looked uncomfortable as he ran his finger round the inside of his shirt collar.

'Hm, just so long as they clean up after it and I don't find dog hairs everywhere,' he said and again Amber grinned.

When she and her uncle had eaten, Amber spent the rest of the evening in the kitchen with Biddy, Mrs Carter and the puppy and by bedtime the new addition to the household had all three of them wrapped around her little paw.

'I might sleep in here in the chair with her tonight,' Mrs Carter mused as the puppy finally fell into an exhausted doze on her lap. 'If it's her first night away from her mother she might fret and I don't want her disturbing Mr Harding.'

'Of course not.' Amber stifled a grin as she winked at Biddy over Mrs Carter's shoulder, and then she set off for her evening stroll along the front.

She had gone no more than a few yards when she glimpsed a young couple strolling arm in arm ahead of her and when she looked more closely, she saw that it was Daisy and young Archie who worked in her uncle's shop. They were staring into each other's eyes, clearly absorbed in each other, and although she was pleased for them, Amber felt a little pang of envy and smiled sadly at the thought that because of the illegitimate child she was carrying, no one would ever look at her as Archie was gazing at Daisy. Once they knew that she had had a child out of wedlock she would be classed as soiled goods and shunned.

Suddenly all the pleasure had gone from the evening and turning about abruptly she made her way back to her uncle's with a heavy heart.

Chapter Eight

August 1845

Barnaby leant down to kiss his wife's cheek and tried to present her with the roses that the gardener had just picked for her, but she turned her face away and pouted.

'I don't *want* them,' she said peevishly, pushing the flowers away. 'The scent gives me a headache.'

'Oh, I'm sorry, my dear, I didn't know.'

Mrs Ruffin frowned at her young mistress. In fairness to the master, he was doing everything he could for her, but nothing was ever good enough for her. In fact, she scowled at him the second he entered the room and once again Ruffy felt quite sorry for him.

'Now there's no need to sound so ungrateful, lass,' she gently scolded. And then to the master, 'Why don't you get one of the maids to put them in the hallway, sir? They'll look a treat in there.'

'Er . . . right, Mrs Ruffin, I will. But is there anything you need, Louisa?'

She turned her head to glare at him her hand resting on the mound of her stomach and he hastily backed away.

'Very well. I'm just going to the shipyard; I have a few things I need to see to so if you need me, I'll be there.'

'Why would I need *you*?' she said cuttingly.

Realising he wasn't welcome, Barnaby hurriedly left the room.

'You were a bit harsh on him weren't yer?' Mrs Ruffin remarked as she plumped up the cushions on the chair Louisa was sitting on at the open window.

'Serves him right!' Louisa answered curtly. 'Just look at the state of me. I've forgotten what it's like to feel pretty. I'm just a fat blob now and still some weeks to go!'

'That'll pass in the blink of an eye. Now put your feet up on this stool. We don't want your ankles swelling up again, do we? An' then per'aps after lunch we could take a stroll round the gardens. A little bit of exercise will do you the power o' good.'

'What! And have the gardeners staring at me as if I'm a beached whale! I think *not*!' Louisa snorted, working herself up into a tantrum.

Ruffy sighed as she collected up the clothes that needed washing. As much as she adored her young mistress there were times lately when she had tried her patience to the limit, so without another word, she swept out of the room leaving her to it. Hopefully by the time she got back Louisa would have calmed down a little.

Later that afternoon the doctor called in to see that all was well and as before he was mildly concerned. The child's heartbeat wasn't strong and Louisa was only weeks away from giving birth. He could only pray that this pregnancy wasn't going to end in yet another stillborn baby because he knew how much it meant to Barnaby to have a child. Still, it was out of his hands, all he could do was keep a check on her and hope for the best, but as he left, he wasn't feeling optimistic.

Once he had concluded his work at the shipyard, Barnaby rode his stallion up to the ruins of Whitby Abbey and tethered him to a tree before going to sit and look out to sea. He usually found a measure of peace here but today it eluded him as he thought of his wife's attitude earlier in the day. She clearly loathed being with child and as much as he hated to admit it, he now realised that it wouldn't be fair to put her through it again, which meant that if this pregnancy didn't end well, the intimate side of his marriage would be over forever and he would never have an heir. He sighed as he watched the waves breaking onto the beach far below him, while the seagulls swooped and squawked above him. There had been a time when he had been so smitten with Louisa that he could think of nothing but her, but over the years his feelings had changed. Once he had found her spoilt nature amusing, but now he found it irritating. Looking back, he couldn't remember ever holding an intelligent conversation with her. Her head was too full of the latest fashions and the characters in the romance novella's she was so fond of reading.

But none of that, he knew now, could excuse his abominable behaviour towards young Amber Ainsley. She had been as pure as the driven snow the first time she had lain with him and had loved him unreservedly, asking nothing in return – unlike Louisa, whose demands for fripperies were constant. And when that had resulted in her being with child, he had callously ordered her to get rid of it as if that little life had meant nothing. Only now did he realise how wrong he had been to do that, because that would have been his child just as much as the one Louisa was carrying, even if it was illegitimate. Time and time again he had stifled the urge to go to Scarborough and track her down just to apologise and make sure that she was all right, but each time he had found some excuse to put it off; probably, he admitted now, because he was so ashamed of himself.

Suddenly he made a decision; her brother Will had told him where he might find her uncle's shop some time ago and once he had tracked that down he knew he would have no trouble finding Amber. He would go to see her as soon as possible – tomorrow in fact – and he would beg her forgiveness. He would also see that she had ample funds until she returned to work, and he would promise her that he would never again take advantage of her. He couldn't expect her ever to forget how badly he had treated her or what he had put her through, but that would be a little salve for his conscience at least. Feeling slightly better he strode back to his horse and after springing lightly into the saddle he turned him in the homeward direction.

He had barely entered the hallway when he met Mrs Ruffin coming down the stairs to fetch a cool drink for her mistress and she asked if she might have a private word with him.

'Of course, Mrs Ruffin, come into my office.' He still found it hard to address her as Ruffy, despite the fact that his wife and the rest of the staff did. 'So what seems to be the problem?' he asked once the door was shut firmly behind them.

'Well . . . I don't quite know how to tell you this,' she said regretfully. 'But the doctor called earlier and he seemed a bit concerned about the baby's progress.'

'In what way?'

'He thinks it feels very small fer the stage Louisa's at and it isn't as active as he'd have liked it to be,' she told him soberly. 'Added to that he said the heartbeat sounds thready.' Seeing the concern pucker his brow, she rushed on, 'Of course it could be that everything will be fine, but I just thought . . .' When her voice trailed off, he mopped his brow with his handkerchief and plopped heavily onto his leather desk chair with a sigh.

'I think what you're trying to tell me is that you fear this child could be born dead like the last two?'

She chewed on her lip before slowly nodding. 'I reckon there's a good chance of it, sir. This is exactly what happened with the last two little mites that were born sleeping. But there, I'm no doctor, so let's just pray that I'm wrong. All we can do is prepare for the worst and hope fer the best, isn't it?'

She slowly turned and made her way out of the room leaving him to sit there staring miserably from the window, feeling as if his heart were breaking. Could this be his punishment for treating Amber as he had? he wondered.

At that moment down in Whitby, Alice Ainsley was just settling herself at the table with a pot of tea and a letter from Amber to enjoy. As yet she hadn't managed to visit her daughter at her brother's house so she looked forward to the letters that Amber wrote on a regular basis. The door into the yard was propped wide open to let the breeze in, and with a sigh of contentment she started to read.

Dear Mam,

Well, so much has happened since I last wrote to yer that I barely know where to start. Do yer remember I told yer about Archie, the young chap that worked for Uncle Jeremiah in the shop? Well, I had a bad feeling that he were looking on me as wife material so I directed him towards a young maid that comes into the shop regular. She lives just up the road an' she's a lovely girl. Anyway, the long an' the short of it is they are now walkin' out together an' I couldn't be more pleased for them. They really do make a lovely couple.

But the biggest surprise is Uncle Jeramiah. A while ago I dropped a hint to him that Mrs Carter would love a puppy and before I knew it he only goes out and buys her one. She's a lovely little thing and Mrs Carter has named her Fancy. But you'll never guess the next bit – now all of a sudden Uncle is going for a stroll each evening after dinner with Mrs Carter when she takes the dog for a walk and they seem to be getting on like a house on fire! Who knows, we might have a wedding in the offing, eh? But we'll have to wait and see.

As for me, well all I can say is I'm so bored!!!! Since Uncle stopped me working in the shop time hangs heavy on me hands and I can't wait to come home and look for a new post.

Alice sighed; Amber was always careful never to mention the baby she was carrying in case one of her brothers or her father saw the letter. They still had no idea that Amber was with child and she prayed it would stay that way. But Alice could read between the lines and it saddened her that she couldn't be with her only daughter to help her through this difficult time.

Still, I don't reckon it will be too much longer now. I can hardly wait to see yer an' the rest of me family again. Till then, take care an' stay safe,
   All my love,
   Amber xxx

As she finished reading, a shadow appeared in the doorway and glancing up Alice saw Molly Preston standing there.

''Ello, lass. My Bertie asked me to call round to see if you'd any news of when Amber might be home.'

Alice shook her head as she hastily returned the letter to its envelope and tucked it into her pocket.

'Not as yet I'm afraid,' she informed her neighbour. 'That was a letter I was readin' off her just then as it happens but she didn't mention when she might be back.'

'Oh, that's a pity, our Bertie is missin' her somethin' awful.'

Alice grinned. 'Well, he didn't appear to be missin' her that much when he come by here last night with young Betsy Piper hangin' off his arm.'

Mrs Preston sniffed. 'Ah, but these lasses who chase after him don't mean a thing,' she said in her son's defence. 'An' who can blame 'em? He is the best-lookin' young man here-abouts, ain't he? But at the end o' the day it's your Amber he's set his cap at as wife material. Ain't it always been took for granted atween the two families that they'd wed one day?'

'I can't say as I've ever even considered it,' Alice said hastily. 'I don't think our Amber is anywhere near ready to think of settling down yet and even when she does, I hope it will be wi' a young man of her choosin'.' But then seeing the hurt expression on her neighbour's face she said quickly, 'Why don't you come an' sit yerself down, Molly. There's a fresh pot o' tea here. What do you say? I might even find a bit o' cake to go wi' it.'

Suddenly Mrs Preston was smiling again; she was never one to turn down a bit of free grub, and so she shuffled over to the table, smelling far worse than any of the fishing nets Alice had been mending that morning, and greedily watched Alice fetch a fresh fruit cake from the pantry.

Chapter Nine

'I shall be away for most of the day today, darling,' Barnaby informed his wife the following morning. She was sitting at her dressing table in a floaty peignoir trimmed with feathers as Mrs Ruffin brushed her shining hair, and her fragile beauty almost took his breath away. Her expression, however, did not.

'Oh, it's all right for *you*, isn't it?' She glared at him in the mirror. 'You can go *wherever* you like *whenever* you like, whereas I am stuck in here like a prisoner!' And then as an afterthought, 'Where are you going anyway?'

'To Scarborough. I have a possible client there. A gentleman wanting a new trawler built.' He crossed his fingers behind his back hoping his face wouldn't give him away. He wished now that he had gone before but with work and one thing and another he had always found a reason to delay the visit.

Louisa shrugged as she turned back to the mirror and attempted to pinch a little colour into her pale cheeks, and feeling that he had been dismissed, Barnaby quietly left the room and hurried to the stable block.

'I've saddled Major for you today seein' as you're goin' a fair distance, sir. He's a stayer is old Major, but don't forget to stop about every five mile or so to gi' him a good drink an' a short rest.'

'I won't, Jimmy.' Barnaby swung himself up into the saddle and within minutes they were trotting down the drive.

It was a beautiful clear day with powder-puff clouds floating in an azure sky but Barnaby was so focused on where he was going that he found little joy in it. Because the weather was mild, he decided to take the coastal path and once he came to a good stretch of grass, he urged Major into a gallop. It was some fourteen miles or so to Scarborough and seeing as the weather was in his favour, he estimated he should be there for lunchtime.

Some five or six miles further on he stopped at an inn for a jug of ale and to give the horse a short rest. He didn't normally drink so early in the day but he reasoned that the drink would not only quench his thirst but steady his nerves for when he finally tracked Amber down – as he had no doubt he would.

As he had hoped, it was approaching lunchtime when the town came into view and he slowed the horse to a trot for the last part of the journey. Once he entered the cobbled streets, he found a stable where he left Major to rest and before leaving, he asked the young groom, 'Would you happen to know where Harding's hardware shop is, young man?'

'Aye, I do, sir,' the young man replied, realising by the cut of Barnaby's fine clothes and the stallion he was to tend that he was speaking to a gentleman. 'It's reet ahead o' you. Just tek your first left then the first sharp right an' you'll come to it on the left o' the street.'

Barnaby touched the brim of his hat and inclined his head before following the chap's directions and within minutes he saw the shop ahead of him. There was a young man outside the front on the pavement sweeping the shop frontage and after checking the sign above the door to make sure that this was indeed the right place, Barnaby approached him with a smile.

'Good morning, sir, or is it afternoon now?' Barnaby said jovially as the young man stood straight and leant on the broom handle. 'I'm looking for a friend of mine, Miss Amber Ainsley. I believe her uncle owns this shop and she's been living with him to take care of him while he's ill.'

Archie narrowed his eyes and scratched his head. 'Aye, Amber's stayin' wi' him all reet,' he agreed. 'But Mr Hardin' ain't been ill so far as I know.'

'Oh . . .' Barnaby was slightly confused but hiding it quickly he went on, 'Then I must have got it wrong. Is she here? I'm sure she'll be pleased to see me. I bring her news from home.'

Archie stared at him suspiciously for a moment but then deciding that the man looked perfectly respectable he shook his head. 'No, she ain't here, sir. Amber ain't worked in the shop for a while now. She'll be at Mr Hardin's house.'

'I see.' Barnaby frowned as he stroked his chin. 'Then I wonder if you might point me in the right direction? Amber did give me the address but when I stabled my horse back there, I realised that I'd come without it and I really don't want to have to go back without being able to tell her mother I've seen her.'

Again Archie hesitated but only for a moment. 'Mr Harding's house is named "Marine View". It's in Royal Albert Road.'

He proceeded to give Barnaby yet more directions and soon after Barnaby found himself making his way through a labyrinth of little cobbled streets. He could hear the sound of the waves breaking on the beach close by and above him the seagulls mewed and dipped and dived to pick amongst the cobblestones for a juicy worm or any other small particles of food they might find.

It wasn't long before he turned into Royal Albert Drive and found the house. It was not on the scale of Greenacres but it was a fine-looking house all the same and he thought how Amber must have enjoyed staying there after the cramped little cottage in Argument's Yard where she had been brought up. After taking a deep breath he climbed up the steps and rapped on the door with the heavy brass knocker and seconds later he heard the tap tap tap of footsteps beyond coming closer.

'Yes'm, sir?'

He found himself staring into the face of a maid whose mop cap was all askew, but before he could tell her why he was there an older woman in a staid dove-grey gown came up behind her and told the girl kindly, 'Go and start slicing the bread for lunch, Biddy, I'll see to this.' She turned to Barnaby and asked politely, 'May I help you, sir?'

He swallowed so hard that his Adam's apple bobbed up and down before he nodded and said hastily, 'Er . . . yes, ma'am, I'm hoping you can. I've come to see Miss Amber Ainsley.'

'Oh!' To say that she looked surprised would have been putting it mildly. No one had visited Amber in all the months she had been there and this gentleman certainly didn't look like the type a girl from Amber's background would normally mix with.

'Please come in.' She opened the door to allow him to enter the hall and he saw that although it was quite sparsely furnished, it was spick and span. 'If you would tell me who is calling, I'll just inform her you are here,' she told him as he removed his hat.

He shook his head. 'Oh no, please, I've come all the way from Whitby and I'd like to surprise her.'

The woman's small white teeth bit down on her lower lip. It didn't seem right to allow a gentleman and a young unmarried girl to be alone without a chaperone, but then the young girl in question was expecting a child so she supposed there could be no harm done.

'Very well,' she agreed uncertainly, although she still wasn't at all happy about the situation. 'I believe Amber is in the drawing room.'

'And her uncle?'

Mrs Carter raised an eyebrow. 'Why, he is at work of course.'

'Oh . . .' He looked surprised but then with a nod he headed for the door she was pointing to as she went to the kitchen to get a tray of tea for the visitor.

After tapping gently, he inched the door open and there was Amber sitting in a chair at the side of the empty fire grate reading a newspaper. But this young woman was not the young maid he remembered. Her hair was loose and fell in shining waves about her shoulders and her face had a glow to it. Until she glanced up and saw him standing there, that was, and then the colour seemed to drain out of it as she dropped the newspaper and gasped.

81

'Barn— M-Mr Greenwood . . . what are *you* doing here?'
She rose from her seat as she spoke and his eyes instantly fell to the mound of her stomach.

He had suspected that she hadn't got rid of the child after visiting her mother and now his suspicions were confirmed, and strangely he felt elated. That was his child just as much as the one his wife was carrying. She, meanwhile, could only stare at him in horror. She had come to her uncle's to seek sanctuary for two reasons: the first being she was terrified of her father and brothers ever discovering that she was to have a child. They were dependent on their home and living to Barnaby Greenwood and she dreaded to think what might have happened should they ever have found out that Barnaby Greenwood was the father. Should they ever have taken revenge on him they could all have found themselves out on the street with nowhere to live and no way to support themselves. The second reason had been that she felt in Scarborough there would be no chance of ever having to see Barnaby again, and yet here he was.

They stared at each other for a moment, until he said faintly, 'The . . . baby, you decided to keep it then?'

Her chin rose as she stared at him defiantly. 'Not exactly. I have every intention of giving it up as soon as it is born but I thought it at least deserved a chance to live! But don't worry, I want nothing from you!'

Barnaby felt sweat break out on his brow and he took his handkerchief from his pocket and mopped it. 'I see,' he muttered when he was able to speak again. 'So what do you intend to do with it?'

'I hardly think that's any o' your business,' she spat as her glorious eyes flashed. She had no fear of him – after all, she reasoned, he would hardly want her condition to become common knowledge.

It was funny, he thought, as he stood there unsure what to say, he had always thought her attractive, but now dressed in decent clothes and with the glow of a mother-to-be about her she was beautiful and he suddenly realised that he had missed her.

He sat down heavily on the nearest chair just as Mrs Carter entered the room. Amber, she noticed immediately, was gripping the back of a chair and looked as though she could have been facing an opponent in a boxing ring. Placing the tray down, she asked, 'Is this man bothering you, my dear? Would you like me to ask him to leave?' She had become very fond and protective of Amber and had no intention of allowing anyone to upset her, especially now she was so close to giving birth.

'No . . . it's all right, Mrs Carter. This man is Mr Greenwood, he is— *was* my employer and I was just surprised to see him, that's all.'

'I see. Then would you like me to stay?'

Amber shook her head. 'No . . . thank you. I'm sure Mr Greenwood won't be stayin' for long.'

'Very well, I shall be just along the corridor if you should need me.' Mrs Carter shot the visitor a scathing look as she swept out of the room in a rustle of stiff cotton petticoats.

'So, would you like some tea afore you go?' Amber asked shortly. It seemed rude not to offer and now she was curious to find out why he had come.

'I, er . . . yes, yes that would be very nice, thank you.' Barnaby yanked at the collar of his shirt and watched as she waddled across to the tray and strained the tea into two china cups before adding milk and sugar.

She handed him his cup and saucer, and after taking a seat again she asked bluntly, 'So why have yer come, Mr Greenwood? An' how did you know where I was?'

'In answer to your second question, your brother told me that you were caring for your sick uncle in Scarborough. And in answer to the first, I suppose I came to try and ease my conscience and apologise to you. I realise that I behaved shamefully towards you and I just wish that I could turn the clock back. I came to reimburse you for lost wages and to tell you that your job is still waiting for you when you wish to return. And, of course, to also assure you that I shall never act in such an ungentlemanly manner towards you again so you need have no fear.'

'Huh!' Amber tossed her head, her glorious tawny eyes gleaming in the sun that poured in through the window. 'Well, you've done it now but I don't want your money, Mr Greenwood, and I can assure you I shall *never* work for you again.'

His expression tightened. 'May I just point out that all you had to do was say no if my advances were so abhorrent to you and I would have stopped,' he said haughtily.

Amber snorted as her eyes flashed hatred. 'Oh yes, of course I could have,' she snarled sarcastically. 'And you in a position to turn my whole family out of work! And anyway, why would I? You told me you loved me and that one day we would be together for always. And fool that I was I believed every word that you said.'

He looked as if he had been slapped but the conversation was stopped abruptly when Mrs Carter entered the room again after hearing their raised voices.

'Is everything all right, dear?' She glanced anxiously between the two of them and suddenly Amber's shoulder's sagged as she turned towards the window to hide the tears that had sprung to her eyes.

'Yes, Mrs Carter, everything is fine. I believe that Mr Greenwood was just about to leave.'

Barnaby rose from his seat and he too was calm now as he said quietly, 'Please allow me to stay a little longer. I want to help.'

'How can you? What's done is done.' Amber's voice held a wealth of sadness and she didn't care if Mrs Carter knew who he really was any more. Only Nancy back at Greenacres knew who the father of her child was, but she trusted her uncle's housekeeper to keep her secret.

'I accept that,' he said humbly. 'But at least let me make things a little easier for you. I ask again what you intend to do with the child once it is born.'

'I intend to deliver it to the poorhouse. At least it will be cared for there,' she said dully. 'There can be no question o' me keepin' it, can there? We'd both suffer. I'd be known as a fallen woman an' the bairn would always be known as an illegitimate bastard an' it don't deserve that. Poor soul didn't ask to be born, did it?'

Barnaby stood there looking thoughtful before saying, 'Then let me be responsible for it. It is my child too, after all. I can arrange for it to go to a loving family and be fostered. Surely that will be better than being left to the mercy of the poorhouse. Everyone knows that many children left there rarely reach their first birthday because of lack of proper care.'

Mrs Carter intervened then when she addressed Amber to say, 'It does sound like the best solution for the child, Amber. Won't you consider it?'

Amber shrugged and remained silent before asking, 'And how would we do that?'

'If you could get word to me when the child has arrived, I would arrange for it to be fetched and placed with a family. And I promise that I would choose wisely. That way you can get on with your life safe in the knowledge that it has gone to a good home.'

She sneered. 'An' meantime you'll no doubt be makin' the most o' your *other* baby? The legitimate one that'll be born wi' a silver spoon in its mouth. I heard me an' your wife are expectin' our babies round about the same time.'

He had the grace to look embarrassed. 'Er . . . yes, I believe you are. But surely that is irrelevant. We obviously both want what is best for the child you are carrying.'

'Just consider it, Amber.' Mrs Carter shot a look of such disgust at Barnaby that he visibly cringed. But even so she could see the sense in what he was suggesting.

'I'll think about it,' Amber murmured, still refusing to look at him. She wanted to run at him and rake her finger-nails down his handsome face, but what good would that do? 'An' when I've made me mind up whether or not to take you up on the offer, I'll write an' let you know.'

Realising that he could do no more to persuade her for now, he lifted his hat and gave a stiff little bow to Mrs Carter before removing a small bundle of rolled notes from his waistcoat pocket and placing them on the table that held the tea tray. 'For any expenses that may be incurred,' he said quietly and with what dignity he could muster he left.

'Well!' Mrs Carter said when they heard the front door close behind him. 'What a turn up for the books! You could knock me down with a feather. Whyever didn't you tell us that it was your employer who had taken advantage of you? Your uncle will be incensed when he finds out.'

'No!' Amber shook her head. 'He must never know,' she said decisively. 'No good could ever come of it if he caused a fuss. Like I just told him, all me family rely on him fer their jobs an' I don't want them to suffer.'

Mrs Carter looked concerned but she nodded all the same. 'Very well. It will be as you say but I urge you to consider his offer, for the baby's sake at least. Won't you be able to have a clearer conscience if you at least know it is in a decent home?'

Amber remained stubbornly silent as, her mind in turmoil, she stood at the window watching the father of her child striding away along the street.

Chapter Ten

'Mrs Ruffin told me that you wished to see me, my dear?' Barnaby said as he entered his wife's bedroom early one misty September morning. Already there was a hint of autumn in the air and there was a fire roaring in the grate.

Louisa was languishing on the window seat in a loose gown of yellow silk that pooled around her. 'Yes. I've been thinking, Barnaby, and I have decided that I don't wish our child to be born here. This room has seen its share of dead babies and I wish to go somewhere there are no unhappy memories.'

'I see. And did you have somewhere in mind?'

She nodded. 'Yes, I would like to go to my parents' holiday home in Scarborough. They did say we could use it whenever we wished and it is quiet and peaceful there.'

Barnaby glanced at Mrs Ruffin with concern writ on his face. Louisa was very close to her time now so surely it wouldn't be wise for her to be travelling any distance. But Mrs Ruffin merely shook her head. She knew of old that what her young mistress wanted she would get so what would be the point of arguing with her?

'I see.' Barnaby clasped his hands behind his back as he began to pace up and down. 'But, darling, the place is no more than a cottage – a very nice cottage admittedly but I don't think your parents have visited it for years. It would need a thorough airing and cleaning and there would be no room for many of the staff.'

'I only want Ruffy with me this time when the baby comes,' she said petulantly, like the spoilt little girl she was. 'And a midwife, of course. I'm sure there will be one there who you could organise to attend.'

He scratched his head and sighed. 'And if I can manage to arrange all this, when would you want to go?'

'As soon as possible,' she answered decisively. 'Ruffy will look after me and do the cooking, won't you Ruffy, dear?'

When Mrs Ruffin nodded, Barnaby knew that he was beaten. It was ironic now that he came to think about it. He had two children due to be born to two different mothers at around about the same time, and now they would be born in the same area – although of course he would only be able to acknowledge one of them. The thought brought a scowl to his face. It was a week since he had visited Amber in Scarborough but as yet she hadn't given him an answer to his offer of finding a home for their child. If she chose not to agree to his idea, he would never know what had become of the baby and he found that this concerned him – not that there was much he could do about it but he hoped that she would look favourably on his idea.

For now, however, he had more than enough to organise if his wife persisted in going to the cottage. He would have to go there as soon as possible in order to employ some locals to prepare the house and get some shopping in and then he would have to enquire about having a reliable midwife on standby. Just when he was so busy at the shipyard as well, he thought glumly, but it couldn't be helped. It occurred to him that if he was going to Scarborough again, he might as well call and see Amber, and although he didn't relish the welcome he might receive it made sense.

The very next day he rode to Scarborough and went straight to Louisa's parents' holiday cottage. They had clearly paid a local to come in and tend the gardens as the lawns were neatly cut and the last of the summer flowers were blooming in the gardens. The cottage had a thatched roof and the sun and salt spray had weathered the outer bricks to a mellow honey colour. Here and there, ivy, honeysuckle and wisteria, no longer in flower, clambered up the walls and across the tiny leaded windows and it reminded Barnaby of a picture he had seen on a large box of chocolates he had once bought for Louisa. It was certainly a pretty place, although the inside looked dusty and tired. It was furnished with rather grand pieces of furniture that Louisa's parents no longer used in their enormous home. They looked slightly out of place in a cottage but were comfortable and practical all the same so he made enquiries at the houses nearby until he found Mrs Reed, a local woman who, for a generous fee, was prepared to go in and give it a good clean. She also recommended a good midwife who he would go and see as soon as he had Louisa settled in.

'Me an' me daughters will 'ave the whole place shinin' like a new penny fer yer wife when she arrives, sir,' she promised. 'An' durin' her stay I'll come an' fetch all her dirty laundry an' tek it back all washed an' ironed fer 'er an' all, if yer like?' Barnaby nodded and satisfied that she would keep her word he gave her the spare key, paid her a princely sum to be going on with and went back to the cottage to have a final look at what Louisa might need to bring.

In a way, he could see why she might want to come here. Perched high on a hill it overlooked the sea and there were no other residences close by, which gave it privacy. After Greenacres it appeared small to him, although it was still a sizable home, boasting four good bedrooms and an indoor water closet upstairs, and downstairs, a good-sized parlour and a large kitchen. Satisfied that he, Louisa and Mrs Ruffin would be comfortable there he locked the door and after mounting Major he turned him towards the town. Tomorrow, he decided, he would send one of the grooms ahead with a carriage containing the baby's crib and Louisa's clothes, for he had no doubt that she would insist that Mrs Ruffin pack enough gowns to dress a dozen women for at least a year. In truth he could ill afford to be away from his businesses at this time as he was surprisingly busy with orders, but it couldn't be helped if he was to be present for the birth of his child. A pang of guilt shot through him as he thought of the other child that would be born shortly. There could be no celebrating that birth but he had made Amber Ainsley a promise and if she would allow him to, he intended to go through with it. He just hoped that she had made her mind up one way or another. Time was running out and he needed to start making enquiries if he was to find a home for the child.

Scarborough was bustling with late holidaymakers when he arrived in the town and after finding a stable where he could leave his horse to be fed and watered, he set out for

Royal Albert Road. It was Mrs Carter who answered his knock at the door and she gave him a granite stare.

'You'd better come in . . . *sir.*' She held the door wide and as he stepped into the hallway, he removed his hat and gave a little bow. 'Amber is in the drawing room if you'd care to come through. I'll just tell her you are here.'

After announcing the visitor Mrs Carter left the room and Amber rose to greet him, although the look she gave him was hardly what might have been termed as welcoming.

'Good afternoon, Miss Ainsley.' His fair hair was tousled and the sun shining through the window reflected the colours in his gaily patterned waistcoat, but his smart appearance and good looks were lost on Amber. All she saw was the man who had duped her and forced her into the unfortunate position she found herself in, so she merely glared at him.

'I was in the area,' he hurried on, 'and so I thought I would call and see if you had given any more thought to my suggestion of finding a foster home for the child.'

She could have told him that she'd thought of little else but instead she nodded towards a chair and he quickly sat down. Her first instinct had been to tell him to go to the devil, she would make her own arrangements for the child, but as Mrs Carter had pointed out, surely she would have an easier conscience if she at least knew that the baby was to be placed with people who would love and care for it.

And so taking a deep breath she nodded. 'Yes I have, an' yes you can go ahead.'

His face broke into a wide smile and she found herself thinking back to the happy times they had spent together – not that it would cut any ice with her. She had seen both sides of him now and she would never forgive him for what he had done to her.

'Very well, I shall start to make enquiries immediately.' He smiled again but when she didn't respond he asked tentatively, 'And have you decided what you are going to do when you leave here?'

'That ain't none o' your concern,' she said sharply, flicking a lock of her shining curls across her shoulder.

'But I feel that it is,' he pressed. 'Surely if you don't wish to return to Greenacres you will let me find you a suitable position elsewhere?'

'I'm quite capable o' lookin' after meself, you just concentrate on lookin' after the baby you foisted on me.'

He recoiled but she showed no remorse. As far as she was concerned, she owed him nothing, least of all respect, and the sooner he was gone the better she would feel. She no longer feared for her family's jobs because she knew that he wouldn't want her pregnancy to become common knowledge and she now held the power to destroy his marriage and his reputation. He had ruined her life – for what decent man would want her now that she was soiled goods? Even so, she wasn't seeking revenge, she just wanted this whole sorry episode in her life to be over. 'So how will I let you know when the baby has arrived? Shall I send word to Greenacres?'

'No, as it happens, I shall be staying here in Scarborough. If you could get word to this address.' He quickly took out a piece of paper on which he had written the address of the cottage, and after handing it to her he slowly rose. It seemed that there was no more to be said. 'I shall wait to hear from you then,' he said uncomfortably. 'And may I say that I hope that all goes well for you, Amber. Good day to you.' And with a stiff little bow he turned on his heel and let himself out.

An hour later he set off back to Whitby feeling wretched. Now he had to find someone who would care for his illegitimate child who could be trusted to keep their mouth shut, for he knew that if word ever got out about it Louisa would petition to leave him. *But would that be such a bad thing?* a little voice inside him asked. *If Louisa had been more of a wife to me, I would never have felt driven to take advantage of a maid.* But even so, he knew that this was no excuse and he urged Major into a gallop to try and escape his guilty conscience.

Three days later when everything they might need had been sent on ahead by coach, the Greenwoods and Mrs Ruffin set off for Seaview Cottage in Scarborough. Mrs Ruffin and Louisa rode in the coach, with Jimmy, Barnaby's faithful groom, driving while Barnaby rode alongside on Major. They had agreed that Jimmy would remain with them in the room above the single stable at the cottage until they returned to Greenacres – whenever that might be. Mrs Ruffin, meanwhile, as well as looking after Louisa, would do the cooking and cleaning, whilst Mrs Reed would see to their laundry. Louisa seemed happy with this arrangement, although Barnaby wished that she would have agreed to stay at home where the doctor he knew and trusted was at hand. Still, as always, her wish was his command.

As they set off, the skies were grey with a threat of rain in the air, and they had not gone very far when Louisa started to complain every time the carriage went over a bump or a rut in the road.

'I shall be black and blue by the time we get there,' she wailed as Mrs Ruffin looked on unsympathetically.

'Well, it was you as wanted to come,' she pointed out unfeelingly and Louisa pouted.

'I didn't know the roads were going to be so rough, did I?' She crossed her arms across her swollen stomach, wrapped her cloak more closely about her and stared sulkily from the window, which suited Mrs Ruffin just fine as it meant she could close her eyes, settle back against the soft leather squabs and take a nap.

The next Mrs Ruffin knew of it they had stopped at a coaching inn for refreshments. As Barnaby helped his wife down from the carriage, she stared at the inn disapprovingly.

'I hope they do hot chocolate here,' she whined. 'How much farther is it now? I don't recall it being such a distance!'

'We're about halfway. All being well, we should be there shortly after lunch and Mrs Reed has agreed to have a meal waiting for us.' He tucked her small hand into his arm and side by side they entered the inn. There were a number of people inside, many of them farmworkers who had taken a break to sneak a quick tankard of ale, and they stared at the couple curiously. The air was fuggy with tobacco smoke and Louisa noticed that the sawdust on the floor didn't look any too clean.

'I hope the water closet is cleaner than this room is,' she said with her nose in the air. 'Surely, we could have stopped somewhere a little more salubrious, Barnaby?'

He stifled a sigh as he led her to a table at the side of an inglenook fireplace where a log fire was crackling. 'I'm afraid if we hadn't stopped here, we would have had to go on for at least another hour,' he told her as patiently as he could. 'And you did say that you needed to relieve yourself.' He left her then to go to the bar to order a tankard of ale for himself and Jimmy, and a pot of hot chocolate for Louisa and Mrs Ruffin.

'Well, I must say this is nice,' Mrs Ruffin said as she took a seat and removed her gloves. 'It's like going on holiday, isn't it?'

Louisa sniffed disdainfully. 'I hardly think so, I only chose to go to the cottage because . . .'

When her voice trailed away, Mrs Ruffin felt a rush of sympathy for her. She knew that her young mistress didn't want to give birth to this child back at Greenacres in case it went the same way as the previous two she had lost and she could understand it, so she was prepared to be patient with her.

The hot chocolate was surprisingly tasty when it came, served by the landlady who was a great Amazon of a woman with ruddy cheeks, hands like hams and a ready smile.

'Off on 'oliday are yer, me lovelies?' she queried.

Louisa chose to ignore her and looked away, so, embarrassed at her mistress's rudeness, Mrs Ruffin told her, 'Yes, something like that. And thank you, this looks very nice.'

Half an hour later they were ready to set off again and within minutes Louisa was complaining loudly once more.

It had started to rain by then so the carriage was forced to slow down, which added time to their journey. But at last Scarborough came into view and soon the carriage drew up outside the cottage.

Louisa had been just a young girl the last time she had visited it with Mrs Ruffin and her parents, and she was quite excited to be having a change in her routine. 'It's bigger than I remember it,' she said approvingly after climbing down from the coach. 'I think we shall be very comfy here, Ruffy, very comfy indeed.'

She hurried on ahead of everyone, and when she entered the large kitchen she was not disappointed. As promised by Mrs Reed, everywhere was clean as a new pin and the tempting aroma of a large cottage pie was issuing from the range. There was a fire crackling in the grate and everywhere looked warm and cosy.

Mrs Ruffin followed her in while Jimmy and Barnaby took the carriage round to the stable.

'It all looks lovely,' Mrs Ruffin said approvingly as she helped Louisa take off her bonnet and cloak. 'But come along, you must be hungry and that pie smells delicious.'

Jimmy and Barnaby soon joined them and Louisa was appalled when she saw that Jimmy was going to join them for their meal. She opened her mouth to object, but as though he could read her mind, Barnaby shot her a warning glance and she angrily snapped her mouth shut, for then at least.

The meal was plain but tasty and everyone but Louisa enjoyed it. 'I would think this is the sort of meal that would be served to the staff back at Greenacres,' she said ungratefully.

Mrs Ruffin almost choked on a mouthful of food. 'Well, you'd best get used to it,' she warned, waving her fork at her. 'Because I don't pretend to be a cook and once I'm doing the cooking you might look back on this and wish you could have more of it!'

'I'm sure we shall be grateful of anything you wish to serve us, Mrs Ruffin,' Barnaby said hastily with another warning glance at his wife.

Colour flamed in Louisa's cheeks and she slammed her knife and fork down, suddenly wondering if coming here had been such a good idea after all.

Once the meal was over, Barnaby and Louisa went into the parlour where a cheery fire was burning while Mrs Ruffin cleared away the dirty pots and Jimmy went to look at the room above the stables, where he would be sleeping for the duration of their stay.

'I can't believe that you expect me to eat at the same table as our groom!' Louisa fumed as Barnaby struck a vesta and lit a cigar.

'Why ever not? We can hardly expect him to sit in the stable to eat his meals, and it was *your* idea to come here,' Barnaby pointed out. Louisa wasn't used to being spoken to that way and promptly burst into noisy tears making him feel dreadful.

'I'm sorry, darling,' he apologised. 'But you must understand this place is only a fraction of the size of Greenacres so you'll have to get used to seeing more of Jimmy while you're here.'

She dabbed ineffectively at her eyes with a scrap of lace handkerchief before turning in a swirl of cotton petticoats and heading for the door. 'I'm going to my room to rest!'

she declared. 'And I just hope that woman you hired to clean the place has put all my clothes away properly!'

Once she'd gone, Barnaby let out a weary sigh and sank into a fireside chair. Their stay at the cottage certainly hadn't got off to the best of starts and he had an awful feeling that it wasn't going to get any better.

Chapter Eleven

The following Monday afternoon, Amber was sitting in the parlour quietly reading when she heard a knock on the front door. She made to heave herself out of the chair but Mrs Carter got there before her and when the parlour door opened, she gasped with delight.

'*Mam* . . . what are you doing here?'

'That's a nice greetin', I must say,' Alice said although she was grinning from ear to ear. 'Can't a woman come an' visit her own daughter, eh?' She plonked down onto the nearest chair, her hat askew. 'Phew, I could fair do wi' a nice cuppa.'

'I'll go and organise one right away,' Mrs Carter said obligingly as she shooed Fancy ahead of her. She was always escaping from the kitchen, especially when she knew Jeremiah was due home from work, and most nights he got a royal welcome.

'So, how are you, lass?' Alice asked, her expression more serious now.

'Oh, you know . . .' Amber shrugged as she tried to sit comfortably. It was getting harder by the day and she felt like a beached whale.

'You certainly look well.' Her mother couldn't help but notice that Amber's hands, which were usually chafed and swollen from all the hard work she used to do at Green-acres, were now smooth and soft and her face was glowing with health thanks to the good food Mrs Carter had insisted she eat.

'Uncle Jeremiah and Mrs Carter have been very good to me.'

'Hm, an' are you still plannin' on takin' the infant to the foundlin' home?' Alice had spent sleepless nights fretting about the poor baby. It would be her first grandchild after all and had the circumstances been different, she would have been looking forward to it.

'Actually . . . no, I ain't anymore.' Amber flushed. 'The, er . . . father o' the baby has offered to have it fostered out to a good family. I was still fer takin' it to the foundlin' home but then me an' Mrs Carter were out one evenin' an' we saw the children from there. They were bein' taken for a walk an' they seemed . . . oh, I don't know, sad, I suppose. They were dressed in these plain brown shapeless dresses an' the girls all looked as if someone had put a basin on their heads an' cut round them. It weren't that so much that upset me though – it were the look in their eyes, they all looked so . . . hopeless.' She shook her head to clear the memory. As much as she had hated the thought of Barnaby Greenwood having anything to do with the child, she had known the evening she saw those children that she had made the right decision for the child's sake.

'So, the father . . . he must have some money if he can afford to have the child fostered out?' Alice looked at her daughter long and hard, and Amber felt herself flushing. 'An' would I be right if I were to take a guess an' say that I

101

think the father o' this bairn is Barnaby Greenwood?' Alice was no fool and she had come to that conclusion some time ago. It had to be him or one of the staff who worked at the big house, for Amber rarely saw anyone else apart from on her days off, and once he'd started turning up at her house, her suspicions had hardened.

Amber nodded miserably, there was no point in lying, and Alice sighed. 'But yer *mustn't* tell me dad or the lads. They must never know about this baby, let alone who the father is!' Amber pleaded desperately.

'Huh! Do you really think I'd be so daft?' Alice snorted. 'Why, if word were to get out one or t'other of 'em would make mincemeat of him. He should be ashamed of himself, takin' advantage of a young girl like that. But have you given any more thought to what you're goin' to do once this is all over?'

'I had thought o' workin' wi' the herrin' girls,' Amber admitted. 'But the herrin' season is almost over now so I'll have to think o' somethin' else. One things fer sure though – I won't be goin' back to Greenacres, even though the gaffer has assured me that he'll not set his hands on me again!'

She stared miserably towards the window for a moment before admitting, 'I had thought o' headin' fer London. They reckon there's lots o' jobs to be found there.'

'Huh!' Alice snorted in disgust. 'Oh aye, o' course there are, an' the streets are paved wi' gold, ain' they? That's why many o' the young lasses that head there end up sleepin' rough in shop doorways or goin' on the game. No, you can forget that idea, me girl.' And then seeing her daughter's downcast expression she reached out to squeeze her hand.

'But don't fret, lass. Somethin'll turn up, you'll see. You know the old sayin, "When one door shuts, another door opens." Let's just concentrate on gettin' this baby here safe an' sound an' then we'll decide what's to be done.' It hurt her to see her daughter so low, so she went on with a grin, 'An' what's brought about the change in Martha Carter, eh? I barely recognised her wi' her hair done softer like that an' a bit o' lace on her collar. She's always been as plain as a pikestaff but she looks quite attractive now. Would this be down to your uncle or is there another gentleman friend somewhere in the picture by any chance?'

'Actually, I think—' But Amber got no further for at that moment the person they were discussing appeared bearing a tray of tea and a jam and cream sponge cake still slightly warm from the oven.

'Here you are, Mrs Ainsley,' she said affably as she set the tray down. 'This should keep you going until dinner time. Jeremiah will be so surprised to see you. You will be staying for dinner, won't you?'

'Well, as it happens, I were hopin' you might be able to find me a bed for the night,' Alice told her. 'I could catch the mail coach back to Whitby first thing in the mornin' then an' be back in time for when the menfolk get back from sea.'

'That will be no trouble at all,' Mrs Carter assured her. 'I'll go and get the spare room ready for you right away and give you two some time to have a good catch up.'

'Ooh, Jeremiah now, is it?' Alice chuckled when she'd left the room. 'Am I missin' somethin' here?'

Amber nodded. 'Yes, as I told you in me letter, it started when I suggested to Uncle Jeremiah that I thought Mrs Carter

103

would like a pet,' she giggled. 'I guessed right from the day I got here that she had feelin's for him – it was as plain as the nose on your face. Anyway, he turns up wi' little Fancy, the dog, an' next thing they're takin' him for walks together. Then recently Uncle suggests that Mrs Carter should join us for dinner an' they seem to be gettin' on like a house on fire.'

'If that's the case I couldn't be more pleased fer him.' Alice smiled. 'She's a good woman is Martha Carter. She were married briefly a long time ago, I believe, to a fisherman but his ship went down in a storm. Not long after that your uncle bought this house an' she came to live wi' him as his housekeeper an' she's been here ever since. Nothin' would please me more than to see 'em get together for they've both led lonely lives one way or another. But now what about a slice o' that cake, eh? It's makin' me mouth water.'

Just as predicted, Jeremiah was delighted to see his sister when he arrived home that evening and dinner was a merry affair as they chatted non-stop.

'Couldn't you stay for another day or two, Alice?' he asked but she shook her head.

'Much as I'd love to, I can't. I've got to be back for when the men drop anchor else they'll think I've run off an' left 'em,' she told him and he nodded understandingly. He knew how devoted his sister was to her family and thought that this was just as it should be.

After dinner Alice joined her brother and Mrs Carter for a stroll along the front with the little dog gleefully running ahead of them on his lead and as Amber watched them go from the window, tears pricked at the back of her eyes as she realised that there would never be anyone special in her life now. Who would want her when they knew that she'd given birth to an illegitimate baby? With a sigh she returned to sewing the tiny nightdress that Mrs Carter had insisted the baby should have. They'd stitched a number of clothes between them now, although Amber knew that she would never get the chance to see the child wearing them.

There were tears when her mother took her leave early the following morning. 'Oh, I wish I could be here to help wi' the birth,' Alice fretted. 'Promise you'll send word the minute it's born, won't you? I'll burn the letter then, just in case your dad or one o' the lads reads it,' she promised.

After she'd left, Amber felt totally bereft, wondering how she would manage to give birth without her mother by her side.

Just one-week later Amber came down to breakfast looking pale with dark shadows beneath her eyes, and instantly concerned, Mrs Carter asked, 'Didn't you sleep well, dear?'

'Not really,' Amber admitted, rubbing her back. 'I think I must have lay funny. I've had a dull backache all night.'

'I see. Well, sit down and have a nice hot cup of tea and some breakfast.'

Amber did as she was told but found she couldn't eat a thing. Soon she was prowling up and down, and Mrs Carter began to feel a little nervous. Never having had any children of her own she wasn't sure what signs to look for when a baby was about to make an appearance but she had a feeling that this might be the beginning of Amber's labour. She was just relieved it was a Saturday. Jeremiah would be home just after lunchtime so at least she would have moral support, if nothing else.

'Would you like me to send Biddy to fetch the midwife to have a look at you?' she offered.

Amber shook her head. 'No, I'm not having pains. It's just this damn backache. It'll probably go off in a minute.'

But it didn't go off and by mid-morning she felt worse.

Mrs Carter was hovering by the door when Jeremiah returned and the minute he stepped in, she told him, 'I think Amber is close to having the baby but she doesn't want me to send for the midwife yet.'

'I see.' Jeremiah looked almost as panicked as she did and heartily wished that Amber's mother was there; she'd know what to do whereas he and Mrs Carter didn't have a clue.

At that moment, as Mrs Carter was hanging his hat and coat on the hallstand, they heard a low moan issue from the parlour, and hurrying into the room they found Amber hanging on the back of a chair with a pool of water on the floor between her feet.

'I . . . I'm so sorry,' she panted. 'I reckon me waters have just broke all over your clean rug.' She herself had heard many babies come into the world in Argument's Yard. The people lived in such close proximity to each other that it would have been hard not to, so she had a good idea what to expect and she knew the worst was yet to come.

'Shall I send Biddy for the midwife?' her uncle asked as he tried not to panic, but still Amber shook her head.

'No, not yet. First-time mothers can be hours havin' the baby an' I ain't had no real pains yet.' The words had barely left her lips when she suddenly gasped and doubled over. She felt as if someone was tightening a steel band about her stomach and the severity of the first pain took her breath away.

As Jeremiah guided Amber to a chair and gently pressed her down into it, Mrs Carter bustled back in all of a fluster with a mop and bucket.

'So what do we do now?' Jeremiah asked, trying to conceal his panic.

'We need to time how far apart the pains are,' Amber told him and he instantly unhooked his gold Hunter watch from his waistcoat and checked the time. 'An' per'aps Mrs Carter wouldn't mind gettin' the bed ready.'

Once the pain had died away Amber felt better and began to wonder if perhaps it had been a false alarm but ten minutes later another pain had her gripping the arms of the chair.

'It's all right,' she told her uncle who had gone alarmingly pale. 'No need to send for the midwife till they're at least five minutes apart.'

It was five o'clock in the afternoon before Biddy was duly sent to find Nurse Bonnet, the midwife her uncle had employed to deliver the baby. Amber had as yet refused to go to bed but when the little woman appeared she bossily ordered her upstairs and much to his relief told Jeremiah, 'An' you can stay downstairs, if you please, sir. The birthing room is no place for a gentleman, although I'd be glad of Mrs Carter's help if only to fetch me hot water and towels.'

'Of course.' Mrs Carter gave a faltering smile, although she was quaking in her shoes. She'd never attended a birth before and had no notion what to expect, but she had an idea it wasn't going to be pleasant.

Nurse Bonnet had come highly recommended. She was a tiny woman almost as far round as she was high with white hair and faded blue eyes. Over the years she had delivered hundreds of babies so at least Jeremiah felt that his niece was in safe hands.

'Reet then, lass, get your arm round my neck an' we'll get you into bed,' she told Amber in a no-nonsense voice and, too afraid to refuse, Amber obliged.

As the evening progressed Jeremiah paced up and down in the parlour, too worried to even concentrate on his newspaper or take Fancy for a walk. Slowly the wails from upstairs were becoming louder and closer together and he had never felt more helpless in his life. But he trusted Nurse Bonnet and that gave him a measure of comfort. Biddy had been running up and down all night with jugs of hot water and towels and now she looked worn out, but her work wasn't over yet nor would it be until the baby arrived.

Ten and eleven o'clock chimed on the grandfather clock in the hallway and then midnight, by which time Jeremiah was convinced something must be terribly wrong.

'Run up and ask Nurse Bonnet if she wants me to fetch the doctor,' he urged Biddy.

She was back in no time. 'Nurse says everythin' is goin' along fine, sir, an' it shouldn't be long now.' And then suddenly another sound floated down the staircase and they stared at each other. It was the sound of a newborn baby's cry and Jeremiah was sure nothing had ever sounded so sweet.

'Thank God,' he whispered as he went to stand at the foot of the stairs. Minutes later Mrs Carter appeared with a tiny bundle wrapped in a white shawl in her arms and started down the stairs towards him.

'It's a little girl, Jeremiah.' Her voice was full of wonder. 'A very *beautiful* little girl.' As she gently folded the shawl back, he found himself staring down into a tiny face. 'And look, the midwife calls this an angel's kiss.' She pointed to a small heart-shaped birthmark on the infant's thigh.

'She is truly special then. And Amber?'

'Doing fine. She was so brave,' she said with a catch in her voice. 'But now would you mind coming into the kitchen with me to hold her while I prepare some water for her bath.'

'Of course.' Once in the kitchen Jeremiah sank down into Mrs Carter's favourite chair and when she placed the newborn in his arms he smiled down at her, his joy at her birth tinged with sadness.

'I don't think it's going to be as easy for Amber to give her up as she thought it would be,' he said quietly and Mrs Carter nodded in agreement.

'I know. She wouldn't even look at her and she was crying so hard she couldn't catch her breath, but what else can the poor lamb do? She wants to feel she's doing the best for the baby.'

They both fell silent.

'Well . . . there is something . . .' he said hesitantly.

'Oh yes, and what would that be?

'They could both stay here with us!' When Mrs Carter stared at him in amazement, he hurried on, 'It makes sense, doesn't it? The few people who have met her since she came to stay here believe she is a young widow. They need never know any different.'

'Hm, I suppose we could put the idea to her,' she agreed pensively, although deep down she had an idea that Amber wouldn't agree to it. Other people might not know but Amber would, and the girl had morals.

Once the baby was bathed and dressed in one of the tiny nightshirts Amber and Mrs Carter had made, she was carried upstairs to her mother but the moment Mrs Carter entered the room with her, Amber turned her head away.

The midwife was just about to leave and if she thought it strange that the new mother was showing no interest in her baby, she didn't comment on it. 'Right, that's me done then. You know where I am if you should need me,' she told them, and keen to get home to her feather bed she quickly took her leave.

'Surely you want to see her, even if it's only just the once,' Mrs Carter urged as she stood at the side of the bed, but again Amber stubbornly refused.

'It's only going to make it harder,' she said in a wobbly voice. 'Now please take her away and send word to Mr Greenwood that she is ready to leave . . . It's better this way. There's no point in delaying it.'

And so with a heavy heart, Mrs Carter took the little one back downstairs. It appeared that Amber had made her mind up and she doubted that anything would change it.

Chapter Twelve

Nurse Bonnet had no sooner arrived back at her home and put the kettle on for a well-earned cup of tea when there was a loud banging on the door. She sighed. It looked set to be a very long night if yet another of her mothers-to-be had gone into labour!

She found Barnaby Greenwood standing on the step with a look of panic on his face. 'It's the baby, Nurse.' Despite the fact that there was a cold wind blowing in off the sea she saw he was in his shirtsleeves. 'I think it's coming. We're staying in Sea View Cottage up on the headland.'

'I know where you are reet enough,' she answered wearily. 'I'll go an' get me bag an' I'll be with you shortly. Meantime, get her into bed and get me plenty of hot water and towels ready.'

He inclined his head before racing off back to his horse and after hopping lithely into the saddle he galloped away as if the hounds of hell were after him as the nurse went back inside to prepare anything she might need for the next birth.

He had just arrived back at the cottage when he saw a cloaked figure approaching the front door and when he reined his horse to a shuddering halt, he saw that it was Mrs Carter.

'I've come to tell you that the baby has been born.' She stared at him disapprovingly.

'I see . . . was it a boy?'

'A girl, actually.' Her dislike of him was oozing out of her every pore. 'A very beautiful little girl, as it happens.'

'I see. Then I shall be there to collect her within the next few hours.'

'And you will . . . you will ensure that she goes to a good home?'

'On my honour!'

His words did nothing to reassure the woman. As far as she was concerned this was a married man who had taken advantage of a young girl in his employ and she doubted he had an ounce of honour in his body. Even so, it wasn't her place to comment on it so after nodding her head she pulled her cloak more closely about her and set off back down the steep hillside as Barnaby took his horse round to Jimmy in the stables before going to his wife.

'I reckon we should be sending for the doctor,' Nurse Bonnet said early the next morning. Louisa had been straining for hours with no sign of the birth being any nearer.

'She'll not have a doctor near her for love nor money,' Mrs Ruffin told her as she clung to her beloved young mistress's hand. 'She swears it was the doctor's fault that she lost her last two babies and she made me promise that I wouldn't let one into the room this time. That's why she didn't want to be at Greenacres for the birth.'

'I see.' The midwife stared down at the writhing figure on the bed and shrugged. 'In that case, I can only do the best I can, but I warn you, I will not be held responsible if anything should go wrong.'

'I understand,' Mrs Ruffin said gravely but as another contraction seized her mistress, she turned her attention back to her, wishing with all her heart that she could take her place.

As the minutes ticked away, Barnaby grew anxious as he paced the floor. He had just received word that his child had been born to the young maid and now within hours he would be a father again if his wife managed to produce a live child. It seemed ironic that suddenly he would be the father to two children when for years he had longed for just one!

Three days later, Amber stood on the doorstep of her uncle's house saying her goodbyes.

'I still think it's far too soon for you to be leaving,' Mrs Carter fretted whilst Biddy stood close behind her softly crying. Amber had said her goodbyes to her uncle before he left for work and she was finding that leaving them all was proving to be far more difficult than she had thought it would be.

'I shall be fine,' she assured Mrs Carter, although she really didn't feel it. Her breasts were heavy with milk and each time she thought of the little girl she had sent away she wanted to cry.

'Well at least let Biddy come with you to the mail coach and carry your bags for you,' Mrs Carter pleaded, but again Amber shook her head.

'No . . . thank you, but I'm quite capable of carrying them myself. And . . . well, thank you so much for all you've done for me over the last few months. I shall never forget it, or any of you.'

'It's been a pleasure and don't be a stranger.' Mrs Carter leant forward and gently kissed her cheek.

Worried that she'd break down if she delayed any longer, Amber turned abruptly and began to walk away. She looked back just once at the end of the road to see Mrs Carter and Biddy still standing on the step waving frantically and after lifting her hand she hurried on. It was time to go home and get on with her life.

'Ah, here you are then, lass.' When Amber stepped into the gloomy cottage her mother rushed forward and drew her to a chair before questioning tentatively, 'It's all over then?'

Amber lowered her head and nodded. 'Yes, it was a girl. She was born three days ago.'

'A girl!' Tears pricked at Alice's eyes as she thought of the granddaughter she would never meet, but forcing a smile to her face she said cheerily, 'Right miss, well you're goin' to rest fer the next few days an' don't try an' argue – I insist. An' then we'll go from there, eh?'

Later that evening a tap on the door woke Amber from a doze and when Alice went to answer it she found Bertie Preston standing on the step.

'Me mam said she saw Amber earlier on, Mrs Ainsley. Is she back from her uncle's?'

'Er . . . yes, she is.'

Without waiting to be invited, he pushed past her to see Amber sitting in the chair trying to straighten her hair.

'So yer back then.'

Amber raised an eyebrow and he chuckled. 'Daft question, eh? But why didn't yer let me know yer were comin' back?'

Amber frowned. 'I didn't know I had to,' she said tartly and had the satisfaction of seeing two spots of angry colour flame in his cheeks.

He took a deep breath and stepping towards her asked, 'So, do yer fancy comin' fer a walk? It's time you an' me got on the same page – about where we stand, I mean,' he ended when he saw her puzzled look.

'The same page?' She stared at him blankly. 'But we're mates, Bertie, we've always been mates.'

He shook his head and shot an uncomfortable glance at Alice. 'I reckon we're a lot more than that, lass,' he told her. 'Leastways, you're much more than a mate to me. I allus thought that once we were old enough, we'd . . . you know? Get wed.'

Amber's eyes stretched wide. 'I don't know what gave you that idea,' she gasped. 'I certainly didn't. I'm not thinking of marrying anyone for some long time – if ever!'

He chuckled again as he looked at her flushed face. 'Then it's high time yer did start thinkin' about it,' he said. 'You could do a lot worse than me. I'd be good to yer an' make sure as yer never wanted fer owt, so give it some thought, eh?'

Before she could answer he turned abruptly and went out the way he had come, leaving Amber and her mother to stare at each other in amazement.

'As if I'd ever be interested in the likes of Bertie Preston,' Amber snorted and was shocked when her mother lowered her eyes.

'I dare say you could do worse,' she muttered. 'An' considerin' what's happened . . .'

'Considerin' what's happened you think I should be grateful to accept anyone as will have me, is that it?' Amber's eyes were blazing with anger and hurt.

'I didn't say that!' Alice said loudly.

'No, you didn't, but it's what you meant.' Springing out of the chair Amber climbed the stairs to her little room in the attic and after throwing herself on the mattress she sobbed.

When her mother came downstairs the next morning, she was shocked to see Amber already up and dressed in her oldest clothes with a warm shawl crossed over her chest and tied at the back. She had scraped her hair into a ponytail in the nape of her neck and tied it with string and she was wrapping her hands in strips of sacking.

'What are you doin'?'

Amber looked up. 'I'm gettin' ready to go to work,' she informed her mother coolly. 'I noticed that the Scottish herring girls are still here in the harbour an' they're always glad of any help as the ships come in.'

Every year, from July to the end of September, when the herrings shoaled along the shoreline, the Scottish herring girls – or the gippers, as they were known – arrived in force to gut and pack them. While they waited for the fishing boats to come in, they were a regular sight about the town as they strolled out with the young men, much to the disgust of the local girls.

'Do you realise how hard that work is?' Alice asked, appalled. 'You're only days after giving birth and you should still be in bed by rights not goin' to work.'

Amber did know how hard the herring girls worked. They were out there in all weathers for poor pay, but she stuck her chin in the air as she finished binding her hands.

'I'm young an' strong,' she said calmly. 'An' any sort o' work I have to do to keep meself is better than havin' to marry a bloke I don't love.' And with that she turned and left as Alice bit down worriedly on her lip.

The stench of fish hit Amber as she neared the harbour and already she saw the herring girls were there getting into groups of three.

'Is there a place for me?' she asked hopefully, approaching the nearest group.

The girl looked her up and down. 'Have yer ever done this before, lassie?' She had a broad Scottish accent but she seemed friendly enough.

Amber shook her head. 'No, but I'm a very fast learner an' I ain't afraid o' hard work.'

'Then join Isla and Bridget over there an' we'll gi' you a trial.'

She pointed to two girls further down the harbour who were rolling the barrels they would need into place. Amber walked over to them, and after introducing herself they handed her a sharp knife.

Lifting a herring, Isla instructed, 'Hold the fish like this an' give one long slash like so.' The knife flashed in the weak sunshine as she sliced straight down the fish's belly from throat to tail. 'Then take out the intestines an' they go in this barrel 'ere.'

Amber knew that nothing was wasted and that the barrels of intestines would be sold to farmers to make fertiliser.

'Then the fish goes in one o' these barrels, an' when you 'ave a nice tier yer cover 'em in salt and start the next layer till yer get to the top. Which barrel the fish goes in will depend on its size, see? The cooper'll keep his eyes open to check yer puttin' 'em in the right one so try an' get it right.'

She pointed to a man who had a wooden gauge in his hand. He was the one who came along row after row, measuring the fish to ensure that they were all of a similar size and Amber wondered how hard it could be. However, after an hour of bending over gutting fish after fish she soon realised it was back-breaking work, and the raw smell was making her heave.

'You'll get used to it,' Isla told her with a grin as she saw the look on Amber's face and Amber managed a weak smile in return. The cooper had already told her off for not getting the right size fish in the right barrels and she was nowhere near as fast as Isla and Bridget, who were gutting at least twice as many fish as she was. 'An' you'll get faster,' the girl said encouragingly, but Amber doubted she would ever be as quick as they were. Already her hands were blistered and covered in small cuts from the knife and she wasn't sure she would ever want to eat fish again for as long as she lived. She was still sore down below and her breasts were heavy and swollen with milk, which didn't help her mood.

By the time the girls stopped to eat lunch, Amber felt ready to drop but she was determined to carry on and sat quietly nibbling the hunk of bread and cheese she had hastily wrapped before leaving home. The trouble was, even that stank of raw fish now and after a while she laid it aside as her stomach revolted.

Things got worse in the afternoon when the wind picked up and it started to rain, and soon she was drenched to the skin, cold and shivering. And yet the Scottish girls continued to laugh and joke as they worked on and Amber could only admire them. They certainly were a hardy lot. By four o'clock in the afternoon the brightness had gone from the day but still they worked on, determined to finish their task. At last, all the fish were gutted and packed and the girls began to disperse to their lodgings to prepare for the next day.

'Be here fer seven in the mornin',' Bridget told her with a cheery smile.

Too tired to even reply, Amber nodded and turned towards home, so weary she could barely put one foot in front of the other.

'Good heavens above, look at the state o' you, lass,' Alice cried when Amber stumbled through the doorway. Her two older brothers and her father were still at sea and expected home the next day and the younger two were away working on the railways now, so once again it would be just her and her mother that evening. Amber had been pleased when her mother had written to her a couple of months before to tell her that Will and Ted were leaving the shipyard. At least that was two of her family who would no longer be reliant on Barnaby Greenwood for an income!

Amber collapsed into the chair at the side of the fire and as her clothes began to steam, the rank smell of fish became overpowering.

'Phew, you'd best get out into the yard an' take them off,' her mother ordered, wrinkling her nose. 'Then we'll get you into somethin' dry afore you catch your death o' cold.'

Amber did as she was told and after washing in a bucket of warm water her mother had ready for her, she sat at the side of the fire wrapped in a blanket, shivering as she started to peel the rags from her hands. A lot of skin came off with them and her mother was horrified as she stared at the raw, bleeding flesh.

'Aw, me poor lass.' She shook her head as she bustled away to fetch more warm water to bathe them.

'Isla, that's one of the girls I'm working with, said it would help if I soaked 'em in the urine in me chamber pot,' Amber said weakly, although the thought of doing anything so disgusting didn't appeal to her at all. 'It hardens 'em up, apparently. They've gone soft cos I ain't been workin' fer awhile.'

'Well, I don't think you should go back tomorrow,' her mother muttered as she gently bathed her hands.

'They'll be gone within a couple o' weeks. Anyway, there ain't so many herrin's bein' caught now so the girls will be movin' on. I might as well try an' stick it out for that long at least.'

'An' then what do you intend to do?' Her mother raised an eyebrow. 'I hope you ain't thinkin' o' goin' with 'em?'

'I ain't decided yet.' Amber snuggled further down into the blanket and by the time her mother had tipped away the dirty water she had already fallen into an exhausted sleep.

Chapter Thirteen

Amber had been working with the herring girls for almost a week. It was a cold, drizzly late September day with a biting wind blowing in off the sea. Despite all her mother's pleas to end the job, Amber had struggled on, although that morning, she had been secretly relieved to hear that the girls would be moving on the following week. Both Isla and Bridget had asked her to move on with them but as much as she had enjoyed their company she wasn't so sure this was a life she would want to live for very long.

Every night when she got back to the cottage in Argument's Yard, she would find her top drenched in milk and she was still bleeding heavily, but at least while she was busy, she didn't have time to think of the child she had given away. And she flatly refused to talk to her mother about it. It was only at night when she lay in bed listening to the wind in the rafters of the cottage that she allowed her tears to fall. Her biggest regret now was not allowing herself to see the baby, and she constantly wondered what she looked like. Did she favour Barnaby Greenwood with his blue eyes and fair hair, or did she look like herself with strawberry-blonde hair and tawny eyes? She would never know now but deep down the sensible side of her told her that it was perhaps for the best.

She was just dropping a fish into a barrel when she became aware of horse's hooves on the cobbles of the harbour and when she looked up what little colour she had in her pale cheeks drained away and she quickly looked down again. It was Barnaby Greenwood. He was the owner of the fishing trawler that had come in that morning so he was no doubt there to ensure that all was well. She just prayed that he wouldn't spot her.

Her prayers went unanswered, however, when a short time later she became aware of someone standing close by, and glancing down and to the side she saw a fine pair of soft leather riding boots. With a sigh she slowly looked up and met Barnaby's eyes.

'Amber . . . Miss Ainsley, I thought it was you,' he said, obviously feeling very awkward. 'What are you doing here?'

She was aware that Isla and Bridget were listening intently and felt herself flush.

'What does it look like? I'm gibbing the fish,' she answered shortly. He was no longer her employer so she saw no reason why she should speak to him respectfully.

'I see.' He looked guilty as he gently smacked his riding crop against the side of his leg. Amber looked terribly ill. She had lost weight and her eyes, which had dark smudges beneath them, seemed to have sunk into her face. As for her poor hands, they were a mass of blisters and cuts, and he couldn't help but feel that this was all his fault. 'But you do know that your job is still open at Greenacres?' His voice was kindly, almost imploring, but it cut no ice with her. This was the man who had ruined her life as far as she was concerned.

'I've no wish to come back to Greenacres,' she answered coldly, her eyes flashing as she met his gaze. She desperately wanted to ask him how her baby was and if she had settled with the family he had found for her? But of course, she couldn't.

'But you do know that the herring girls will be moving on next week?' he went on persistently. 'I trust you are not thinking of going with them?'

She wondered why he should care? After all, he hadn't cared when he had turned his back on her.

'I haven't decided what I'm doing yet.' She slit another fish open and deftly threw the intestines into the offal bin.

'Well . . . if you should decide you wish to come back do come and see me.' He bowed then, as if he was speaking to someone of his own class, and turning about, he strode back to his horse.

Isla and Bridget started to titter. 'So who were that then, lass?' Isla asked enviously. 'Weren't that the owner o' the trawler?'

'Yes, it was,' Amber said shortly.

'Ooh, fancy you knowin' him.' Isla sighed. 'He's ever so handsome, ain't he?'

'I can't say as I've noticed.' Amber was in a thoroughly bad mood now and sensing that she was upset the other two girls exchanged a puzzled glance and got on with what they were doing. Barnaby Greenwood was not mentioned again until they all sat on the harbour wall to eat their lunch.

'So how come you know the gaffer, then?' Isla asked curiously and Amber sighed.

'I used to work for him and his wife in their house. I was the laundry maid.'

'So what made you leave there to do a job like this?' Isla asked persistently.

123

Thankfully Amber was saved from having to answer when she spotted yet another person she knew trotting along with a large wicker basket on her arm, and dropping her bread and cheese she picked her way through the crowd of girls.

'Nancy . . . over here!'

Nancy had been heading for the market place, no doubt with a list of things Mrs Boswell needed, but when she heard her name called, she stopped and turned, her face breaking into a wide grin when she spotted Amber.

'Amber.' Dropping her basket, she gave her friend a hug then wrinkling her nose she quickly stepped away from her. 'Phew, you don't half pong!' She grinned. Then becoming serious again she drew Amber towards an alley where they couldn't be overheard and whispered, 'Is it all over then? You had the baby, I mean?'

Amber nodded as she wrapped her arms about her waist to try and get warm. 'Yes, a couple of weeks ago. It's all taken care of now.'

'You poor cow!' Nancy said sympathetically. 'But don't worry, your secret is safe wi' me. As far as anyone back at the house knows, you've been off lookin' after your sick uncle. But why ain't you come back to the house an' your job?'

'If I never see that man again it will be too soon for me,' Amber ground out bitterly. 'An' if I came back I'd have to see him every day.'

'But I doubt he'd be daft enough to try an' set hands on you again,' Nancy pointed out sensibly. Then leaning closer she confided, 'Between you an' me I don't reckon he'll have time to. The missus is comin' back from her parents' cottage in Scarborough tomorrer. She nearly died givin' birth, apparently, an' the master's come back to organise a nanny for her for when she gets home.'

'Oh, she's had the baby then?' Amber's voice was flat as she thought of her own baby.

'Ner, not one baby, two! A boy an' a girl by all accounts.'

The colour, or what there was of it, drained from Amber's face as she leant heavily against the wall. *Twins!*

Nancy nodded. 'Aye, a boy an' a girl, an' it sounds like one o' them ain't very well, though I don't know which one. The missus is so poorly they've had to arrange a doctor to travel back in the coach with her.'

'Well at least the master got his son in the end.' Amber couldn't keep the bitterness from her voice and Nancy gave her a sympathetic smile as she bent to retrieve her basket.

'Right, I'd best be off else Mrs Boswell will be on me tail like a blood'ound,' she said. 'But do consider comin' back, *please*. It ain't the same at Greenacres wi'out you. I've missed you somethin' rotten!'

'I've missed you too and I'll think about it,' Amber said, although she had no intention of doing any such thing. She watched Nancy walk away before turning about and going back to work.

'The skipper reckons we've only got another two or three days work left 'ere,' Bridget informed her that evening as she flipped the last of the iridescent herrings she was gipping into a barrel and began to cover it with coarse salt. 'Have yer given any more thought to movin' on wi' us, lassie?'

'I appreciate the offer but I think I'm going to try my hand at something else now,' Amber told her apologetically. 'I'm really grateful that you let me work with you but I doubt I shall ever get as fast as you and Isla.'

Soon after she set off for home and as she turned into Church Street she saw Bertie Preston swaggering towards her in his Sunday best.

'Phew, lass.' He made a big show of pressing his nostrils together. 'Yer reek to high 'eaven.'

'It's because I've been working hard. You should try it sometime,' she responded sarcastically.

'I don't 'ave to kill meself to earn a bob or two,' he said smugly. 'I live off me wits an' like I said, if yer'd let me put a ring on yer finger, you'd never want fer owt.'

Amber sighed and moved on. She was just too tired to even try and make conversation with him and just wanted to get into the warm.

When she entered the cottage, she was grateful to see the tin bath full of steaming water in front of the fire.

Her mother smiled at her. 'I thought I'd get it ready for you afore the men come in,' she told her kindly. 'Come on, lass, strip off now an' while you're havin' a soak, I'll bring you a nice hot cup o' tea. How does that sound, eh?'

'Like bliss!' Amber's hands were so chapped and sore that it took her some time to undo the buttons on her blouse and undress, but at last her clothes lay in a heap at the side of the tub and as she slid into the water she sighed with contentment.

'The word's goin' round that the mistress up at Greenacres has had twins,' her mother told her a few minutes later as she passed her a steaming mug.

Amber nodded. 'I know. I saw Nancy and she told me. I saw Mr Greenwood an' all this mornin'.'

'Oh yes, an' what did *he* have to say for himself?' Alice's voice was scathing.

'He offered me my old job back an' it took me all me time not to tell him he could stuff it up his arse!' There was a wicked twinkle in Amber's eyes and within seconds both she and her mother were giggling.

'Eeh, it's good to have a laugh,' Alice said as she mopped at her eyes with the bottom of her pinafore. 'But on a more serious note, what are you goin' to do when this job is done? You ain't the sort to sit about the house, an' as you know jobs are scarce round here.'

Sombre again, Amber nodded. 'I know, but somethin' will turn up,' she said optimistically, and for then the subject was dropped.

The girls were due to move on the next day and as Amber worked alongside them she suddenly realised how much she would miss them. They had formed a friendship and although the job had been back-breaking it had taken her mind off recent events.

'Yer could allus change yer mind an' come wi' us, lass,' Isla encouraged, but Amber smiled and shook her head.

'Thank you, but I reckon it's time I decided what I want to do wi' me life now.' She sighed as she looked out over the sea of masts bobbing eerily in the fog that had settled over the harbour. In a few days it would be October and she knew the job would be even more unpleasant when the really bad weather set in.

It was dark by the time she wearily set off for home and she had just walked along Bridge Street and turned into Church Street when she saw a tall, well-dressed figure striding purposefully towards her and her heart sank. It was Barnaby Greenwood and it was too late to avoid him now because she knew he had seen her, so with her chin held high she walked on until they drew level with each other.

'Ah, Miss Ainsley, I was just coming to see you,' he said courteously and she scowled at him.

'And why would that be? I don't reckon we have anythin' to say to each other anymore,' she replied boldly. Just the sight of him turned her stomach now after what he had put her through.

He lowered his head for a moment but then looking up again he said quickly, 'Actually, I wished to speak to you about something that may be to your advantage.' He was dressed in a top hat and a thick woollen overcoat and as she stared at his fine clothes, she became aware of how poorly dressed and smelly she was and flushed. 'The thing is,' he hurried on, afraid that she might set off again without hearing him out, 'I heard of a job yesterday that I thought might suit you – not at Greenacres,' he said hastily as he saw her scowl. 'A good friend of mine is taking his wife to visit her family in London until after Christmas and unfortunately their nanny has been taken ill so they are looking for someone to accompany them to care for their two children. It would only be a temporary post until they returned, but would it be of interest to you?' He had hated seeing her bent over gibbing the herrings and was looking for a way to assuage his sense of guilt.

Amber narrowed her eyes. 'I ain't never been a nanny,' she pointed out shortly and he shook his head.

'That wouldn't matter in the least, I assure you. The Temples merely want someone trustworthy; they will be happy to tell you what's expected of you and the pay is more than generous. The only thing is, they leave in three days' time. This Saturday, in fact, so they would need an answer.'

Amber opened her mouth to tell him to clear off but then paused. Would she be cutting her nose off to spite her face? She actually liked the idea of visiting London; she'd never gone farther than Scarborough and this sounded like a job that would be much more pleasant than standing out in the freezing cold gutting herrings. *After all*, she reasoned, *how hard could it be to look after two little children?*

'I should have to discuss it wi' me mam,' she told him cautiously. 'So could I give you an answer tomorrer? I ain't promisin' anythin', mind.'

'Of course not, I quite understand.' He smiled, but she was indifferent to his charms now and it didn't make her like him any more.

'May I come for your answer tomorrow then?'

'Yes, in the evenin' at the cottage,' she answered. 'I'm doin' me last day wi' the herrin' girls tomorrer.'

'Very well, thank you, Miss Ainsley.' He removed his hat and gave a little bow before turning and striding away.

As Amber climbed the steps to Argument's Yard, her mind was reeling. This was a turn up for the books and no mistake, although she had no idea why he should want to help her now after the way he had treated her.

When she entered the cottage, the warmth wrapped itself around her like a blanket and her chapped cheeks and hands began to glow as she hurried towards the fire. The smell of a beef stew simmering in the big black pot on the fire made her stomach rumble and as Alice rushed off to pour her a cup of tea, Amber told her of Mr Greenwood's offer.

'London!' Alice was horrified. 'Oh, I ain't too sure as I'd want you goin' there, lass,' she said worriedly. 'I've heard tell it's a den o' thieves an' they'd slit your throat for sixpence! There's pickpockets, prostitutes an' all manner o' lowlives there.'

Amber giggled. 'I doubt it would be like that in the area Mr Greenwood's friends would be visitin',' she pointed out. 'They're gentry so I dare say Mrs Temple's parents live in a big swanky pad somewhere. An' it is only till after Christmas. So what do you think I should do? He reckons they'll pay well an' that would give me some time to decide what I want to do next.'

'Hm.' As Alice handed her her tea she stared thoughtfully off into space for a minute, before saying, 'But what about your clothes, lass? Will they be fancy enough fer the likes o' them? Even your best skirt an' blouse is darned now.'

'I dare say they'd supply a uniform for the time I'm with 'em. An' I do have the clothes Uncle Jeremiah bought for me.'

'Ah, I hadn't thought o' that. Well . . . all I can say is, if you like the sound of it, I won't stand in your way but it'll be sad that you ain't here fer Christmas. Me an' your dad an' the lads will miss you. I don't think there's ever been a Christmas when we ain't all been together before. At least . . . not since . . .' Amber knew that her mother was thinking of Brian, the child she had lost to pneumonia some years before. Her mother still visited his tiny grave at least once a week. Alice pulled her thoughts back to the present and shaking her head she went on, 'Still, I dare say I'm gonna have to get used to that. Our Amos an' young Lilly Price 'ave been walkin' out together for some time now an'

130

he slipped it out t'other day that he's savin' up to buy her a ring. Happen a change o' scenery will do you good an' all, after what you've just gone through so if you want to do it you can go wi' me blessin'.'

'An' what about me dad?'

Alice chuckled. 'You just leave your dad to me, lass.' Her eyes strayed to the window where the fog had now come down so densely that she could barely see beyond the glass. 'The boat should be back be now,' she fretted. 'I just hope they ain't stuck out at sea in this fog.'

Over the years Amber had watched her mother worry about exactly the same thing time and time again. Not that she was any different to any of the other fishermen's wives. They all knew what a risk their menfolk were taking when they sailed off and they all offered up a prayer of thanks each time they returned safely.

'They'll be fine, Mam.' Amber sat back in her seat to enjoy her tea, for now too bone weary to even get out of her filthy clothes and wash. She had a lot to think about.

Chapter Fourteen

'Would you like me to get Nanny to bring the babies through to see you?' Mrs Ruffin asked as she leant over the bed to tuck the covers more closely about Louisa's thin frame. They had arrived home the day before and Louisa hadn't stood up at all well to the journey. She was bleeding heavily again; so much so that Mrs Ruffin had insisted the doctor should be sent for.

Louisa scowled. 'Not at the moment,' she said. 'I don't feel strong enough just yet.'

Mrs Ruffin secretly wondered when she would be. Since the day the babies had arrived her answer had been the same every time she was asked.

'Perhaps if you were to get up for a little while each day and sit in the chair by the window it might build your strength up?' she suggested tentatively but Louisa pouted and shook her head, setting her curls bobbing on her shoulders.

'No, I told you I'm not well and the babies are so . . .' She frowned as she tried to think of the right words to describe them. *'Noisy* and *sicky,'* she said disgustedly. She really couldn't understand why everyone seemed to be making such a fuss of them. All the staff and especially Barnaby were besotted with them. And it wasn't even as if they could do anything yet apart from drink milk, yell and fill their binders. She could only begin to imagine what he would be like with them when they could potter about.

The door opened and Barnaby appeared with a bunch of fresh-cut flowers he had asked the gardener to pick from the hothouse.

'I thought these might cheer you up,' he told her with a smile, handing them to Mrs Ruffin, who hurried away to put them in a vase in water.

Louisa glowered at him. 'I think it will take a lot more than a few flowers to do *that*,' she told him ungratefully. 'You *do* realise that I almost died having those babies, don't you?'

'Of course I do, darling.' He pulled a chair up to the bedside and made to take her hand but she snatched it away.

'Actually, I'm glad we have a few moments alone because there's something I must say to you.'

'Of course.'

He stared into her face and with her chin in the air she went on, 'The thing is, the doctor has told me that if I were to attempt to have any more children it could kill me.'

He nodded, his face sombre. 'I'm quite aware of that.'

'Good, then you will realise that we must never . . .' She sought for the right words before ending, 'We must *never* lie together again. It isn't worth the risk. And after all, you have not one but two children now so surely you are happy with that.'

Barnaby nodded resignedly. Their love life had never been the best and he knew that she had only endured it now and again for his sake, but she was right, it wasn't fair to risk her health again. Of course he knew there were ways and

133

means to prevent pregnancy, but if he was honest, given her obvious horror of the act, lying with Louisa had not been pleasurable for some time.

'I am more than happy with the family you have given me,' he said sadly. 'Although it saddens me that we will not be intimate again.'

'Speak for yourself,' she said tartly. 'It certainly doesn't sadden me! In fact, I can tell you now, I find the whole process messy and uncomfortable. No, I will stand firm on this, Barnaby. From now on you are to stay to your own room.'

'As you wish.' His face set, he stood and looked down on this woman who he had once idolised, and then with a curt nod he turned and left the room. His next stop was the nursery where he found the nanny he had employed to care for the children changing the boy's binding whilst the wet nurse from the town fed the girl. His face instantly softened as he asked, 'And how are they today, Nanny?'

'Oh, the lass is as good as gold, sir,' the nanny, a plump, middle-aged woman with a kindly face replied. 'But the boy is still quite fractious.' She finished fastening the boy's binding and after adjusting his tiny nightshirt she handed him to his father, thinking, *It's a good job one o' the parents shows an interest in the little mites. The mother certainly don't.*

Barnaby cuddled the tiny boy close, feeling a rush of love the like of which he had never felt before. Oh, he had thought he loved Louisa, but had he really? a little voice in his head asked. Or had he merely been infatuated with her ethereal beauty?

Before their wedding he'd soon discovered that her beauty was pretty much all there was to her. She enjoyed being admired, pampered and kissed but that was as far as it went. In the early days of their marriage, he'd convinced himself that things would improve with time, but they hadn't and it was this that had made him seek his pleasures elsewhere. Not that this was any excuse for the way he had treated Amber Ainsley. Time and time again he wished he could go back and undo the wrong he had done her – the day he had seen her gipping herrings on that cold quayside he had felt like the lowest of the low. He cringed when he remembered the scorn in her eyes when she looked at him, and the worst of it was that he really couldn't blame her.

Bringing his thoughts sharply back to the infant in his arms, he stared down at him. He was the double of himself, with fair downy hair and blue eyes, whereas the girl's hair was a darker blonde and already her eyes seemed to be changing colour and he suspected that they would be dark.

'You'd never believe these two came from the same womb, let alone that they were twins, would you?' the nanny remarked as she took the full, contented girl from the wet nurse's arms. The boy was tiny and quite scrawny whereas the girl was plump with long silky eyelashes that rested on her chubby cheeks as she contentedly blew milk bubbles.

'I just wish he was as fond of his milk as she is,' the woman went on as she sat the little girl on her lap and began to tap her back to wind her. 'This little madam would suckle till the cows came home if you let her, whereas his lordship here has to be encouraged to take every ounce. And already they're different in nature an' all. She's a sweet, contented little soul whereas he cries a lot – not that he ain't a bonny little thing,' she added hurriedly when Barnaby raised his eyebrow. Standing up, he gently laid the boy into one of the cribs that stood on either side of the fire and then took the girl and held her against his chest. She really was the sweetest, prettiest baby he had ever seen, and once again a feeling of love surged through him. It was just as well, he thought wryly. Because his wife had made it more than plain that there would be no love forthcoming from her again.

'Have you thought of any names for them?' the nanny asked.

Barnaby shook his head. 'I don't think Louisa has been well enough to give it much thought yet,' he admitted.

'Hm, I heard she had a really bad time of it at the birth.'

He nodded. 'Yes, she did, she can't even remember it – she was semi-conscious by the time he arrived.'

'Poor soul, let's hope she picks up soon,' the woman said sympathetically. She took the now slumbering child from his arms, crooning to her as she gently laid her in her cot, forgetting that Barnaby was even there.

Once downstairs he ran his hand distractedly through his hair as he thought of the forthcoming visit he would pay to Amber that evening. He hoped she would accept the job he had offered. The Temples were long-term friends of his and he knew that she would be well looked after with them, even if the position was only temporary. It would certainly beat gutting herrings!

It was dark that evening when Barnaby reached Arguments Yard and when he tapped on the door of Amber's home, she almost instantly answered it and stepped outside to speak to him, explaining, 'Me dad an' me brothers are in an' I don't want 'em askin' too many questions. Shall we walk, else we'll be settin' the tongues waggin'.'

She pulled the thick woollen shawl draped across her shoulders more tightly about her and he noticed that she must have bathed since she got home from her last day with the herring girls as her hair was still damp.

When he said nothing, she seemed to think she owed him some sort of explanation and went on, 'If me dad saw you here, he'd start to ask too many questions. For instance, why are you botherin' to do this for me? An' I think we both know what he'd do if he knew the answer to that, don't we? He'd kill you stone dead as soon as look at you!'

Barnaby felt the heat build in his cheeks. He wasn't used to being spoken to this way by people he employed and yet he didn't retaliate because he knew he deserved it.

'But let's face it, surely anything has got to be better than gutting herrings,' he said quietly.

Amber sniggered bitterly. 'Oh aye? So you think it were fun when I worked in the laundry at the house, washin' all your dirties, do you?' She would never have dared speak to him in such a way before this but now she felt she owed him nothing and she certainly had nothing to lose. But then her voice softened a little as she asked tentatively, 'Have you heard how me baby is?'

Avoiding her eyes, he strode on beside her until they came to the harbour where they stood watching the waves slap against the quayside. It was yet another foggy, murky night and bitterly cold. 'I can promise you that she is doing very well indeed and being very well cared for,' he said quietly and just for a moment he saw pain flash in Amber's eyes as she glanced at him. But almost instantly her chin was up again and he asked, 'Have you given any thought to the job I offered you?'

She snorted. 'I've thought o' nothin' else an' yes, I'll take it. It'll do me good to get away from here for a while.'

'Good.' He nodded. 'But I did make it clear that this was only a temporary position? The Temples' two boys are going away to boarding school in the New Year when they return from London so they'll have no need of a nanny then.'

She shrugged. 'When one door shuts another door opens so they say, so I'll cross that bridge when I come to it.'

She had guts, he had to give her that, he thought admiringly, staring at her from the corner of his eye. Most girls would have folded after what he had put her through. A picture of her as he had last seen her, bending over the barrels of herrings within days of giving birth to their daughter, flashed before his eyes and he couldn't help but compare her to his wife who had never done a day's work in her whole life.

'Then perhaps you could present yourself at the Temple residence tomorrow morning at ten o'clock when Mrs Temple will receive you to tell you what your duties will be and provide you with suitable clothes.'

Her face flamed as she glanced down at her shabby skirt. 'They live—'

'I know where they live,' she cut in ungraciously. 'About half a mile further on from Greenacres.'

'Yes. Now, is there anything else I can help you with?'

She glared at him as she held something towards him and he automatically took it from her. Glancing down, he was shocked when he realised it was the roll of notes he had given her when he had visited her at her uncle's, as well as the golden guinea he had given her to get rid of the unborn baby.

'But I gave you this as—'

'I don't want your money,' she said proudly, her glorious eyes flashing. 'It goes against the grain to take this job, seein' as you arranged it, but then some of us have to work for a livin'. We ain't all married into money.'

She saw him flinch. Everyone knew that Louisa had brought the money to the marriage. Admittedly Barnaby had already owned two fishing trawlers when he met her, but Louisa's father had provided the money that had helped him to build his businesses up.

'Then I shall put it away and should you ever need it you only have to say.' He slipped the money into his pocket and as Amber turned to walk away, he called, 'Would you like me to see you home?'

She stopped abruptly and there was a sneer on her face as she turned and answered, 'Why? Are you worried someone might take advantage o' me?' She gave a mirthless laugh that made his blood run cold. 'I reckon it's a bit late to be worryin' about that, don't you?' And with that she walked away, leaving him standing there shamefaced.

She was walking along Church Street when she saw Bertie Preston swaggering towards her and she gave a silent groan. After having to speak to Barnaby Greenwood, he was just about the last person she wanted to see that evening, but he had seen her so there could be no avoiding him.

''Allo me lovely.' As he drew level with her, he reached out in a familiar fashion to twist one of the curls lying on her shoulder around his finger and she instantly stepped back.

'You can pack that in, Bertie Preston, I ain't in the mood,' she told him sternly and Bertie laughed. He was looking very smart and she had no doubt he would be off to a card game somewhere.

'So when will yer be in the mood?' he asked teasingly. 'An' when are yer gonna let me make an honest woman o' yer? I don't know why yer don't just agree to it. Yer know we were meant to be together.'

'Says who?'

Bertie shrugged. 'Everybody! Even our mams allus took it fer granted we'd get wed when we were of an age, so why don't we just do it? I've got enough tucked away to keep yer, an' there's old Mrs Besom's cottage just come empty now she's passed away. Think on it – yer wouldn't 'ave to work again.'

Amber sighed and made to walk on but he caught her arm and now his voice had an edge to it as he told her, 'I shouldn't be too long makin' yer mind up, gel. There's plenty o' lasses hereabouts as would jump at the chance o' bein' me wife.'

'I suggest you give one o' them the honour o' becomin' Mrs Preston then,' she said harshly and hurried away. Deep down she knew she shouldn't be so hard on him. Bertie might be a rogue but he was likable with it and as her mother had told her, she supposed she could do far worse. The trouble was she didn't love him and she would never love anyone now. She blinked back tears as she wondered if Bertie would still be so keen to wed her if he ever discovered she had just given birth to Barnaby Greenwood's child.

Chapter Fifteen

As she turned into the tree-lined driveway, Amber paused to stare at the Temples' beautiful house She was still hesitant to accept the post seeing as it had been Barnaby Greenwood who had secured it for her and she didn't want to be beholden to him for anything. But common sense took over, so taking a deep breath, she passed the coach house and set off. The leaves were fluttering from the trees and a cold wind was blowing but after working with the herring girls, Amber was used to the cold now. She glanced down at her hands. They were still cut and sore and she wished that she'd had some gloves to wear. But gloves were for toffs so all she could do was hope that Mrs Temple wouldn't notice them. They certainly didn't look like the hands of a nanny.

As she emerged from the trees and neared the round marble steps that led up to two enormous oak doors, a gardener carrying a scythe appeared from the side of the house and she asked him, 'Excuse me, would you happen to know where I'm to go? I've come to see Mrs Temple about a position.'

His face broke out in a broad smile and he thumbed across his shoulder. 'Yer'd best go this way then, lass. Follow the path round an' you'll come to the kitchen an' the housekeeper'll sort you out.'

She smiled her thanks and hurried on the way he'd pointed to find herself in a large yard where some brilliant white sheets were flapping on a line in the wind. She passed a room with steam floating out of the door and saw a young, red-faced girl at a large sink scrubbing away at a sheet as if her very life depended on it. Beyond that was a large stable block where beautiful thoroughbred horses poked their heads over the top half of the doors, and beyond them she saw a large orchard. And then she spotted the door she wanted. She could hear the sound of pots and pans clattering as someone scrubbed them and rightly assumed that this must be the kitchen. Nervous now, she tentatively tapped on the door and seconds later it was opened by a young maid in a rough apron – the kitchen maid no doubt.

'I've come to see Mrs Temple,' Amber told her and the girl ushered her inside without saying a word. A rosy-cheeked cook was standing at an enormous table rolling pastry and at sight of Amber she raised an eyebrow.

'If it's a maid's job yer after I'm afraid yer out o' luck, lass,' she said, not unkindly. 'We don't need no one at present.'

Amber shook her head. 'Oh no, I'm not here for a maid's job. I have an appointment with Mrs Temple at ten o'clock. I've come for the nanny's position.'

The woman's eyes stretched wide as she glanced at Amber's down-at-heel boots and her shabby skirt and shawl. The lass looked clean enough, but she certainly didn't look like nanny material, the cook thought.

Amber shuffled uncomfortably under the cook's regard, wishing she'd worn the boots her uncle had given her, but she hadn't wanted to ruin them on the long walk to the house.

Luckily, before the cook had the chance to comment, a tall, slim woman with fair hair swept into the kitchen and as her eyes settled on Amber she asked, 'Are you Miss Ainsley?'

'Yes, ma'am.'

'Ah good, you are punctual so that's a good start,' the woman said. 'I'm Mrs Brewer, the housekeeper, and if you'll come this way, I'll show you in to Mrs Temple. She's in the drawing room.'

Nodding towards the cook, who was watching with interest, Amber followed the woman into a large hallway that was even bigger than the one at Greenacres and very tastefully furnished with gilt-framed pictures and mirrors on the silk-wallpapered walls. The keys on the chatelaine about Mrs Brewer's waist clanked together as she walked and the full skirts of her stiff bombazine gown swooshed over the highly polished tile floor.

'Wait there,' she told Amber, pausing at a set of double doors, before disappearing through them, only to reappear seconds later to hold one of the doors wide and tell Amber, 'Mrs Temple is expecting you. I shall be back shortly.'

As Amber entered the room she felt as if she was walking into a lion's den for she had no idea at all what to expect. But she needn't have worried. As Mrs Temple rose from her chair she gave her a wide smile and ushered her towards the chair opposite hers.

'Do come and sit down. It's Amber, isn't it? Or would you prefer to be called Miss Ainsley?'

'Oh no,' Amber said hastily as she perched on the edge of the leather wing chair. 'Amber is fine, ma'am.'

Mrs Temple looked to be in her early thirties and was very attractive indeed. Amber had seen her pass through the town in her fine carriage on a few occasions but close up she realised she was even prettier than she had realised. It had been the talk of the town when she had married her husband, a wealthy barrister, some twelve years before, for he was at least twelve years her senior and everyone had gossiped that it wouldn't last. But the Temples had proved them wrong and it was clear to see that this woman in front of her was a very happy one.

'So, what has Barnaby— I'm sorry, I mean Mr Greenwood, told you about my two little terrors?' There was a twinkle in her eyes as Amber stared back at her blankly. The woman's hair was very fair and tied into two small bunches of ringlets above her ears and the blue shot-silk day gown she was wearing was the exact colour of her eyes. A row of perfectly matched pearls was strung about her slender throat and matching pearl earrings adorned her ears. She was, Amber thought, quite simply one of the most beautiful women she had ever seen.

'He, er . . . he ain't told me much about 'em at all, 'cept to say that they need someone to be their nanny till after Christmas.'

'I see.' Helen Temple's mind was racing as she wondered what her parents would think of this young woman's dialect. It was broad Yorkshire, but then she supposed it was a problem that could be overcome. She could sit in when the boys had their twice weekly elocution lessons and it wasn't as if her parents were going to see a lot of her anyway.

'Then I shall tell you about them,' she said with a smile. 'And before you leave you must meet them. They're both quite lovely, but then I'm their mother so I would say that, wouldn't I? Henry, or Harry as we call him, is almost ten, and George is almost nine. But I should warn you, just like most young boys they can be very mischievous so you will have to let them know who is in charge right from the start or they'll run rings around you, I'm afraid. My husband always says I'm far too lenient with them but then he isn't much better himself.' She gave a tinkling laugh and just for a moment Amber's face was transformed as she smiled back. This woman made it very hard to remember there was a class divide between them.

'But now while we have a chat, we shall have a cup of tea. It's a little early for elevenses but who cares?' Rising she went to the side of the large marble fireplace where a cheery fire was roaring up the chimney and pulled a silken rope. Soon yet another maid in a starched white apron and a cap, both trimmed with broderie anglaise, appeared and dipped her knee.

'Yes, ma'am?'

'Tea for two, if you please, Binny,' Mrs Temple told her. 'Oh, and you might tell Cook we wouldn't be averse to some of those lovely shortbread biscuits she made yesterday to go with it, if there are any left.' She grinned at Amber as the maid left, confiding, 'They're Master Harry's absolute favourite and I've no doubt he's been cadging them off the cook. He can wrap her around his little finger. But now, let's get down to business . . .'

For the next ten minutes they discussed Amber's wages, which Amber thought were very generous indeed, and what duties she would be expected to perform, and then Binny appeared wheeling a little tea trolley loaded with a silver teapot, bone china cups and saucers and a number of fancy pastries on a plate, along with some of the shortbread biscuits.

'Do help yourself,' Mrs Temple encouraged as she strained the tea into the delicate cups, and feeling much more relaxed than she had when she'd arrived, Amber willingly did as she was told. It wasn't often she got to have such delicacies. Eventually, when they were done, Mrs Temple again pulled the silken rope and when Binny appeared she asked her, 'Could you fetch Master Harry and Master George down from the nursery, please, if they've finished their lesson.'

'Oh, they have, ma'am, I just saw Mr Bowler leaving,' the nurse informed her. Mr Bowler, Amber was to learn, was the boys' tutor who came in daily to teach them.

Amber sat quietly for a few moments, admiring the lovely room, until she heard the scuffle of footsteps outside the door on the tiled floor and two young boys, who looked remarkably like their mother, exploded into the room.

They were both giggling and jostling each other but at sight of Amber they stopped abruptly and stared at her.

'Now boys, do remember your manners,' Mrs Temple told them severely, although her eyes were smiling. 'This is Miss Ainsley. She's coming to London with us and she will be your nanny until you leave for school in the New Year.' Mention of the school took the twinkle from her eye and Amber guessed that it must have been her husband's idea to send them there. She certainly didn't look too happy with the idea.

The boys, meantime, were eyeing her curiously. She certainly didn't look anything like any of the other nannies they had had. They had all been older and much more smartly dressed than the young woman in front of them now.

'How do you do, Miss Ainsley,' they chorused at a frown from their mother and Amber gave them a broad smile that showed off the dimples in her cheeks.

''Ello, lads. I'm sure we'll get along just fine.'

Their eyes stretched wide as they heard her speak and they would have broken into laughter if a glare from their mother hadn't stopped them.

'Very well, you may go back upstairs now,' Mrs Temple told them. 'I'm sure Mr Bowler will have left you some homework to be doing and I shall be checking it later this afternoon to make sure you've done it.'

'Yes, Mamma,' they both said miserably and with a nod towards Amber they quietly trooped out of the room.

'So, have you had much experience of boys?' Mrs Temple asked.

'Well . . . I've got four brothers, if that counts.'

Mrs Temple smiled and nodded. 'Then I'm sure I shall have no need to tell you how boisterous they can be. But now I shall summon Mrs Brewer and she will fit you out with suitable clothes. Can you be here on Friday evening? We shall be travelling early on Saturday morning so it would be easier if you were already here to help get the boys up.'

'Of course, ma'am.' Amber inclined her head and when the housekeeper appeared she followed her to the back of the house where she unlocked a door that led into a small room where a number of uniforms were hanging.

'Now then, let's see, you look about the same size as the last but one nanny the boys had,' she said thoughtfully as she looked Amber up and down and so saying she lifted a gown down and held it against her. 'Try that one on,' she urged, heading for the door. 'And I shall be back in a minute.'

The dress was a fine wool in a soft blue-grey colour and when Amber slipped it on, apart from it being a little long, it fitted as if it had been made for her. There was a detachable cotton collar and cuffs and a very full skirt and Amber felt very grand in it.

'Perfect apart from the length,' Mrs Brewer observed when she came back. 'Will you be able to shorten it yourself or should I get Mrs Temple's seamstress to do it?'

'Oh, I can do it,' Amber quickly assured her.

'Good, there's another identical one here and of course you'll need the petticoats to go beneath it and some new boots and a cloak.' By the time Mrs Brewer had finished there was a pile of clothes and Amber wondered how she was going to carry them all.

'You can leave them here and I'll have them packed for you ready for Saturday,' Mrs Brewer offered. 'Just take the two gowns that need shortening.'

And so soon after Amber set off for home feeling a lot more optimistic about her new post than she had when she'd arrived.

'I reckon Harry an' George are goin' to be a bit of a handful,' she told her mother when she got home.

Alice chuckled. 'Show me a little lad as ain't. Why, I can remember I used to threaten our Amos an' Reuben wi' all sorts when they were little. They fell out like cat an' dog an' I'd threaten to bang their bloody heads together if they didn't pack it in, yet look at 'em now! Thick as thieves they are. So, just stand firm, lass, an' let the little buggers know who's boss from the start.' The smile slid away then and she said, 'I were talkin' to Mrs Preston earlier on an' she were sayin' Bertie ain't too 'appy about you goin' at all.'

'I don't know why,' Amber snapped. 'I've never given him any reason to believe there's anythin' atween us so if he wants to think there is then that's his lookout!'

'All right, all right, leave me head on,' Alice soothed. 'I were only sayin'.' And bending her head she got on with kneading the dough on the table while Amber set about altering the hems of her new gowns.

In no time at all Friday rolled around and as Amber kissed her mother goodbye there were tears in Alice's eyes. 'Eeh, it feels as if you've only just got back from your Uncle Jeremiah's,' she said sadly. 'An' now here you are off again. Still, I suppose I should get used to it. All me chicks will fly the nest eventually.'

'Oh Mam, I'm only goin' till the New Year,' Amber pointed out with a grin, and hoisting her bag up she gave her mother one more kiss and set off.

In one way she was glad to be leaving the area, if only for a short while, because she'd found every time she saw a woman with a baby she'd wonder if it was hers. She hadn't wanted to know where Barnaby was going to place her daughter when she was born, but now she bitterly regretted not finding out. It was odd to think that she wouldn't even know her if she did see her because she had refused to even have a glimpse of her after she had given birth. But it was too late for regrets now, she told herself, and perhaps far better for the baby never to know that its own mother hadn't wanted it. Taking a deep breath, she straightened her shoulders and moved on. It was time for the next chapter in her life to begin and surely it couldn't fail to be better than the last?

Chapter Sixteen

'When Helen Temple called to see me yesterday, she mentioned that you had recommended the girl who used to work here as our laundry maid to be her temporary nanny,' Louisa said to Barnaby as he sat beside her bed on his daily visit to her room. He had resigned himself to the fact that he would never share her bed again and had mixed feelings about it, but he kept them to himself.

She raised her eyebrow. 'Why would you do that?' she questioned. 'And why did she leave here?'

Barnaby swallowed his surprise. He hadn't expected news of Amber's new job to reach Louisa so quickly but he supposed he should have realised that gossip spread like wildfire. He was painfully aware that Mrs Ruffin was watching him intently and although he was quaking inside his voice was calm when he answered.

'I believe she left to go to Scarborough to care for her sick uncle for some time and she probably didn't think we would keep her job open for her because I saw her working with the herring girls in the harbour when I visited one of our trawlers one day. Anyway, Philip Temple had mentioned that they were looking for someone to go to London with them to look after the boys for a couple of months, and so

I mentioned it to Miss Ainsley. I believe their last nanny walked out again.' He gave a wry grin. 'As you know, those little terrors never manage to keep a nanny for long. Philip is hoping that a boarding school will calm them both down. Helen is dead set against it, of course, but I think Philip put his foot down this time.'

'Yes, I did get the impression that Helen isn't happy about them going,' Louisa agreed. 'But I still find it rather strange that you would suggest a former laundry maid should go to London with them. I'm sure the girl will be totally out of her depth.'

Barnaby shrugged, keen to change the subject. 'Oh, she'll cope, no doubt. Most of their nannies have been much older and the boys have run rings around them. It could be that someone younger will keep them in check. But anyway, enough about that. I've received a reply to my letter from Dr Franklin in Harley Street in London today. He's agreed to come and see you, so let's hope there's something he can do to get you up and about again.'

Louisa pouted. 'Such as what? Dr Lewis has tried everything but nothing has helped so far. I think I shall have to resign myself to the fact that I am an invalid now.' In fairness, Louisa hadn't recovered at all well from the birth and she looked pale and wan, nothing like the beauty he had fallen in love with. Her once lustrous hair was thin and wispy and she seemed to have no energy, despite the delicacies that cook prepared to try and tempt her to eat. Occasionally she would get out of bed to sit in a chair by the window for a short time but most days now she rarely rose.

'Well, it won't hurt for him to come and have a look at you,' Barnaby said with a smile. 'And have you seen the babies today?'

She shook her head, avoiding his eyes. She really couldn't understand why he was so besotted with them.

'No . . . I don't feel strong enough,' she said petulantly and Barnaby frowned.

'But, darling, if you don't start to spend a little more time with them soon you won't bond with them,' he pointed out.

'So? It was *you* that wanted them,' she responded resentfully. 'And now it has cost me my health.'

Seeing that she was building up to a tantrum, Barnaby stood up quickly and asked, 'Is there anything I can get for you before I go to the shipyard?'

She sniffed and turned her face away, and with a sigh he quietly left the room. He hadn't been lying when he said he had to go to the shipyard, but first his steps led him towards the stairs that led to the nursery and when he entered, he found the nanny just changing the little girl's binding.

'Ah, here you are, sir, I've been meaning to speak to you,' she said pleasantly as she glanced up. 'Only, well, the thing is it's quite hard to address the babies when they don't have names. Have you and the mistress decided on any yet?'

He hesitated. He'd raised the matter many times with Louisa but each time she had told him she was too tired to make a decision so now he decided that he would do it.

'Yes, we have as it happens, Nanny.' He smiled as he stroked the little girl's plump cheek. 'This little one will be called Charlotte and Louisa for her middle name after her mother, and that little chap there will be called David and Barnaby after me.'

The nanny beamed as she crossed to the crib that contained David where the smile slid away.

'Beautiful names,' she said approvingly. 'But I have to say I have concerns about this little one. He doesn't seem to be thriving like Charlotte is. He sleeps for most of the time and even when I wake him for a feed he has to be encouraged. His wet nurse is concerned too, although Dr Lewis can find nothing obvious wrong with him as yet.'

'I'm sure he'll catch up eventually,' Barnaby muttered as he stroked the little boy's tiny hand. He really was very small compared to his sister. She had been over eight pounds at birth, whereas David was just below five pounds, so he reasoned that it was bound to take a little time for him to catch up with her. Even so, as he left the room, he found himself getting concerned so he turned his mind to work and tried not to worry. He had enough to fret about with Louisa without worrying about the baby too.

At the Temples' house all was hustle and bustle as the servants loaded the mountains of luggage onto the two waiting carriages. Part of the journey would be by train and the rest by carriage so Amber was aware that there was a long journey ahead and judging by the state of high excitement the boys were in it wasn't going to be an easy one. Amber, the two boys and Mr Temple's valet were to travel in one carriage, whilst Mr and Mrs Temple and her lady's maid travelled in another.

'Are you sure that we need to take quite so much luggage, my love?' Philip Temple asked as the boys ran amok around him. 'I think you've got Betty to pack everything but the kitchen sink.'

His wife, who was looking beautiful in a pale-green velvet travelling costume with a matching hat giggled. 'It isn't all luggage, darling. A lot of it is presents. We can hardly make the boys wait for them until we get back, can we? They must have some to open on Christmas Day. And there are some for Mamma and Papa too, so don't be so grumpy.'

He grinned – he could never begrudge her anything and worshipped the very ground she walked on so he was aware that even if she'd decided to take the whole house brick by brick, he would have allowed it somehow.

'Oh, very well. Come along then, into the carriages or we'll never get there.'

Amber took a seat next to Mr Wadsworth, the master's valet, and the boys clambered in to join them, hanging out of the window to wave to the staff who had collected on the steps to see them off. And then they were off and at last the boys sat down and stared at Amber curiously.

'You look different today to what you did when we met you,' Harry observed and Amber smiled.

She was now clad in one of the lovely gowns Mrs Temple had supplied her with and a warm cloak and felt quite the lady.

'It's probably what I'm wearin'.'

Harry dug George in the ribs and giggled rudely. 'Why do you talk so funny?' he enquired and Amber felt her cheeks grow hot.

'That's quite enough of those rude comments, Master Harry,' Mr Wadsworth scolded. 'Where are your manners?'

Mr Wadsworth was a tall, grey-haired, stately gentleman and Amber flashed him a grateful smile as for the first time she wondered if she had made a mistake taking this job. It appeared the boys were going to be a real handful.

Mr Wadsworth regarded Amber seriously. 'If you don't mind me saying, Miss, I think you should start as you mean to go on, if you follow my meaning?' He inclined his head towards the two boys who were play fighting on the seat opposite.

Amber nodded, knowing he was right. So, hoping to assert her authority she said firmly, 'That's enough o' that boys! One o' you will get hurt in a minute!'

Harry gave her a scathing look. 'You can't tell us off,' he goaded. 'You aren't that much older than me!'

'Oh, yes I can, an' age doesn't come into it,' Amber responded sharply. 'I was chosen by your mother to take care of you and if you don't heed me words, I'll tell both your parents that your behaviour has been appallin'.'

George instantly sat back in his seat whilst Harry made a great show of putting his chin in the air, scowling fiercely and folding his arms tightly across his chest. But at least they were quiet, for then at least.

'Well done, Miss Ainsley,' Mr Wadsworth whispered and Amber felt as if she had won a small victory.

'We're here, we're here!' The boys whooped when the carriage that had taken them from the train station pulled up outside their grandparents' house in Mayfair. It had been a horrendous and lengthy journey and Amber was utterly exhausted, but even so she stared from the window at the house in awe. London was like another world compared to

Whitby and up to now she wasn't at all sure that she liked it. At the station she had been mesmerised by the amount of people rushing to and fro, and by the volume of traffic on the roads. There were hackney cabs, private carriages, dray horses pulling huge carts and all manner of vehicles, and to someone who was used to nothing louder than the sound of the waves breaking on the shore, the noise was deafening. The air smelt strange too – foggy and sooty – and she felt a million miles away from home, although she had to admit to herself that the house looked very grand.

It was in a crescent that skirted a park and was three storeys' high. Two bay trees pruned into fancy shapes stood either side of a shiny red door with a brass lionhead knocker on it, and the steps leading up to it were solid marble. A low, fancy wrought-iron railing ran along the front of it with steps leading down to the kitchen where snow-white lace curtains hung at the windows. The carriages had scarcely pulled up when the door was opened by a maid in a starched frilly white apron and seconds later a woman who looked like an older version of Mrs Temple erupted out of the door and hurried to the carriage in front to greet her daughter.

'Helen, my darling, how I have missed you.' Heedless of who might be watching the woman hugged her daughter and kissed her soundly on the cheek and before Amber could stop them the boys suddenly threw open the carriage door and raced to embrace the woman.

'*Grandmamma!*'

'*Oh, my little loves!*' The woman threw her arms about them and wrapped them in a fierce embrace before leading them indoors, leaving Mr Wadsworth and Mr Temple to supervise the unpacking of the luggage while Amber stood there feeling completely out of her depth.

'Come along, my dear,' Mr Temple said, taking pity on her as he hefted a large bag up the steps. 'I'm sure my wife will show you where to go.'

It was organised chaos in the hallway with the boys running riot as various members of staff stopped to greet them and the bags were brought in.

'Daisy.' Mrs Jennings, Mrs Temple's mother, beckoned to one of the maids. 'Would you take Miss Ainsley up to her room, please? She's to go in the one next to the boys.'

'O' course, ma'am.' The maid dipped her knee and with a cheeky wink at Amber, she led her up a sweeping staircase to a galleried landing. There were doors dotted all along it and stopping outside one, the girl told her, 'This'll be your room, Miss. Would yer like me to 'elp yer unpack? It'll be no bovver at all.' Her accent was broad cockney and Amber was struggling to understand her.

'No, thank you . . . Daisy, ain't it? I can manage fine.' Could she have known it, Daisy was finding her dialect difficult to understand too. She followed Daisy into the room and was pleasantly surprised. It was quite large and beautifully furnished, decorated in varying shades of pale greys and pinks, which made it feel very calming.

'So you're the latest nanny, are yer?' Daisy asked and when Amber nodded, she chuckled. 'The latest in a long line, eh? Them pair o' little devils never manage to keep one fer more than a couple o' months.'

'Well, my position is only temporary until they start boarding school in the New Year,' Amber informed her as she undid the ribbons on her bonnet and slid the cloak from her shoulders.

'Just as well, I doubt you'd 'ave stuck it fer much longer than that,' Daisy said with a grin. 'But would yer like to see the boys' room, an' will yer want any 'elp wiv their unpackin'?'

Amber nodded and followed her from the room to the next door along. This one was decorated in shades of blue and a cheery fire was burning in the grate with a large guard placed around it. 'This is the room the young 'uns usually use when they come to stay,' Daisy told her. 'But now, if yer sure there's nuffin I can 'elp yer wiv I'd best gerr on else the missus will 'ave me guts fer garters.'

Amber smiled at her and as the girl bustled away she felt as if she had made at least one friend here. Daisy looked to be about the same age as herself and after all the heartache of the last few months she was like a breath of fresh air.

Minutes later the boys' luggage was carried up to her and she spent the next hour unpacking their clothes and putting everything neatly away. She was just about finished when the door burst open and the boys sailed into the room.

'The maid is bringing us afternoon tea up here, and you're to have yours with us,' Harry informed her. 'Because the grown-ups want a few minutes to themselves.' He was a good-looking young fellow with curly blond hair and bright-blue eyes, and already it was plain to see that he was going to be very handsome when he grew up. He was going to be tall too because he already reached just past Amber's shoulder.

Seconds later a maid appeared bearing a laden tray. There were dainty cucumber and ham sandwiches, tiny pork pies, a large pot of tea and a selection of cakes and pastries. The maid placed it on the table by the window and Harry asked politely, 'Shall I pour one for you, Miss Ainsley?'

Amber was in the process of folding their pyjamas and she smiled at him. Perhaps they did know how to behave after all. 'Yes, thank you, Harry. I shall be with you in a second.'

She finished what she was doing and joined them, pleased to see that they were sitting quietly. 'Oh, I can't tell you how much I've been lookin' forward to this,' she said as she lifted the delicate cup and saucer and took a long drink. Suddenly she clutched at her throat, trying to catch her breath as her eyes watered and the boys began to giggle helplessly. It was then she saw the pepper floating on the surface of her drink and she glared at them. She would have liked to shout at them but she couldn't get a word out of her stinging throat.

'Th . . . at wa . . . sn't f-funny!' She managed to croak eventually. They showed no signs of remorse whatsoever and now Amber understood why so many of their nannies had left. Even so, she behaved with as much dignity as she could muster as she reached for another cup and poured herself a drink and thought back to the advice she had been given – start as you mean to go on! Perhaps it was time to do just that!

Chapter Seventeen

Thankfully, by bedtime the boys were tired and once Amber had ensured they were tucked up in their beds and had all they needed, she slipped next door to her own room. The maid had been in and lit the oil lamp. She had also made up the fire in the small grate and turned back the bed so the place looked warm and cosy. Amber yawned. She was worn out, what with all the travelling and trying to keep the boys in order, and all she wanted to do was sleep. Quickly she undressed and hung up her gown, then after washing in the water the maid had left ready, she slipped her nightgown over her head and clambered onto the bed. She was so weary that she was sure she would be asleep as soon as her head touched the pillow, but as she pushed her legs down the bed, they connected with something disgustingly wet and squidgy and she shrieked as she leapt out again. Throwing back the covers back to see what it was, she heard laughter on the landing outside her door, and rushing to it she thrust it open to find the boys in their nightgowns with tears of mirth streaming down their cheeks.

'Thought that was funny, did you?' she barked, heedless of who heard her. And lunging forward she took the boys by their ears and began to haul them back towards their own room.

'*Ow! Ow!* Get off me,' Harry shouted, slapping out at her ineffectually.

At that moment Mr Temple appeared from his room further down the landing. 'What the *hell* is going on here?' he demanded. 'You're making enough noise to waken the dead!'

'Shall I tell him, or shall *you*?' Amber spat as she shook the two boys, making them screech louder than ever. 'Actually, sir, these two thought it were a huge joke to put a wet sponge in me bed,' she told her employer. 'An' that were after almost chokin' me by puttin' pepper in me tea earlier on!'

'I see.'

Mrs Temple appeared at his shoulder and glanced worriedly towards the boys as she saw that Amber was holding each of them by an ear, but her husband put his arm out and ushered her into the room.

'I suggest we deal with this matter in the morning before we wake the whole household,' he said with authority as he glared at the boys. 'Meanwhile, you two get yourselves to bed this instant, and Miss Ainsley, I suggest you ring the bell in your room and the maid will supply you with dry sheets.'

'Yes, sir.' Amber reluctantly released the boys and looking aggrieved they rubbed at their sore ears before slinking back into their room.

Amber realised now that she shouldn't have got so physical with them but she wasn't sorry. Mr Temple could dismiss her for all she cared. She'd be damned if she'd let those two little devils get the better of her.

Once back in her room she reluctantly rang the small bell to the side of the fireplace, hating having to disturb any of the maids so late at night. Had she known where the linen cupboard was, she would have got the dry sheets herself, but as it was, she didn't have much choice.

Daisy appeared within minutes, and half an hour later the bed was dry and newly made up again.

'Eeh, they're little buggers, them pair are,' she said as she collected the wet sheets into a pile, and then she blushed. 'Sorry, miss. Me mouth tends to run away wiv me. Me ma allus says it'll be the death o' me one o' these days.'

Amber shook her head. 'It's all right, Daisy. I agree wi' you. If I don't get the sack in the mornin' I reckon I'm goin' to have to start puttin' me foot down wi' 'em else they'll be runnin' rings round me, the little blighters. I have to say Mrs Temple didn't look none too pleased wi' me at all.'

'That's 'cos she's the one as ruins 'em,' Daisy confided. 'An' that's why Mr Temple wants 'em sent away to school to learn a bit o' discipline.' She stifled a yawn and smiled apologetically. 'Sorry, miss. It's been a long day. Is there anythin' else you'll be needin' afore I turn in?'

'No, you get off to bed, an' thanks, Daisy.'

Once the girl had gone Amber clambered into bed again and lay watching the shadows flicker across the ceiling. Although it was quite late at night it was still very noisy outside and she couldn't get used to it. A great wave of homesickness swept over her as tears started to form in her eyes and suddenly she almost hoped she would be dismissed the following morning. Just as her mother had once warned her, London was turning out to be nothing like she'd expected and she longed for the peace of the tiny cottage where she had been brought up. Thankfully at some point she slept, although in her dreams she could hear her baby crying and she woke the next morning with tears on her cheeks.

'So, who is going to explain what went on then?' Mr Temple asked sternly as Amber and the boys stood in front of him in the drawing room after breakfast the next morning.

'It was our fault, Father,' Harry confessed with his head bowed and Amber was so shocked that her eyes widened. Unknown to her the boys had had a conversation earlier and they were actually quite impressed with the way she had stood up to them. None of their other nannies had ever dared to do that and they didn't want her to leave. She was so much younger and much more fun than the others had been.

Harry went on to confess more fully what they had done, ending with, 'And we are very sorry and we'd like to apologise.'

'Then do it.'

They both turned to face Amber and told her meekly, 'We apologise for our bad behaviour, Miss Ainsley.'

When Amber nodded, not quite knowing how to react, Mr Temple said with a glower, 'Very well, we'll let it go this time. But I don't want to hear another word about you playing any more silly pranks, do you hear me?'

'Yes, Father,' the boys said quietly in unison and he pointed at the door. 'Right, now go and get your breakfast and be thankful that I haven't confined you to your room for the day.'

Needing no second bidding the boys scooted off to join their mother and their grandmother in the dining room and inclining her head towards him, Amber made her way back upstairs and began to tidy the boys' room. She wasn't quite sure where she was supposed to breakfast until Daisy appeared with a tray a short time later.

'I wasn't sure what yer'd want, miss,' the girl told her with a cheery smile. 'So I've put a bit of everythin' that were goin' on. Just leave what yer don't want. An' cook says to tell yer that yer more than welcome to join the staff in the kitchen fer breakfast, if yer'd prefer it to havin' it in yer room.'

'That's reet kind of yer, Daisy,' Amber answered and then suddenly corrected it to, 'That's very kind of you, Daisy.' She supposed she should at least make an effort to speak as the boys did – for the time she was working with them at least.

'So what 'ave the little terrors got in mind fer today?' Daisy asked pleasantly as she placed the tray on the table by the window.

'They ain— haven't really said yet,' Amber answered as she eyed the food. There looked enough on the plates to feed her and the boys and she knew she wouldn't be able to eat even half of it, but it was kind of Daisy to have thought of her.

'I 'eard the mistress an' Mrs Temple sayin' they were goin' shoppin',' Daisy told her as she turned to leave and with a cheeky grin she confided, 'They do a lot o' that when Mrs Temple comes to stay. I dare say yer ain't got as many shops at the coast as we 'ave 'ere?'

'I couldn't really say seein' as I haven't seen much o' London yet,' Amber answered as she poured herself a cup of tea.

Daisy nodded. 'In that case, if yer can wangle any time off I'll 'ave to take yer sightseein'. I'm off next Sunday so we'll 'ave to see what we can do. Ta-ra fer now.' And with that she was off as Amber sat down to tackle the gigantic feast the girl had brought her.

As it happened, later in the week, which luckily passed with the boys on their best behaviour, Amber discovered that they were to go to church on Sunday morning with their mother and grandmother and then they were going to have lunch with them, so Mrs Temple told Amber that she wouldn't need her services until late in the afternoon.

They were now into November and as she and Daisy set off on Sunday morning, the streets were shrouded in a thick yellow fog and it was bitterly cold.

'Oh, this is horrible,' Amber said as she pulled her scarf up over her mouth.

Daisy, looking quite resplendent in her Sunday best, which included a very pretty bonnet trimmed with silk flowers, giggled. 'We call it smog an' yer get used to it when yer live 'ere,' she told her. 'I don't mind it meself. It's the snow I don't like. Do yer get snow in Whitby?'

'We get it up on the moors but not so much at sea level,' Amber answered, thinking how different Daisy looked out of her uniform. 'Where are we going?

'I thought I'd take you into the city to see the shops,' Daisy answered good-naturedly. 'Although most of 'em will be shut o' course, wiv it bein' a Sunday. Still, we can 'ave a look in the winders.'

Amber was lost in seconds as they moved on, although Daisy seemed to know the whole place like the back of her hand.

'This is Oxford Street,' Daisy informed her eventually as they turned into a street that seemed to stretch for miles. There were shops all the way down on either side and Amber was shocked. She had never seen so many all at once in her life. There were huge department stores with beautiful mannequins in the windows modelling everything from day dresses to evening gowns, shoes, bags and all manner of things, and dotted in between were jewellers' shops displaying rings, bracelets and necklaces set with jewels in all the colours of the rainbow. Apart from a few people who were window shopping like her and Amber, the street was surprisingly quiet.

'Crikey, we only 'ave one dress shop in Whitby,' Amber told her. 'An' it ain't a quarter as big as any o' these.'

They strolled on for quite a while till eventually Daisy asked, 'There's a coffee shop 'ere that's open, look. Shall we treat usselves to a cup o' tea and a slice o' cake?'

'Why not?' Amber found that she was quite enjoying herself and soon they were seated at a table in the window. A little maid came to take their order and they spent another pleasant half an hour chatting and enjoying themselves. The light was beginning to fade by that time, so reluctantly Amber told her, 'I think we should be heading back now. I don't want to get into Mrs Temple's bad books.'

As they left the café and began to walk back the way they had come, Daisy asked curiously, 'So 'ave you got a boyfriend back 'ome?' She'd noticed a sad look in Amber's eyes on many occasions and wondered if it was perhaps because she was missing a sweetheart she'd left behind. But before Amber could answer, a man dressed in little more than rags with straggly dirty hair ambled towards them with his hand outstretched pleading, 'Spare a penny or two fer a poor 'omeless bloke, ladies?'

He reminded Amber of Trampy Ned, an old man who lived in and around Whitby, and she began to delve into her bag, but Daisy put her hand out to stop her and told him smartly, 'N,o we ain't. Now be on yer way else I'll call a copper, matey!'

The man turned with a scowl as Amber looked towards Daisy in dismay. 'But the poor chap was down on his luck,' she said with concern. She always tried to spare a little for Trampy Ned back at home.

Daisy snorted. 'Now look 'ere, you'll 'ave to 'arden up if you're to be 'ere fer any length o' time. This city is crawlin' wi' people like 'im an' most of 'em will spend anyfin' yer give 'em on drink or drugs. The place is rife wiv pickpockets an' all, so just make sure you allus keep your 'and on your bag. I should 'ave warned you before. They're so good at what they do you don't even know they've robbed you till you come to get your purse.'

When Amber looked shocked, Daisy chuckled. 'Don't be fooled by the posh shops.' She shook her head. 'London is a den o' vice. There's more prostitutes 'ere than anywhere, I reckon, an' if you were to come out of an evenin' you'd see 'em all standin' on street corners toutin' for business.'

'Really?' Amber looked around nervously but Daisy was quite calm.

'Don't worry, you're quite safe wiv me,' she reassured her. 'An' you ain't likely to be out much on your own at night, are you? So you'll be fine. I was just tellin' you, that's all.'

They did a detour on the way back so that Amber could get a glimpse of the River Thames and once again she was disappointed. On the pictures she had seen of it the water had been blue but in reality she saw that it was a sludgy brown colour with a lot of rubbish floating on it.

'You wouldn't fancy fallin' in that, would you?' Daisy grinned, then said, 'Tell me all about Whitby.'

'There's nothing much to tell really,' Amber told her. 'Most of the people who live there are fishermen, includin' me dad an' two o' me brothers. The other two work on the railways.'

'Oh, an' you didn't get to answer me question – is there a boyfriend back there waitin' for you an' how long 'ave you worked for the Temples? I must admit I was surprised when I first saw you, most o' their nannies were much older.'

'In answer to your first question, no, I don't 'ave a boy-friend,' Amber said a little tetchily. 'An' in actual fact I didn't get this job till a couple o' days before we all set off to come 'ere.'

'So what did you do before that?'

Amber sighed, a little tired of all the questions. 'Actu-ally, I was workin' at the harbour wi' the Scottish herrin' girls before that. But the job came to an end when they moved on so I took this one. It's only till we get back to Whitby, though. The boys will be goin' off to boarding school then, an' before you ask – no, I ain't decided what I'll do next.'

'Oh!' Daisy looked disappointed. She'd hoped that she'd see more of Amber in the future when the boys visited their grandparents but it didn't look like that would happen.

'Well, you could allus get a job 'ere,' she suggested but Amber shook her head.

'I suppose I could but to be honest I've missed me home. I reckon London is a bit busy for me. Still, I'm sure somethin' will turn up.'

Daisy nodded in agreement and they hurried on their way, keen to get back to the house before darkness set in.

The next weeks passed in a blur. The boys kept Amber busy and she was pleased to be included in the sightseeing trips that their parents and grandparents took them on. She saw Buckingham Palace and the Houses of Parliament and many famous landmarks that she had only ever heard about. Then suddenly Christmas was almost upon them and her feeling of homesickness intensified. She had never been away from her family for the Christmas celebrations, but then, she thought, she was earning good money and it was only for the one year, after all. She also thought of her baby and wondered what sort of first Christmas she would have, but the thought was so painful that she tried to push it away.

The week before Christmas a huge Christmas tree was delivered to the house. It was so tall that it almost reached the high ceiling of the drawing room where it was placed in a large barrel of earth, and Amber and the boys spent a happy afternoon decorating it with their grandmother's beautiful glass baubles and hundreds of tiny candles.

'You've done a lovely job of that,' Mrs Temple praised when she came down to dinner, standing back to admire it.

'But would you get the boys to change now please, Amber? They'll be dining with the family this evening.'

Amber didn't mind at all. When the boys dined with their family, she had her meals with the staff in the kitchen and she got on well with them. In fact, it was soon more than obvious that Thomas, one of the young grooms, was smitten with her.

'You lucky devil,' Daisy sighed enviously. 'I wish it were me he were sweet on. Don't you like 'im?'

'He's very nice,' Amber told her cagily. 'I just don't want a boyfriend.'

Daisy raised her eyebrow but didn't comment. All she ever thought about was getting married, having her own little home and having babies, but then she supposed it was each to her own and thankfully she stopped teasing about it.

A couple of days before Christmas, Mrs Temple allowed Amber to have a few hours off to go and do a little Christmas shopping and she set off with Daisy in a happy mood. Amber bought small gifts for each of her family and once again, as she thought of being away from them at Christmas, she felt a severe wave of homesickness. She had decided some time ago that she would never want to live in London. Compared to Whitby it was sooty and noisy and nothing like she'd imagined it would be. She missed being able to stroll up to the ruins of Whitby Abbey on a balmy evening to watch the ships out at sea and feel the wind in her hair. And she missed the sounds of the waves lapping on to the beach and the good clean salt air. But she also wondered what she would do when she got home.

It was hard to believe that not so long ago she had been happy in her job at Greenacres, until the master had started to take an interest in her and everything had changed. Now she knew that her life was never going to be the same again. She would never be able to trust another man and fall in love and even if she did, she knew that it could only end in tears when they discovered that she'd given birth to an illegitimate child. So what did the future hold for her? At the moment it looked very bleak indeed. Not a day went by when she didn't think about her baby and yet deep down she knew that she had done the right thing by letting her go. What sort of life could she have offered the child? But it didn't stop her hurting, and so she just took it a day at a time as she counted down the days until she could go home again.

The one good thing to come out of this job was that after a not so good start she had now got a good rapport going with Harry and George and surprisingly she knew that she would miss them when the job finally finished.

When she and Daisy got back from their shopping trip, Amber took the gifts she had bought up to her room to find Harry waiting on the landing for her. She smiled and went to walk on but he fell into step beside her asking, 'Did you get everything you wanted?'

'Yes. I found me mam a lovely shawl on the market and I got me dad a new pipe. He likes to sit outside the cottage of an evening and have a smoke when the weather allows. Then I got socks fer me brothers. Theirs have always got 'oles in 'em.'

He courteously carried the bags to her bedroom door for her before saying pensively, 'George and I will miss you when we go away to school, Ainsley.'

'I shall miss you too,' she responded. 'But I'm sure you'll love it at school when you settle in.'

She paused to take the parcels back off him and blushing, he asked, 'Will we ever see you again?'

'Oh, I'm sure you will. You'll be coming back to yer 'ome fer the holidays an' seein' as we live in the same town, we're bound to bump into one another at some point.'

He nodded and with his shoulders drooping he sadly made his way back to his room leaving her with a frown on her face. If she wasn't mistaken the boy had developed a little crush on her. But it didn't trouble her unduly. She had no doubt he would soon forget about her once he started school.

Chapter Eighteen

'How would you like me to carry you down to dinner in the dining room tomorrow? It will be Christmas Day after all,' Barnaby suggested to Louisa as he stood at the side of her bed on a cold and frosty evening.

She turned her face away. 'When will you get it into your head that I'm not well enough to get up? Why don't you spend the day with your children? They're the ones who seem to demand all your attention nowadays.' Her voice was dripping with sarcasm.

Barnaby glanced at Mrs Ruffin, who was pottering about the room dusting the furniture, but she merely shrugged and he felt the colour flame in his cheeks. He had done everything he possibly could to please Louisa since they had brought the babies home. Only the week before the Harley Street doctor Barnaby had been corresponding with had come to the house to see if there was anything that could be done to help her regain her health. But after examining her the man had shaken his head.

'I'm afraid your wife's condition appears to be as much mental as physical,' he had told him in hushed tones. 'There is nothing that can be done about the continued bleeding, although I do feel it might help if she could resume her normal lifestyle as much as she's able to. Lying in bed never did anyone any good. She'll lose muscle power and become even more depressed.'

'So what can be done? There must be *something*!'

The doctor had shaken his head. 'Your wife is of a very delicate constitution and she informed me that she never wanted the babies in the first place. She seems to resent you for that and blame you for what is happening to her now.'

'I'm quite aware of that, sir.' Barnaby had strode to the window with his hands clasped behind his back feeling helpless. 'Do you think it would help if I insisted she got up?'

'I fear that would do more harm than good. Believe me, I have seen this happen to women of a certain class more times than I care to remember. Some women have no inclination to become a mother and I'm afraid, from what I have gathered, your wife is one of them. All you can do now is gently persuade her to get up when she feels able to, although I fear she will never again be as she was. And I suppose I don't have to remind you that another pregnancy could well be disastrous for her, do I? I'm sorry I can't give you more positive news.'

Once the doctor had left, Barnaby had made his way up to the nursery on legs that felt like lead. He had found the nanny tidying the nursery whilst the babies slept in their cribs and as he gazed down on them he felt infinitely sad. He had imagined that their birth would bring him and Louisa together again, but all it had done was drive them further apart and he was wondering if he was paying now for his wickedness in the past.

Charlotte was continuing to thrive, but the same couldn't be said for David. Despite the wet nurse's best efforts, he was still a puny, sickly child who spent the majority of his time whining, whilst Charlotte was plump with a ready smile for anyone who paid her attention. She already recognised her father and would reach up her chubby arms to him and gurgle with delight each time he leant over her crib. He never tired of being with her or her brother, which he supposed was just as well seeing as their mother had no time for them. Every day the nanny would go to Louisa's room to ask if she would like to see them and every day the answer was always the same – she was too tired.

And so it was that on Christmas Day Barnaby made his way up to the nursery to see his children. 'Any problems, Nanny?' he asked.

The woman shook her head and smiled. 'Not with Miss Charlotte, sir. But I'm afraid I'm still gravely concerned about Master David. I've asked the doctor to call in again to check him over the day after tomorrow. I hope that meets with your approval? Oh, and a Merry Christmas, sir.'

'The same to you,' Barnaby responded, although it certainly didn't feel like the best start to it. 'And of course, please feel free to summon the doctor whenever you deem it necessary.' Barnaby stared down at the little boy. He had always dreamt of having a son, a boy he could teach to play football and swim and ride a pony, but this poor little scrap was so weak he struggled to even feed. 'I shall be at the shipyard for the next few days but perhaps you could let me know what the doctor says when I return home?'

She nodded and not wishing to disturb the babies while they were resting, he left the room. Soon after he mounted his horse and set off for the harbour. A couple of his whaling ships were late returning and he wanted to see if there had been any news on them. The wives of the fishermen were becoming concerned and only the night before they had carried lanterns up to the Abbey where they could watch for them returning. Up until now he hadn't been too worried – the whaling ships were often late in, but now he was becoming uneasy.

The whaling ships were at the most risk for they travelled as far as Greenland in appalling conditions and some were lost and never returned when they were trapped by sea ice or crushed. Those that did return would bring their catches of whales, polar bears and seals back and there would be furious activity in the large boiler houses along the quay where the whale blubber was turned into oil. The whale bones would then be cleaned and sold to make women's corsets, so there was little waste and much higher pay for the men who had risked their lives to catch them.

Barnaby had known men to lose fingers and toes through frostbite and many had been washed overboard in storms at sea. But the boats that were late at present were concerning him more than most because he knew that Amber Ainsley's father and two of her brothers had sailed in one of them to earn a little extra money for Christmas. This was foremost in his mind as he reached the hill that led down to the harbour. Here he reined his horse in and stared out across the great expanse of sea, looking out for the tall masts of the ships from which the sailors would watch for icebergs or whales in the freezing Arctic oceans. But he was disappointed. So he carefully guided his horse down the frosty hill.

As he rode into the harbour, he saw many of fishermen's wives gazing out to sea, their faces strained. Dismounting, he tethered his horse and went to join them. Some of them had hungry-looking children clinging to their skirts, their faces gaunt and their noses red with cold. Others held babies in their arms while the older women stood huddled into drab woollen shawls, their faces anxious as they looked for a sight of their men returning. An arrow of guilt pierced through him; they should have been at home celebrating Christmas with their families. He knew they would probably be relying on the wages the men had earned to feed them and making a hasty decision he strode towards his office, which was nestled next to one of the boiler houses.

'Winterton, give me the key to the safe,' he ordered the young clerk who was sitting at his desk. Normally he would have had the day off but because of the missing ships he had agreed to work. Now the young man jumped to attention as he fumbled in the desk to do as he was asked.

Minutes later Barnaby withdrew a bag of coins from the enormous metal safe and after tucking it into his pocket he handed the key back to Winterton, telling him brusquely, 'Make sure that is put away safely, then get yourself off home to your family. There's nothing more you need to do today.' With a nod he strode out into the cold again.

As he approached the first woman he came to, the little girl at her side shrank further into her mother's side and stared at him suspiciously.

'Mrs Larkin, isn't it?' He ruffled the little girl's hair and was rewarded with a wary smile. It was funny, he thought, until he had had his own children, he'd never taken much notice of anyone else's.

She nodded. 'Aye, it is, Mr Greenwood.'

He pressed a silver coin into her palm. 'Use this to tide you over until your husband returns.'

Tears sprang to her eyes as she clutched the coin. 'Thank you, but I think yer mean *if* he returns, don't yer?' She had seen too many men lost at sea in her time.

'He'll be back, Mrs Larkin,' Barnaby said with a certainty he was far from feeling.

He began to walk amongst them, handing out coins, which would no doubt be spent on a meal for them all that evening. He felt it was the least he could do.

Eventually at the far side of the harbour he came to Mrs Ainsley who bristled when she spotted him coming towards her.

'Good evening, Mrs Ainsley.'

She gave him a curt nod and turned her attention back to the sea.

'I hope you are well?' he said, trying not to be bothered by the woman's reaction to him.

'I will be when me man an' me lads come 'ome.'

From her manner towards him, he realised that she had guessed he was the father of her daughter's child and he felt ashamed as he offered her a silver coin.

'An' what's that for?' Her voice had a cutting edge to it as she glared at him.

'I'm merely trying to ensure that the families of the fishermen have enough to get by on until they get back.'

'Aye, well I 'ave, thank yer very much, so yer can keep yer money.'

'You can consider it a loan until Mr Ainsley returns, if you prefer,' he said patiently but again she shook her head. After what he had done to her lass she could have spat on him as look at him, although of course she knew that she couldn't.

'I, er . . . was wondering if you'd heard how your daughter is getting on with the Temples in London?' he said then. 'She's due back soon, isn't she?'

'In just over a week, an' aye, I have heard from 'er an' she's well.'

'Good, I'm delighted to hear it.' He would have liked to say more but it was like talking to a brick wall so he turned with a sigh. She was the only one who had refused his money and he hoped that she had enough food to get by on – he didn't like the thought of her going without. But there was nothing he could do about it if she chose to be stubborn. 'Goodbye then, Mrs Ainsley, and a Merry Christmas.' The second the words had left his lips he could have bitten his tongue out. Here she was standing in the freezing cold waiting for a husband and sons who might never return and he was wishing her a Merry Christmas. The look she gave him was so scathing that he shrivelled inside and he turned about so hastily that he almost fell over.

Alice stood there until late that morning. Many of the other women with children had made their sad way home to see to their bairns but Alice stayed, hoping against all hope that a glimpse of the ships would appear through the mist.

The house felt strangely quiet when she got back and she stared sadly at her husband's empty chair at the side of the fireplace. Will and Ted had come home the day before to spend Christmas with the family and she saw that they had thought to pop the goose that she had collected from the butcher the day before into the range oven. They had also prepared the Brussels sprouts and the vegetables, so at least they would have a Christmas dinner – not that she thought for one moment any of them would enjoy it. How could they when half of their family was missing, possibly lost at sea?

She nodded towards the two young men who were solemnly staring at her. Then with an effort she raked the fire, which was almost out, and once she had got it blazing again, she set about rolling some pastry to make mince pies.

The following morning found her standing on the quay yet again. The boat was four days late now and everyone's concerns were growing but all they could do was watch, wait and pray.

Boxing Day had no happier start for Barnaby up at Greenacres, for as he sat at breakfast there was a pounding on the door and seconds later Nancy appeared to tell him. 'Your mother an' father in-law are 'ere to see yer, sir. Shall I show 'em in?'

'Er . . . yes, Nancy, please do.' He quickly dabbed at his mouth with his napkin and was just rising when Louisa's parents swept into the room.

'Good morning, Mrs Hamilton-Tate, Mr Hamilton-Tate.' Barnaby gave them a little bow. They looked tired and dishevelled and he realised that they must have travelled through the night in their carriage. 'This is a pleasant surprise,' he lied. 'I wasn't expecting to see you.'

His mother-in-law scowled at him as she undid the ribbons on her elaborate bonnet. 'We didn't expect to see you either, but I received a letter from Louisa asking us to come as soon as possible, so here we are. I believe she is no better?'

'I'm afraid not.' Barnaby sensed trouble. Both Louisa's parents were fiercely protective of her and he dreaded to think what she must have written to them to make them come so quickly.

'So what have you done about it?' Margaret Hamilton-Tate stared at him haughtily.

'Well, I did have a doctor from Harley Street come to examine her,' he said in his own defence. 'But unfortunately, he said that there's nothing to be done. Hopefully time will be the healer.'

'Rubbish!' she scoffed. 'That isn't good enough if my poor darling is suffering. And what about the babies?'

'Charlotte continues to thrive but I'm afraid David isn't quite so hearty,' he mumbled, feeling as if it was his fault. His mother-in-law could always make him feel that way.

'And what about my businesses? Are they doing well? I'll take a look at the books whilst I'm here.' This was from his father-in-law, Robert, and Barnaby clamped his teeth together. Robert never allowed him to forget that he'd had very little when he first met Louisa and that he owed his success to him.

'The businesses are doing fine,' he told him tightly. 'Although a couple of our whaling ships are late coming back and we have grave concerns about them. But I haven't given up hope of them returning safely.'

182

Margaret waved her hand and said irritably, 'Oh, don't start on about business, please. I'm more concerned about my daughter at present. A cup of tea and some breakfast wouldn't go amiss either. We have travelled a long way, you know!'

'Of course.' Barnaby quickly summoned the maid to bring a fresh pot of tea and more food as she settled herself at the table. Soon the room became silent as they ate their meal but the second she had finished, Margaret asked him, 'Would you kindly accompany me to my daughter's room? And then once I've seen her, I would like to see my grandchildren.'

Barnaby nodded but couldn't help but notice that the urgency to see her daughter had only struck after his mother-in-law had eaten her eggs and drunk at least three cups of tea.

As soon as she entered Louisa's bedroom, Margaret rushed forward, leaving Barnaby hovering behind her at the door. 'Oh, my poor darling!' she cried when she caught sight of her daughter in the bed. She hardly recognised her as the beautiful young woman she had once been. Louisa's once lustrous thick hair now hung in limp cats' tails about her gaunt face and she was so thin that Margaret gasped. 'Are they feeding you?' she cried, appalled.

Mrs Ruffin bristled. 'I've tempted her with every tasty titbit I can think of,' she said, highly affronted. 'But she won't eat, so what do you suggest we do? She doesn't eat enough now to keep a sparrow alive, but we can't force feed her.'

Louisa began to cry as she clung to her mother like a little girl. 'Barnaby has been such a beast to me,' she sobbed. 'He put having children above my welfare even though he knew that I am not strong. I've told him now that he must never come to my bed again. The doctor has told me that it could kill me if I ever become with child again.'

'Then you have done quite right,' her mother assured her. If she were honest, she had never been keen on the physical side of marriage either, which was why Louisa had been an only child. Then turning to Barnaby, she said sharply, 'I suggest you leave the room. You are clearly upsetting her!'

Barnaby clenched his fists and turning about, he barged out of the room, slamming the door behind him so hard that it danced on its hinges. He had never really seen eye to eye with his in-laws. They had never made a secret of the fact that they didn't think he was good enough for their daughter but today he could quite willingly have strangled Margaret.

Meanwhile Margaret was telling Mrs Ruffin, 'I think it's high time my husband and I called in a good doctor to take a look at her. There must be something that can be done.'

'In fairness, Mr Greenwood has already had a doctor here from Harley Street,' Mrs Ruffin told her. 'And he couldn't come up with a cure, but I have noticed . . .' She paused and bit her lip before saying tentatively, 'Well, I have noticed over the last few days when I washed her that although Louisa is losing weight everywhere else her stomach seems to be a little swollen.'

'Let me see,' Margaret demanded bossily and when Louisa drew the covers back and lifted her nightdress her mother saw that Mrs Ruffin was right. 'Are you quite sure that you're not pregnant again?' she asked worriedly.

Louisa shook her head. 'Of course I'm not. I haven't allowed Barnaby to come anywhere near me since the twins were born,' she said indignantly.

'In that case I definitely am going to get another doctor to take a look at you. In fact, I shall go to your father and tell him to organise it immediately.' And with that she swept from the room leaving Louisa looking more than a little frightened.

Chapter Nineteen

Alice had thought of writing to Amber to tell her that her father and brothers' boat hadn't arrived as yet, but she'd thought better of it. By the time Amber would have received it they might have returned safe and sound, and Amber would have had her last days in London spoilt for no reason. After all, she tried to convince herself, they could sail into the harbour at any minute and then all of their worrying would have been for nothing.

Although reluctant to leave without news of their brothers and father, the boys had now returned to their jobs on the railways, and early the next morning after they had departed, Alice wrapped her warmest shawl about her shoulders and set off to keep her vigil on the quay again. It was already crowded with other wives and mothers when she got there and she could see the pain and fear etched into their pinched faces. She herself was desperately tired as she hadn't slept a wink all night, but she was made of stern stuff and was determined not to give up hope.

There was a thick mist floating on the sea and the cold seemed to bite through her, and as the minutes ticked away into hours, she decided to go home, make herself a hot drink and warm up before coming back again. So she made her weary way back to the cottage where she made the fire up and put the large kettle on to boil. Then she sat staring into the flames, her face strained and anxious as she offered up silent prayers that God would return her loved ones safely back to her. But as the light faded from the day so did her hope of ever seeing them again.

Suddenly the door flew open and, startled, she turned to see Edward and William.

'Hello, Mam!' Ted gave her a hug that lifted her from the seat and when he'd finally put her down, Will did the same. 'We decided we couldn't leave you all alone until we know what's happened,' he told her as he gently stroked a wayward lock of hair from her forehead and once more she marvelled at the way they seemed to have grown. They had been little more than boys when they had left to start their new jobs but now they were muscular and tall like their father, especially Edward, who was the double of Eli when she had met him, and unable to stop them, she felt tears start to bubble down her cheeks. The boys looked worried. They could count on one hand the number of times they'd seen their mother cry in the whole of their lives and as one they rushed to embrace her and offer what comfort they could.

As William put his strong arm about her shoulders, his face was grave. He knew now that something must be badly wrong. None of the fishermen ever missed spending time with their families at Christmas if they could possibly help it.

'I'm shocked at me dad even considerin' goin' on a whalin' ship,' he said. 'He's gettin' a bit long in the tooth for that now, surely?'

Alice glared at him. 'Rubbish! Yer dad is still a good, strong figure of a man, I'll have yer know,' she snapped. Yet deep down she knew that he was right. Only the strongest of the fishermen ever ventured on the whaling expeditions but Eli had insisted he would be fine.

'Anyway, it's only five days late,' William told her reassuringly, not daring to voice what he really thought. 'I've known the ships to come back later than this.'

There was a pounding on the door and Mrs Preston stuck her head into the room.

'One o' the ships 'as been sighted from the headland,' she told them breathlessly. 'It should be comin' into the harbour any time now.' And with that she was gone again as Alice snatched her shawl and hastily followed her out with the boys close behind her.

Breathless and panting they arrived to see the ship just coming into the harbour, but as it drew closer Alice's heart sank. It was *The Mermaid*, and Eli and her sons had been on *The Neptune*.

At last it was moored and as the gangplank was lowered, weary sailors came down it to a rapturous welcome from the waiting families. The captain was the last to descend and racing forward Alice caught his sleeve.

'Is *The Neptune* following, Captain?'

Her face was so hopeful that he felt himself shrivel. Removing his cap, he shook his head sorrowfully. 'I's afraid not, Mrs Ainsley. I can only imagine she must have hit an iceberg that was below the surface. We saw the SOS flares and got to her soon as we could but it were too late by then, she'd already gone down! I'm so sorry.'

Unable to take the terrible news in she stared at him numbly.

It was Edward who asked, 'But surely there were *some* survivors?'

The captain gulped and nodded. 'Aye, there were, but not many, lad. Seven we fished out o' the sea but two of 'em passed away shortly after an' your dad an' yer brothers weren't amongst 'em. I'm so sorry fer your loss.'

He replaced his cap and with a nod moved on into the waiting arms of his wife as Alice and her sons stood there trying to absorb the news. Someone had sent word to Greenacres and minutes later Barnaby Greenwood appeared, his face grave as he jumped down from the horse's saddle and went to seek out the captain of *The Mermaid*.

The younger widows were crying and wailing, and their children, seeing their mothers so distressed, joined in, but Alice just stood there, too numb with shock to show any emotion. Her lovely, kind Eli and her beautiful boys, all snuffed out like the flame of a candle. It was just too much to comprehend.

After a while, Barnaby clambered onto a large coil of thick rope to address the crowd.

'To those of you who have suffered a loss, I give my condolences,' he said with a crack in his voice. He gulped as he tried to pull himself together. The news had shocked him too. 'But rest assured you will all be compensated.'

'Oh aye,' one young wife shouted as tears pumped down her pale cheeks. 'An' what cost a life, eh? A lovin' husband an' father?'

Barnaby stared at her helplessly; he had no answer and had never felt so bereft in his life. He jumped down from the rope and once again he moved amongst the crowds, dishing

189

out coins to the bereaved until, at last, they all filtered away. He stood for a long time on the deserted quay staring out to sea and thinking of all the lives that had been lost. One thing was for sure: for many people, their lives were never going to be the same again and there wasn't a damn thing he could do to make it better for them.

Alice, meanwhile, was being led back along the quay by Will and Ted but she could barely put one foot in front of the other. She felt as if she was caught in the grip of a nightmare as she tried to imagine her life without her beloved husband and sons. They had never been rich in the material sense but she had always counted herself lucky that she and Eli had shared the sort of love that comes only once in a lifetime. And now he and her beautiful boys were gone forever and in that moment the pain was so severe that she could have happily flung herself into the sea to join them, for she didn't want to live without them.

Things didn't improve for Barnaby when he arrived home to find his wife in a full-blown temper. 'Where have you been?' Louisa screeched when he entered her room looking weary and upset.

'Something dreadful has happened,' he said quietly. '*The Neptune* has gone down at sea and only a handful of the crew have survived.'

'So?' she answered shrilly. 'That was hardly an excuse to go running off like that leaving me here to entertain Mamma and Papa when they've come all this way to see us. It's not your fault if the ship has sunk, is it?'

Barnaby stared at her for a moment as if he was seeing her for the very first time, and he didn't like what he saw. 'Didn't you hear what I said? There are dozens of men dead! What about their families? How are they to live with the main breadwinner gone? And many of them have young children.'

She shrugged her thin shoulders. 'That's hardly *your* concern,' she told him with a toss of her head. 'And since when have you worried about your workers? They were well paid for what they did and they knew the chances they were taking.'

'Now, Louisa sweetheart. Don't go working yourself up into a tizzy,' Mrs Ruffin, who had been watching the scene with a worried frown, urged.

'Oh, shut up and leave me alone, the pair of you!' Louisa turned her back on them and with a sigh Barnaby left the room.

As he descended the staircase, he saw his father-in-law standing in the hall, a glass of brandy in his hand, staring up towards him with his eyebrows raised. 'Trouble?' he asked.

Barnaby sighed to himself, realising he would now have to tell his father-in-law about the loss of the whaling ship. After all, although it was Barnaby who had built the businesses up to be thriving concerns, his father-in-law was still the major shareholder. Once or twice Barnaby had offered to buy him out but Robert had scoffed at the idea.

'No point, old chap,' he would tell him jovially. 'After all, everything's going to go to your children one day, isn't it? So we may as well leave things as they are.' And with that Barnaby had to be content, although he felt it was unfair.

191

'We've lost *The Neptune* and most of the men on board. The captain of *The Mermaid* suspects she hit an iceberg that was floating beneath the surface. Before she sank, they sent up a flare but by the time *The Mermaid* got to her it was too late.'

Robert stroked his chin. 'Damn bad luck,' he remarked with a shake of his head. '*The Neptune* was a fine ship.'

Barnaby stared at him as if he couldn't believe what he was hearing, before saying shortly, 'Yes, it is. Especially for all the men who lost their lives, and for their families.'

Just like his daughter, Robert seemed less concerned about them than the loss of the ship.

'Aw well, there's nothing can be done for them now, is there?'

'Not for the men,' Barnaby agreed hotly. 'But we could help their families financially. Most of the men had young children.'

Robert shrugged as he swirled the brandy in his glass before taking another swallow. 'We'll have to have a think about it,' he remarked and walked back into the drawing room as calm as you like.

Barnaby clenched his fists and stormed off to his study, wondering exactly what sort of cold-hearted family he had married in to.

Down in Argument's Yard Alice sat staring numbly into the fire as her sons swung the sooty-bottomed kettle over the fire to boil for some tea. As yet their mother hadn't shed so much as a single tear but they weren't surprised. They could see she was in deep shock and guessed that the tears would come later. They just wished Amber was there to comfort her.

'When will Amber be home, Mam?' William asked.

'What?' She stared at them blankly for a moment before answering, 'Oh, not for another eight or nine days. As I told you, she's been working as a nanny for the last couple of months or so.'

'Aye, but where?'

'London.'

They both looked shocked. They had assumed that her new position was local and had wondered why their sister hadn't at least visited them over Christmas, but they hadn't liked to question their mother when she was so worried about their father and brothers. 'And how did she come to hear about a job like that?'

'Barnaby Greenwood told her about it. She's gone wi' the Temples from up on the headland.'

'An' why would he think of offerin' the job to our Amber?' It was Edward who spoke now. 'She is goin' up in the world, ain't she?'

'It's only a temporary position,' Alice told him so quietly that he had to strain to hear her. 'She'll be back soon as New Year is over.'

'Oh aye, an' then what's she gonna do? Will she go to work back at Greenacres?' He was aware that a lot of responsibility would fall to him and William now with three wage earners gone. He and Edward would have to send some of their wages back each week to their mother, otherwise how was she to live and pay her rent? Still, there would be time for talking about practical issues when they'd had time to come to terms with what had happened, but soon, unfortunately, they would have to return to their jobs.

Many of the people in the town were grieving and those who had lost loved ones knew that Christmas would never be the same for them – it would always mark the loss of their nearest and dearest. However, they got on with life as best they could and three days later a poster in the town hall informed everyone that there was to be a memorial service for the deceased. There could be no burials, they had all already gone to a watery grave, so this was the best they could do for them.

The service was to take place in St Mary's Church on the East Cliff and it was a sombre crowd that climbed the one hundred and ninety-nine steps that stood adjacent to the Donkey Road that trailed up to the abbey and the church.

Alice and her sons wore their darkest clothes – they couldn't afford to buy black especially for the occasion. Alice still hadn't shed a tear, nor had a drop of food or drink touched her lips since the night they had learnt the terrible news. Now she was weak and the boys each took an arm and helped her to climb the steep steps.

The church was crowded and, as Alice looked down the aisle, she saw Barnaby Greenwood sitting with his head bent in his family's pew at the front. Next to his was the pew that belonged to the Lord of the Manor, Nathaniel Cholmley, and Alice felt a wave of resentment. Many of the young bereaved wives with small children had already been forced to leave their cottages and take themselves and the children off to the workhouse, but Barnaby Greenwood would never have to worry about facing such a fate, would he? she thought bitterly.

'Amber should be here,' William said brokenly, interrupting her thoughts.

Alice shook her head. 'There's no post over Christmas so there was no way o' lettin' her know,' she told him in a hushed voice. 'An' anyway, there's no point in upsettin' her afore we have to. There's nothin' she could do.'

The service started and as the names of the dead were solemnly read out by the vicar it finally hit Alice that she would never see her lovely sons and husband again and at last the tears came in a wave that threatened to choke her.

'We'll make sure as you an' Amber are all right, Mam,' the boys assured her, feeling helpless but she shook her head. They were young with their whole lives in front of them. One day they would marry and have children of their own and she didn't want them to have to be responsible for her and Amber as well.

'We'll be absolutely fine,' she assured them as they led her from the church. 'Amber will get another job an' I ain't quite past doin' a job o' work meself yet, so you just worry about yerselves.'

The young men exchanged worried glances. They knew how stubborn their mother could be, but now wasn't the time to upset her any more than she already was so they wisely held their tongues as they guided her home.

Chapter Twenty

As the carriage rocked along the bumpy roads, Harry sat as close to Amber as he could, his head lowered, until eventually, he said quietly, 'I can't believe we won't see you again after today.'

'O' course you'll see me,' she told him. 'Like I told you, you'll be coming home from school for your holidays and we'll probably see each other then.'

'But it won't be the same,' he said mournfully.

The boys had been a handful at times, but once Amber had stood up to them and showed them that she wasn't going to allow them to get the better of her, they had shown her a grudging admiration. It was hard to believe they were on their way home. The time seemed to have flown by and already Amber was wondering what she was going to do next. Barnaby Greenwood had assured her that there would always be a job for her at Greenacres, but she knew that she couldn't go back there after what had happened. She also knew that she would never want to live and work in London. It had been nowhere near as romantic as she had thought it would be and she was looking forward to breathing the clean, fresh sea air again, and seeing her mother. She had missed her and hoped that she would be able to find a job that ensured she could still live at home.

She wondered if her father, Amos and Reuben would be at home when she got back. She knew they'd been due back for Christmas but it could be that they had sailed on another trip by now.

For the first part of the journey the boys had been chatty but as it progressed, they both dozed, which gave Amber time to think and her thoughts turned to her baby as they often did. Only the day before she had wrapped the boys up warmly in thick coats, hats and mittens and taken them to the lake in the park to sail the little boats that their grandparents had bought them for Christmas. The sight of the nannies pushing the perambulators about had brought a lump to her throat. Her little girl would be four months old now and she still thought about her every single day. Her biggest regret was refusing to see her. At least if she had she would have a memory of her to cling to. But as it was all she knew about her was what she had heard the midwife say about her having an angel's kiss on her thigh.

'Amber, have we got much further to go?' It was Harry who had woken from his doze.

Amber started. 'Not too far now,' she told him kindly. 'An' I believe we're goin' to stop at an inn soon for somethin' to eat an' drink.'

George was still fast asleep and Harry said quietly, 'Me an' George don't want to go away to school, you know, but father thinks it will be good for us.'

'And I'm sure it will,' Amber answered. 'You'll settle in in no time, an' think of all you'll learn. Why, wi' a good education you can be anythin' you want to be when you grow up.'

It was early evening by the time they arrived back at the Temples' residence and Amber went straight to her room to collect her things together. There was no point in delaying so she supposed she should leave as soon as she was ready. When she came downstairs, Mrs Temple was waiting for her. She led her into her husband's office where she paid Amber her wages, adding a hefty bonus.

'You've been wonderful with the boys,' she praised, shaking her hand. 'Thank you so much for stepping in at such short notice. I know the boys have enjoyed their time with you. In fact, I think they will miss you.'

'Thank you, and I shall miss them too,' Amber responded.

They left the office to find the boys waiting for them in the hallway. They would be leaving for their new school the next morning and both looked thoroughly miserable.

'Take care of yourselves,' Amber told them as they shyly stepped forward to give her a cuddle, and she was surprised to see that there were tears in their eyes. Despite not getting off to the best of starts they had become firm friends and she was sincere when she said that she would miss them. Caring for and nurturing the boys these past few weeks had brought out a side of her that she hadn't known was there. At least, she had thought it was the boys who had unearthed her maternal side, but she had also noticed that her mind had been straying to her baby more and more, so perhaps it was her daughter who had brought about the change in her. She was a mother now. Was someone caring for her baby as she had cared for Harry and George?

Amber made for the door and set off down the drive, as the boys and Mrs Temple stood on the steps waving, and although she was sad to say goodbye to them she also felt excited at the prospect of seeing her family again.

She had just turned into Church Street when someone shouting her name made her look around and there was Bertie Preston rushing towards her with a broad smile on his face.

'Ah, so the wanderer has returned again, has she?' He gave her a cheeky grin. 'What wi' you rushin' off to take care o' your uncle then goin' off as a nanny to the Temple lads for Christmas, I've 'ardly seen owt of you fer months. I hope you're home to stay now?'

Amber really wasn't in the mood for Bertie but not wishing to be rude she merely shrugged and kept on walking. 'Who knows what the future holds, eh? I suppose it all depends on what job I get next.'

He scowled at her. 'But surely now you're ready to think o' settlin' down?' He sounded aggrieved. 'You know I'm ready to get wed whenever you are.'

She stopped so abruptly that he almost bumped into her. This, she decided, had gone quite far enough.

'Look, Bertie, you're a nice chap an' all that, an' I'm sure there's any number o' girls that would jump at the chance o' bein' your wife, but I don't want to get wed. Not now – not ever if it comes to that – so I'd best set the record straight once an' for all!'

His face darkened. 'Oh, I see. I ain't good enough for you now that you're hobnobbin' wi' the gentry, is that it?'

'Of course it ain't!' Amber sighed with frustration. What would she have to do to convince him she wasn't interested? 'I don't even know where you got the idea that there was ever anythin' between us.'

She could see that he was put out but it couldn't be helped and after giving him a curt nod, she hurried on

199

leaving him standing there. Hopefully now he would have got the message.

As she turned into Argument's Yard and saw the dull glow of the oil lamp through the curtains in the cottage, she felt a little rush of happiness. This humble cottage was the only home she had ever known and she was happy to be back.

On entering she saw her mother sitting darning in the chair by the fire but instead of the warm greeting she had expected Alice simply stared at her and Amber knew immediately that something was badly amiss. There was a large clothes horse with damp clothes steaming in front of the fire and the whole place stank of wet washing.

'Hello, Mam.' She gave a tentative smile as she placed her bag down by the door. 'Everythin' all right, is it?'

'No, lass, I'm afraid it ain't.'

Was it her imagination or did her mother suddenly look older? Amber wondered as she went to take a seat opposite her. She looked like the weight had dropped off her as well.

'What's up?'

Alice licked her dry lips and gently told her about what had happened to her father and brothers. Amber's face crumpled as she thought of them all. Her gentle, kind dad, Reuben's cheeky smile and Amos's teasing nature. They were all gone and she would never see them again. It was a lot to take in and she began to pray that she was in a nightmare. Surely she would wake up soon and everything would be as it had been. And yet as she stared at her mother's strained face, she knew that it was true and tears started to pour down her cheeks.

'B-but why didn't you let me know? I would have come home!'

'There wasn't time,' Alice pointed out. 'An' what could you have done, lass?'

'So how have you been managin'?'

'Will and Ted are goin' to send me a bit o' their wages each month, although I'm not happy about it, an' I've started takin' in washin' an' ironin' from the big houses up on the hill. That brings in a bit. We'll scrape by somehow. Especially if you can find another post.'

'I will,' Amber promised brokenly, although as yet she had no idea what she could do. No doubt by now some of the widows whose husbands had gone down with *The Neptune* would be vying for any jobs that were going and they were always scarce enough as it was. Anxiety set in. It was more important than ever to find something – anything. Amber bowed her head. It felt as if her whole life had fallen apart over the last months; first with the baby and now losing her father and brothers, but she knew this wasn't the time to give in to self-pity. Her mother needed her and somehow, although she just wanted to sit and cry, she was determined that they would get by.

Bright and early the very next morning, Amber set off across the frosty cobblestones to begin her job search, but by lunchtime she was chilled to the bone and thoroughly disheartened. She had even tried the local inn saying she was prepared to work behind the bar, cook, clean, anything, but the answer was always the same. There was not a job to be had anywhere and now Amber started to panic. What would become of them if she didn't get work? A vision of the workhouse flashed before her eyes and she shuddered. But at least she could deliver the washing and ironing her mother would have ready.

Once home, she loaded it all onto an old cart the boys had made years ago, each pile safely wrapped in a clean towel, and set off up the hill to the nice houses that looked down across the harbour. How she had always dreamed of living in one of them, she thought wryly, and now she would just be grateful to be able to earn enough to keep the cottage roof over their heads.

At each house, she went to the back door where the housekeeper would check that the work was up to standard before paying her a pittance. Her mother had written her a list of where each pile was to go and halfway through the deliveries Amber was mortified to discover that her next drop-off was at Greenacres.

For a long time she stood at the end of the drive, shivering as she tried to force herself to go on. It had started to snow and it was settling fast, making it difficult to pull the cart, and she dreaded facing the staff she used to work with. But there was no other option so she clamped her teeth together and set off. At the moment her mother needed every penny she could get to survive and she couldn't afford not to.

'Well, bless my soul if it ain't our Amber,' the cook said jovially when Amber timidly tapped at the back door. 'What brings you here, lass?'

'I'm just deliverin' the clean washin' an' ironin' for me mam.'

'Then pull that cart over there in the shelter an' come on in afore you catch your death o' cold,' the kindly woman ordered her. 'I'll get you a nice hot cup o' tea while Nancy goes to find Mrs Boswell.'

Amber did as she was told and minutes later, she gratefully sank down onto a chair at the side of the enormous kitchen table, glad for a brief respite out of the bitter cold. It was so hot in there that her damp clothes instantly started to steam.

The cook carried a mug of tea to the table for her, clucking her tongue sadly before saying, 'We all heard what happened to your dad an' your brothers, God bless their souls. I'm so sorry, lass.'

'Thank you.' Amber sipped at her tea, not quite knowing what to say but thankfully Nancy appeared and grinned from ear to ear when she saw Amber.

'Oh, it's so good to see you,' she said as she hurried forward to give her a hug. 'An' ain't it strange that you're still doin' the laundry for Greenacres one way or another. The new laundry maid what took your place came down wi' the flu last week an' from what we've heard she's reet poorly. Won't you consider comin' back?'

Amber had no time to answer for Mrs Boswell had swept into the room and she too offered Amber her condolences on the loss of her family.

'I've brought the clean laundry back, Mrs Boswell,' Amber told her, rising from her seat. 'I'll just go an' bring it in for you to look at.'

'There'll be no need for that,' Mrs Boswell assured her kindly. 'I know it will be quite acceptable if you and your mother have done it. Just leave it over there and I'll go and get your payment.'

When Amber went back outside it was snowing harder than ever and as she was manhandling the large pile of laundry from the cart, Barnaby appeared around the side of the building and stared at her in amazement.

'Amber . . . Miss Ainsley,' he said eventually. 'What brings you back here?'

She stared at him with loathing. 'I only came to bring the clean washin' me mam has done,' she told him shortly.

'I see.' Rushing forward he lifted the heavy load before she could object and headed for the kitchen with it, but just before he entered, he paused to tell her, 'You do know your job is still open here if you want it, don't you? With two babies in the house now, we could do with more than just one laundry maid.'

Ignoring him, she opened the door and when he passed through it, she re-entered the kitchen where Mrs Boswell was waiting with her payment. As she accepted the money Amber saw Barnaby flush with embarrassment, and keen to be gone she told them, 'Thank you, I'd best get on now. I have other deliveries to make.'

'Ah, can't you stay for just a while longer?' Nancy pleaded. She had missed her and was reluctant to see her go so soon, but now that the master was there she could tell Amber couldn't get away quickly enough.

'We'll have a get together very soon,' she promised as she left, closing the door firmly behind her.

She had barely reached the end of the drive when she heard footsteps pounding behind her and glancing over her shoulder, she saw Barnaby racing towards her.

'I'm glad I've caught you,' he said breathlessly. 'I just realised that Mrs Boswell didn't give you enough for the work you and your mother have done.' He opened his palm and as she saw the coins gleaming there, she shook her head, her eyes flashing with hatred.

'We've been paid the goin' rate an' we don't need your charity!' she snapped, before moving on again, dragging the heavy cart behind her.

Barnaby stood and watched helplessly until her slight form had been swallowed up by the snow.

It was late afternoon and fast growing dark by the time all the laundry was delivered and as Amber pulled the cart down the hill leading into Whitby town she was sure she had never been so cold and weary in her life.

Once she reached the cottage, she left the cart at the little woodstore at the back. As she opened the back door, however, she got a lovely surprise when she saw her uncle sitting at the table drinking a mug of tea.

'Uncle Jeremiah!' Her face lit up at the sight of him. 'Whatever are you doing here?'

He beamed at her. 'I've come to offer my condolences for the loss of the boys and Eli. I just received your mother's letter. And I've also come with what I hope you will think is good news,' he told her. 'And also with a proposition that I hope you and your mother will like!'

When Amber and her mother stared at him curiously, he blushed like a schoolboy. 'The thing is,' he began. 'Martha – that's Mrs Carter – and I . . . well, I know this will sound ridiculous at my age, but we have decided to get married.'

'Why, that's *wonderful* news, Uncle Jeremiah.' Amber rushed to plant a gentle kiss on his cheek. 'And I'm not completely surprised.' She smiled. 'While I was living with you I could see how fond of each other you were, even though you hadn't admitted it to yourselves. I'm sure you'll be very happy together.'

He smiled self-consciously. 'Thank you. But now for my proposition.' Knowing how independent his younger sister was he looked slightly uncomfortable about what he was to suggest but he went on, 'Martha and I have talked about your sad situation and realise that it will be hard for you to manage now, and so we were wondering . . . Would you consider coming to live with us? As Amber will tell you, that house is far too big for just the two of us and—'

Before he could go any farther Alice held her hand up. 'That's a reet kind offer and mightily appreciated,' she said primly. 'But me an' Amber ain't quite charity cases just yet!'

'Please, lass, let me finish,' Jeremiah said hastily. 'For a start off, I never for one minute meant to suggest that you were charity cases. The thing is, you'd be doing us a big favour, you see? Because once we're wed we want to travel, which means we'll need someone to look after the house an' keep an eye on the shop while we're not there, and on Fancy and Biddy. And there would be a wage of course.'

Amber smiled as she thought of the little dog who had stolen all their hearts while she was living with them.

'So will you at least sleep on it afore you make your decision? I shall be staying here tonight, if that's all right with you, and you can tell me what you've decided before I catch the coach home tomorrow.'

'Aye, I'll sleep on it,' Alice said quietly as she turned the idea over in her head. It would be a solution to all their problems, she had to admit, and it would mean that the two sons she had left wouldn't have to help her and Amber out financially. 'But now sit yourself down while I warm some soup up for you an' get you a hot drink.'

And after the journey he'd had, Jeremiah was only too happy to oblige.

Chapter Twenty-One

'The doctor I contacted will be coming to see Louisa tomorrow,' Barnaby's father-in-law informed him at dinner that evening.

'Well, as I have already told you, I have had one doctor from Harley Street come out to examine her,' Barnaby replied, trying hard to keep his temper. His in-laws had done nothing but interfere and criticise since they had got there and he could hardly wait for them to leave, although they showed no signs of going as yet. Like his wife, they had shown little interest in their grandchildren, even though they would be the only ones they were ever likely to get, and he was fast losing patience with them. Robert had also pored over the books – it was as if he didn't trust Barnaby to run the businesses properly, so it was no wonder that he was feeling annoyed. Still, he consoled himself, hopefully once the doctor had been and gone, they would leave too and then the house could return to some sort of normality.

He dabbed at his lips and pushing his chair back, rose from the table saying, 'If you'll excuse me, I usually go up to see the children after dinner. Would either of you care to accompany me?'

They both immediately shook their heads as though he had suggested they walk barefoot in the snow, and so with a sigh he left the room.

Upstairs in the nursery the atmosphere wasn't much better. The nanny had come down with a cold and she looked flushed and ill.

'I'm sorry, sir, but I think you're going to have to get someone in to take over until I'm over this; I'm afraid of passing it on to the babies,' she croaked when he entered.

Barnaby sucked in his breath, wondering if things could get much worse. They had recently dispensed with the services of the wet nurse as the babies were being weaned and could take milk from a bottle, which meant that the nanny was in sole charge of them.

His mind worked overtime as he wondered who he could get to temporarily take the woman's place but then she dropped yet another bombshell when she admitted quietly, 'To be honest, I've been finding two babies a little taxing so I've been thinking of going to retire and live with my sister in Gloucester. She is widowed like me and I think we would rub along very well together. Of course, I was going to give you time to find a replacement once I gave you notice, but now I've come down with this . . . Well, I may as well give you notice now.'

'I understand.' He scratched his head as he wondered who he could trust to replace her, but at that moment Charlotte woke and as soon as her eyes lit on him, she gave him a big grin and held her arms towards him to be picked up. Only too happy to oblige he scooped her out of her crib and tickled her under the chin and instantly she rewarded him with a gummy smile. Charlotte was always delighted to see him and she always made his day with her happy little personality. He only wished her brother was the same. A look of concern flitted across his face as he glanced towards David's crib where he slept on, pale-faced and so much tinier than Charlotte that it was hard to believe they were related.

'How has he been, Nanny?'

The older woman gave a shrug. 'Not good, if I were to be honest, sir. As you know, the doctor calls weekly to check him and the last time he came he thought he detected an irregular heartbeat. That would account for the blue tinge about his lips.'

Barnaby had feared something like this and he frowned, feeling helpless. The poor little chap, it was just as well he was so undemanding because he and his nanny were the only ones who ever paid him any attention. Even his grandparents didn't have any time for him, or Charlotte if it came to that. But then his thoughts returned to who could care for them until he could employ another nanny, and the only one he could think of who might be able to do it was young Nancy, the maid.

'I accept your resignation,' he told the woman solemnly. 'But I would appreciate you trying to hold the fort just until I can get someone to take over. Hopefully it will be in the next day or two. I have someone in mind and if she's agreeable perhaps you would be kind enough to show her the ropes?'

'Of course I would, sir, and I'm sorry to inconvenience you.'

He could hear the relief in her voice and after handing Charlotte to her he quietly left the room and went in search of Nancy.

He found her polishing the long mahogany sideboard in the dining room and the second he entered the room she stood up and glanced at him nervously as if he had caught her doing something she shouldn't.

'Sorry, sir. I didn't know you were usin' this room. I'll come back when you've done.' The staff had been taught to only clean the rooms that weren't being used by the family but as she collected the beeswax polish and duster and headed for the door, he held his hand up to stay her.

'No, Nancy, it's quite all right. I was looking for you as it happens and wondered if I might have a word?'

She narrowed her eyes. 'Yes, sir.'

Barnaby quickly told her about the nanny resigning and as he went on her eyes stretched wide again.

'So you want *me* to stand in as nanny?'

When he nodded, she chewed on her lip for a moment. Nancy was one of nine children so in fairness she was quite used to being around little ones and she supposed she could do it if it was only going to be a temporary thing. In actual fact, she decided, it might be quite a nice change from cleaning so after another moment or two she nodded.

'Very well, sir. But only till you find a replacement, eh? An' you'll 'ave to clear it wi' Mrs Boswell.'

'You leave the housekeeper to me.'

She could hear the relief in his voice and suddenly she felt a little sorry for him. It was common knowledge amongst the staff that Mrs Greenwood was giving him a hard time and the way she treated those babies . . . Well, everyone was disgusted with her. It was obvious she had no interest in the poor little mites.

211

'Thank you.' To her surprise he leant over and took the duster and the polish from her, saying, 'Why don't you go on up to the nursery now so that Nanny can start to show you their routine?'

Nancy bobbed her knee and shot from the room like a bullet from a gun before he had the chance to change his mind.

Late in the afternoon the following day, the doctor from London arrived to see Mrs Greenwood. He was a personal friend of the family and very well respected in his profession, so before he went to see Louisa, Margaret fussed over him, serving him afternoon tea and cake and instructing a maid to prepare a bedroom for him, for all the world as if she were the mistress of the house. Barnaby, meanwhile, prowled about feeling like a spare part.

'Thank you, Margaret, my dear, that was most enjoyable,' Dr Darwin said when he'd eaten his fill. 'I've quite thawed out now so if you would kindly show me the way I shall go and have a look at your daughter now.'

'Would you like me to come with you, sir?' Barnaby volunteered but his mother-in-law shook her head.

'That won't be necessary,' she told him imperiously as she led the doctor from the room.

For almost an hour Barnaby paced up and down the drawing room. His father-in-law had gone out riding so all he could do was wait to see what the doctor said.

He heard him descending the stairs with Margaret when he was done with his examination and one glance at his face told Barnaby that it was not good news.

212

'Well?' Barnaby greeted him as he entered the drawing room and the doctor looked at him gravely. 'Do you have any idea what might be wrong with her?'

'I'm afraid I do.' The doctor clasped his hands behind his back and walked to the window. He always found this part of the job, where he had to impart bad news to the family of his patients, very difficult.

'I'm sorry to tell you this,' he said eventually. 'But I fear your wife has a tumour growing in her stomach.'

Barnaby was shocked; he hadn't expected this. 'I see. And what can be done for her?'

The doctor shook his head. 'I'm afraid there is nothing that can be done with a tumour that size,' he said regretfully. 'I believe it could already have been forming before she became with child and now I gauge it to be the size of a small football. Should I attempt to remove it I doubt she would even wake up from the operation.'

'So what you're saying is . . .' Barnaby couldn't even bring himself to say the words.

'I'm afraid so. I'm so sorry, my man.'

'And . . . and how long has she got?'

The doctor shrugged. 'That I cannot tell you. It could be a few years or it could be a few months. It all depends on how quickly it grows. I've prescribed something to ease the pain but I'm afraid apart from keeping her as comfortable as possible there's nothing more I can do. You can seek a second opinion, of course, if you're not happy with what I've told you.'

'No.' Barnaby shook his head and flopped down onto the nearest chair like a rag doll as he tried to take in what he'd been told. 'I trust you, Doctor, and I'm grateful to you for coming all this way to see her.'

Margaret appeared, sobbing, and Barnaby vaguely real-ised he should be comforting her – she was Louisa's mother after all – but somehow, he couldn't seem to make his legs work.

Suddenly Margaret turned on him, her face livid. 'This is *all* your fault.' She pointed a wavering finger at him. 'All you ever cared about was having a son and heir, even though you knew my darling was of a delicate constitution.'

Greatly embarrassed by her outburst the doctor tried to calm her. 'As I pointed out, Margaret, the tumour could well have started to form before the pregnancy,' he said, hoping to calm the situation, but now she turned on him.

'And you can be quite certain of that, can you?'

The doctor stepped back from the fury in her eyes, before slowly shaking his head. 'Well no . . . I can't say for sure but—'

'Then I suggest you don't have any idea what my poor girl has had to go through married to this monster! She has suffered one miscarriage after another, plus two stillbirths. Don't you think most men would have thought that was enough without putting her through it all again? And for *what*?' She snorted as she cocked her head towards the ceil-ing. 'He might have a son but the chances are he'll never raise him! He's a weakling. Why couldn't it have been the girl instead?'

'I really don't think I wish to be involved in this conversa-tion,' the doctor informed her coldly. 'So if you will excuse me.' Nodding at them both, he left the room.

Margaret glared at Barnaby. 'And what will happen now?'

He shook his head as he passed his hands wearily across his eyes. 'I don't know . . . I haven't had time to think! I suppose all I can do is make the time she has left as comfortable as possible. I'm so sorry, Mother-in-Law—'

'And so you should be!' She turned in a swirl of taffeta skirts and stormed from the room, banging the door behind her so hard that it bounced off the wall, leaving Barnaby still reeling from the shock of what he had just learnt. He finally had children but now he was about to lose his wife and guilt flooded through him as he looked at the bleak future that lay ahead.

Chapter Twenty-Two

'So what do you think o' your uncle's idea, lass?' Alice asked early the next morning as she and Amber sat at the table enjoying an early morning cup of tea together. Jeremiah wasn't up yet and she was keen they should have time to talk.

Amber had lain awake half the night thinking about it, and now she answered honestly. 'I think it's a brilliant idea for you. You've always got on well with Mrs Carter and Uncle Jeremiah and Will and Ted could still come and see you when they had time off work, so I'm sure you'd love living there, especially if Uncle and his wife are going to be away a lot – you'd have Fancy and Biddy to keep you company and the shop to keep you busy. But . . .' – she chewed on her lip for a moment before going on in a rush – 'but it wouldn't be for me. I think I'd like to go my own way and there would be too many memories of . . .'

Alice knew she was thinking of her baby and she gave her a sympathetic smile. 'But how could I go an' leave you to manage all by yourself wi' a clear conscience, lass?' she said worriedly.

Amber chuckled. 'Oh, you've no need to worry about me,' she assured her. 'I can go back to work at Greenacres any time I like.' When she saw the frown appear on her mother's face, she hurried to assure her. 'And don't worry, Mr Greenwood won't be layin' another finger on me. I'd be quite safe there.'

Seeing that her mother still looked undecided, she went on, 'Just think of it, Mam, no money worries, no more wet washin' strung all about the place an' no more havin' to watch every penny. This place is full o' ghosts now an' it would do you good to go somewhere for a fresh start. An' I'd come an' see you every chance I got, you can be sure o' that.'

'Hmm, then I'll think about it,' Alice promised as she rose to stir the porridge that was simmering on the small range. She could hear Jeremiah moving about upstairs and she didn't want him to go back to Scarborough on an empty stomach. Meanwhile Amber began to get dressed for outdoors. She would be collecting the dirty washing for her mother from the big houses on the hill this morning, because even if her mother did decide to leave, she would hate to let her customers down.

By the time she went back into the kitchen her mother and uncle were in earnest conversation and he paused to smile at her.

'Your mother has agreed to come to Scarborough to live.' He was clearly pleased with Alice's decision. 'But can't I persuade you to come too? You know you would be very welcome. Martha would love to have you living there again.'

Amber smiled at him. 'I know you would, but I'm a big girl now wi' a job waitin' for me up at Greenacres.' She had no intention of going back there ever again but she wasn't

217

about to admit that to them. 'In fact, I might have a word wi' Mrs Boswell this very mornin' when I collect the laundry.'

'Very well, if you're quite sure. But just remember there will always be a home with us should you change your mind,' he told her sincerely.

After they'd said their goodbyes, Amber began to tug the old cart through the snow towards the hill, finally allowing the tears she'd been holding back to fall. She was pleased for her mother; it would do her good to start afresh somewhere new and she felt sure that she would be happy living in Scarborough, but now she wondered what the future held in store for herself?

She was breathless by the time she reached the top of the hill and she paused to stare down at the town where she had been born. Perhaps it was time for her to seek pastures new as well, she thought. Depending on when her mother decided to leave for Scarborough this could well be the last time she had to do this and she wasn't sorry.

It was almost lunchtime by the time she dragged the cart down the drive at Greenacres and as she approached the kitchen yard, she spotted Barnaby over at the stables talking to the groom. She quickly averted her eyes, hoping he hadn't seen her. The less she had to do with that man the better, as far as she was concerned. But as she knocked on the kitchen door, she heard him approaching. To her relief he swerved away when Nancy answered, and she gratefully entered the warmth.

The cook ushered her towards a chair saying, 'Eeh, come an' get warm, lass. You look perished. I'll get you a nice hot cup o' tea, eh?'

Whilst she bustled over to the stove Nancy joined her at the table to tell her in a hushed voice, 'Ooh, you wouldn't believe what's been goin' on up here! The mistress's parents sent for a fancy doctor from London to look at the mistress an' apparently, she's really ill.'

When Amber raised her eyebrow, she rushed on, 'Some sort o' tumour in her stomach he reckons an' there's nowt that can be done for her, poor thing.'

Amber looked shocked. 'But what about the babies?'

Nancy shrugged. 'That's another thing. Nanny 'as just given the master notice so he's asked me to take over wi' 'em for a while till he can find a replacement. Poor little mites.'

'That's terrible.' As much as Amber hated Barnaby Greenwood she felt sorry for the mistress – doubly so now.

The cook bustled back with a steaming mug for her just then and asked, 'Nancy told you the gossip, has she?'

Amber nodded as she sipped the drink gratefully. 'Yes, it's very sad. And I have a bit o' gossip an' all, as it happens.' She went on to tell them of her uncle's offer to have her mother go and live in Scarborough with him and when she was done Nancy frowned.

'That's good for your mam but what'll you do now?'

'Ah, well, that's where I was hoping you'd be able to help me.' Amber swallowed. She hated asking but what choice did she have. 'I was wonderin' if per'aps your mam might let me stay there just till I found another job.' All attempts at improving her vocabulary had gone out of the window since she'd returned from London and she was now speaking in her broad Yorkshire dialect again. 'I know it's a big ask,' she rushed on. 'But I could pay me way. I've still got some o' the money I earned from the Temples that'll tide me over for a while an' hopefully by then I'll have got another post.'

'Why don't you just come back here?' the cook asked. 'Mrs Boswell's been sayin' we need another laundry maid.'

Amber flushed as she and Nancy exchanged a glance. Only Nancy knew the real reason why she had left her job as laundry maid so hastily and that was the way she wanted it to stay.

'Though you'd 'ave to be quick,' the cook went on. 'I mean, since that ship went down it won't take long to fill the position.'

'Right, with cook's permission, I'll pop down to see me mam this afternoon an' ask her about you're stayin' fer a while,' Nancy said quickly, keen to get the cook on to another topic of conversation. 'Just so long as you know what you're lettin' yerself in for,' she added with a grin. 'They're packed in to that cottage like sardines in a tin, but I suppose it's better than nothin, so leave it wi' me, eh?'

Amber gave her a grateful smile as she quickly drained the rest of the tea then followed Nancy outside to collect the dirty washing from the laundry room. It had been packed into pillowcases and once it had been loaded onto the cart Amber set off for home.

She was nearing the bottom of the hill when she saw Bertie Preston and her stomach flipped. She'd done her best to avoid him since refusing his last proposal but it was clear he had seen her so she kept on towards him.

'Well, well, well, how the mighty are fallen, eh?' he sneered, staring pointedly at the dirty laundry in the old cart. 'One minute a posh nanny to the nobs' kids in London, an' then a washerwoman, eh?' His hat was set at a jaunty angle and beneath his heavy topcoat, which was trimmed with a thick fur collar, she could see an embroidered waistcoat.

'Don't start, Bertie,' she said wearily. 'I've had a long day and I just want to get home.'

'Hm, but it won't be home for long though, will it, if what your mam told my mam this morning is right. Off to pastures new in Scarborough to live wi' your uncle, ain't she? An' then what will you do? I don't suppose you'll be able to afford to keep the cottage on.'

'That's none of your business,' Amber retaliated as colour rose in her cheeks.

He shrugged nonchalantly as he examined his fingernails. 'You're quite right.' He grinned spitefully. 'But it's funny, ain't it? The rapid recovery your uncle has made, I mean? Makes me wonder why you were *really* hidin' away in Scarborough all those months.'

Amber's stomach did a somersault. What was he hinting at? Could it be that he'd found out about the baby she'd been carrying? Dread coursed through her. If he had, just one word from him and it would be all over the town in no time and her reputation would be gone for ever. Even so, her gaze remained steady as she pulled the cart past him avoiding his eyes.

'It's funny an' all that your uncle is gettin' wed to his housekeeper.' His voice followed her along the street. 'I wonder why you had to go an' look after him if they were so close? I'd say there were somethin' fishy goin' on here.'

Amber hurried on, ignoring him, but a bad feeling had started in the pit of her stomach and when she finally turned into Argument's Yard, she breathed a sigh of relief, before glancing over her shoulder to make sure that Bertie wasn't following her. When she saw old Ned hovering in the shadows, despite the fact that every penny counted, she fished in her pocket and handed him a coin. Touching the old woolly hat that covered his wispy grey hair, he limped on his way. Most of the people in the town helped him when they could and Amber and her family were no exception, poor old thing.

She hoisted the first full bag of laundry into the cottage kitchen and her mother instantly began to sort the washing into piles, ready to put into the copper in the corner, which was already bubbling away. Amber's breath caught in her throat when she saw her fish out some soiled baby clothes. Without thinking she snatched them from Alice's arms and held one of the tiny nightgowns to her nose and sniffed it. Seeing the look of pain on her daughter's face Alice quickly took it off her and handed her some soiled bedding and without a word Amber submerged the sheets into the boiling water, blinking back the tears that had come to her eyes.

It was late afternoon by the time they finished hanging the clean washing on the lines strung across the beams, and they sat down beneath it as it slowly steamed in the heat of the fire.

'I saw Bertie earlier on an' he was askin' questions about why I went to stay in Scarborough,' Amber said worriedly. 'You don't think he knows somethin', do you?'

'O' course he don't,' her mother said, reaching out to pat her hand. 'I told your uncle that I'd join him in Scarborough in the next couple weeks or so.' She looked around sadly at the little cottage that had been her home for so many years. 'First though, I'll have to get rid of all me stuff. I had a word wi' Mrs Preston earlier an' told her I were leavin' an' sellin' up, an' that's better than usin' a loud speaker. Everyone will know be now that I've stuff to sell, unless you want to keep anythin', o' course?'

Amber shook her head. 'Even if I did I've nowhere to store it,' she responded. 'And anyway, if you can sell it for a few bob you'll 'ave a bit behind you.'

'But what will *you* do, lass? Please won't you change yer mind an' come with me? I'm sure we'd settle there.'

'Don't you worry about me,' Amber gave her a warm smile as she rubbed some goose fat into her sore hands. 'I had a word wi' Nancy up at Greenacres earlier on an' she's goin' to speak to her mam about me stayin' wi' them for a bit, just until I get on me feet an' find another post.'

Alice looked horrified. '*What?* You're plannin' to stay wi' Sadie Grimshaw? Why, they're packed to the ceilin' wi' little 'uns as it is an' although she's got a heart as big as a bucket she ain't the cleanest o' women, it's a well-known fact.'

Amber chuckled. 'Well, it'll do fer now. It ain't as if I'm intendin' to be there for long, is it? A job is bound to turn up.'

Alice sniffed, clearly displeased with the news, but she held her tongue. Her daughter had grown up into a young woman over the last months, she'd had to, and now she must let her chick leave the nest and fly free. It wouldn't stop her worrying about her, though, and she wished that things might have been different. It was a funny old life and you never knew what was around the corner. She just prayed that it would be something good for Amber. She deserved a bit of good luck after all she'd been through.

When Amber returned the clean laundry to Greenacres a couple of days later Nancy confirmed that her mother was agreeable to her moving in with them. 'But it ain't posh,' she warned. 'An' the little 'uns can be a reet pain in the arse at times. You'll have to share a room wi' me four little sisters. The other two lads that are still at home have got the other room an' me mam an' dad sleep downstairs in the kitchen.'

'I'm sure it will be fine,' Amber assured her gratefully.

'In that case me mam said just turn up whenever you've a mind to,' Nancy responded.

Over the next week, Amber saw the cottage slowly empty as people bartered for the few bits of decent furniture that Alice had. The only thing she kept was the bone china tea set that had been a wedding present to her and Eli from Jeremiah. It was edged with gold and painted with tiny forget-me-nots and she found that she couldn't bear to part with it, so it was carefully wrapped in newspaper and packed in a trunk to be sent ahead to Scarborough. The oak dresser that it had been displayed on, which had been lovingly polished over the years until you could see your face in it, was sold and eventually all that was left were the two beds they slept in, two chairs and a few pots and pans.

'I don't mind leavin' these for whoever gets the cottage next,' Alice told Amber sadly as they sat together in front of the fire for their last evening. 'It might be a young newlywed couple who'll be glad of 'em.'

Amber nodded, feeling thoroughly miserable. It was hard to believe that just one year ago they had all been together, a happy, loving family. Now some of them were dead, the two younger boys were working miles away and somewhere the newest member of the family, her baby daughter, would be hopefully living happily with her new family.

'I'll miss you, lass.' Alice reached out to squeeze Amber's hand, her voice choked.

'And I'll miss you too. But don't think you've seen the last o' me. I shall come to see you just as often as I can. After all, it ain't as if Scarborough is a million miles away, is it?'

'No, course it ain't.' But for both of them, the imminent parting was breaking their hearts.

Chapter Twenty-Three

'Mrs Ruffin, I just wanted to let you know that my mother-in-law has instructed me to hire a nurse for my wife.'

'Then you can just go and tell her that she already has one – *me*!' Mrs Ruffin puffed her chest out until she looked almost twice her size. 'I've already asked that my bed be carried into her room just in case she needs anything during the night so a nurse will simply be in the way.'

'I see.' Barnaby worried his bottom lip with his teeth as he stared back at the woman. Her devotion to Louisa was clear to see and he secretly agreed with her, although trying to get that across to his mother-in-law would be another thing altogether. At one stage they had insisted that Louisa should go home with them, where they said she would have proper care, but the doctor had pointed out that the journey would be too much for her.

'Very well, I shall inform them,' he said quietly and once again Mrs Ruffin noticed the change in him. She was no fool and had known for some long time before the children had been born that the marriage was not all it should be. She knew that her darling was partly responsible for that for denying her husband his marital rights. She had seen the frustration and the anger in him, but since the birth of the children he had been different. Softer and more approachable somehow. There was no doubt whatsoever that he loved his babies but now he was having to face the loss of his wife and possibly his son too, for little Master David wasn't faring any better.

She watched as he made his way up the stairs, his shoulders slouched, and she felt sorry for him, but then she dismissed him from her mind as she went back to her young mistress who was curled up in bed with her little dog tucked into her side.

'I'm afraid we shall have to go home later this week,' Barnaby's father-in-law informed him at dinner later that evening. 'Work commitments, you know.'

'Of course, I quite understand.' In truth, Barnaby was relieved to hear it. His father-in-law had done nothing but interfere in the businesses Barnaby had built up almost from scratch, and because it was Robert's money that had set him up, there was very little he could do to stop him as he was still the main shareholder. His mother-in-law, meanwhile, had caused chaos in the normally smooth-running household with her interference, much to the annoyance of Mrs Boswell.

'But that doesn't mean we will not be back on a regular basis to check that our daughter is receiving proper care,' Margaret chipped in curtly as she cut a slice of succulent roast beef and placed it on her plate. One thing she couldn't fault was Cook's delicious meals nor her cakes and pastries.

'Mrs Ruffin assures me that she will barely leave her side,' Barnaby said quietly. He had learnt that it was best not to argue with either of them and, after all, he asked himself, what more did he deserve than their contempt? Over the last months he had been forced to stand back and take a good long look at himself and he didn't at all like what he saw and now he was reaping the rewards for his wickedness.

When the dessert was served – a delicious treacle tart with thick cream – Margaret helped herself to two portions. It seemed her concern for her daughter hadn't affected her appetite, Barnaby thought wryly. Thankfully, when she had finished, she left the room and Barnaby and his father-in-law retired to the study for a brandy and a cigar. As much as he resented Robert's interference, Barnaby had to admit that he was a very astute businessman.

'So,' Robert said as he clipped the end off his cigar and settled back into one of the two leather wing-back chairs. 'You must have suffered a great loss with the sinking of *The Neptune*.'

'Yes,' Barnaby admitted. 'But not such a loss as the wives, children and mothers of the men who were aboard her. I believe some of them have had to go into the workhouse.'

Robert waved his hand airily. 'That is not your problem,' he said callously. 'Every man who sets out on a whaling ship is aware of the danger they are placing themselves in and they are well paid for taking the risk. If they haven't made proper provisions for their loved ones, it's none of your concern. What you should be concerned about, though, is how much it will cost to replace the ship.'

Barnaby clamped his lips together and didn't answer. Only that day he had seen one of the fishermen's widows standing on the harbour with a clutch of small, gaunt-faced children hanging off her skirts as she begged from anyone that passed by. He had made sure that she had enough to feed them for the next few days at least, but it had done nothing to ease his conscience, for what would happen to them then? And she was only one of many.

'If you'll excuse me, I'll leave you in peace to enjoy your cigar while I go and check on the children.'

Robert raised an eyebrow but said nothing as Barnaby strode from the room and took the stairs two at a time up to the nursery floor.

Inside he found Nancy with David on her lap as she tried to tempt him to take some bread soaked in warm milk – or pobs as they called it – while Charlotte lay on a blanket on the floor kicking her legs and gurgling contentedly. At the sight of her father, she beamed and instantly held her arms up to be lifted. Barnaby scooped her up and held her tightly. It seemed the only time he was happy now was when he was up here with the children.

'How is he today, Nancy?'

'Hmm.' Nancy sucked her teeth and shook her head. 'Not so good, if I'm to be honest, sir. I've spent ages trying to get him to take some o' this pobs but he ain't havin' it. I even put a bit o' sugar on.'

Nancy had actually turned out to be excellent with the children and they clearly loved her already.

'All you can do is your best.' He grinned as Charlotte snuggled into his neck whilst David lay across Nancy's lap, limp and lethargic. The difference between the two children was growing more marked by the day but Barnaby didn't know what to do about it.

'I don't suppose you've had time to advertise fer another nanny yet, have you?' she timidly ventured to ask.

'I'm afraid I haven't, what with my in-laws being here and one thing and another,' he said apologetically.

'Oh, I weren't complainin',' Nancy was quick to tell him. 'But it just so happens I know someone who might be suitable.'

'Really? Who would that be ?' Charlotte had snuggled down into his lap now and her eyelids were drooping.

'It's Amber who used to work here in the laundry,' she said innocently. She knew that Barnaby wasn't aware that she knew of what had happened between him and Amber. 'Her mam is goin' to live in Scarborough wi' her brother so she'll be lookin' for a job an' I reckon she'd be reet good wi' the babies.'

'Amber? If her mother is leaving, where will she live?'

'That's just it.' Nancy gave up trying with the food and wrapped David's shawl about his scrawny little shoulders. 'She's moved in wi' me mam, just temporary like till she can find a job that suits.'

She saw his jaw tense and knew that he didn't like the idea but despite the fact that Amber had made it clear she never wanted to work for him again she felt she owed it to her to try and find her a place to live – that's if Amber wasn't too stubborn to take the job if it were offered.

'I, er . . . don't think that the job would suit Amb— Miss Ainsley. She isn't a trained nanny, is she?'

Nancy shook her head. 'No sir, she ain't, but then neither am I an' I'm copin' well enough, ain't I? An' as you know she didn't do a bad job wi' the Temples' two boys in London. If you'll forgive me sayin', I reckon it'd be nice for the babies to have someone younger to care for 'em. The older, trained nannies seem to be a lot stricter.' Realising that she might be overstepping the mark, she became silent but at least she had planted the seed. Now all she could do was wait and see if it grew.

Much to Barnaby's relief, Louisa's parents left two days later and as the carriage pulled away the whole house and the staff inside seemed to give a sigh of relief. Once he had waved them off, he went straight to Louisa's room and at sight of him his wife started to sob pitifully.

'What do *you* want? You've scarcely been to see me while Mamma and Papa were here.' She snuggled Tumble to her and pouted.

Barnaby could have said it was because whichever of them had been in the room with her had always made him feel so unwelcome, but he didn't want to be unkind so instead he said simply, 'I'm here now and wondered if there was anything you'd like?'

'Oh yes there is,' she said. 'I'd like to rewind time so that those brats upstairs had never been born. I might not be dying if I hadn't had them!'

Admittedly she had never shown any interest in the babies but it was the first time she had openly said how much she disliked them and as Barnaby stared down at her, he hardly

231

recognised her. The woman he had fallen in love with had been beautiful, flirtatious and sweet. Now she was bitter and frail, as if she was fading away before his very eyes, and there wasn't a thing he could do about it. But was he really to blame? he asked himself. He really had loved her when he married her and had been excited for the future and the thought of the children they would have together. But from the start it had become clear that she had never loved him in the way he had her. Had she returned his love, he would never have sought solace with other women.

There had been two other women apart from Amber who he had dallied with during his marriage, although neither of them had meant a thing to him. The women had both been married to much older men and had used him as much as he had used them. And then a picture of Amber flashed in front of his eyes and again the guilt weighed heavy on him. She and Louisa were as different as chalk from cheese in every way. Louisa had been breathtakingly beautiful and pampered with her every wish catered for, whereas Amber, although attractive, was a hard-working girl with rough hands and no pretty clothes to speak of. So what, he wondered, had ever attracted him to her? She had been nervous when he had first made advances to her, probably because she had been fearful of what might happen to her family should she deny him. But then she had given herself to him heart and soul and he had made promises that he couldn't keep – and look what the outcome had been. He had ruined the girl's life and he couldn't put that right either. His shoulders suddenly sagged and without a word he left the room.

'That was a little harsh, my love,' Mrs Ruffin scolded Louisa as she helped her to take a sip of water.

'*Why* was it?' Louisa answered sharply. 'I was only telling the truth!' And with that she turned her back on the woman who loved her as her own child and went into a sulk.

Chapter Twenty-Four

'Any luck, lass?' Sadie Grimshaw asked as Amber entered the kitchen.

The noise in the room assailed Amber and she smiled wearily. Nancy's younger siblings were rolling about on the peg rug in front of the fire making enough racket to waken the dead and the smell of boiled cabbage and stale bodies hung heavy in the air.

Amber shook her head wearily. She had been out since early that morning job-hunting, just as she had every day during the week she had been staying there, but again she'd had no luck, even though she'd walked for miles and ventured much further afield. Even the farms that were dotted across the moors had nothing to offer and now she was seriously disheartened. It seemed much longer than a week since she'd said a teary goodbye to her mother and waved her off on the coach bound for Scarborough, and although Sadie had gone out of her way to make her feel welcome, Amber often longed for the peace and quiet of the cottage that had been the only home she had ever known.

As two of the younger children started to fight, Sadie waved a wooden spoon at them. 'If you bloody pair don't be'ave I'll bang yer bloody 'eads together. Now keep the noise down!'

Amber couldn't help but smile. For all her shouting, Sadie was as soft as butter inside. The children were lovely too, if rather undisciplined. Now each night Amber squashed into one of the two beds in the attic room with Nancy's four sisters, and although it was a bit of a squeeze, she was grateful for the children's warmth because the wind seemed to find every opening in the thatched roof.

Nancy's father was a fisherman, as Amber's own had been, and thankfully the family never went hungry, although their staple diet consisted of fish and boiled cabbage. Sadie wasn't too keen on cleaning either and Amber dreaded to think how long it might have been since the sheets had been changed, or the children's clothes for that matter. But even so, she was grateful that Sadie had taken her in and made her feel so welcome.

Thankfully Amber had been able to give Sadie some of the money she had saved from when she had worked in London to cover her keep, but now she was seriously concerned about what she would do when it was all gone. She could hardly expect Sadie to keep her for nothing and knew that if the worst came to the worst she would have to go to her uncle and try to find a job in Scarborough. But worrying as all this was, the biggest problem she'd had since her mother had left to go to her uncle's was Bertie Preston. He seemed to be hounding her and he was scathing each time he saw her.

Amber picked her way through the tangle of little bodies rolling around the floor and made for the fire where she held her hands out to the heat of the flames. They were blue with cold and as the feeling started to return to them, she flinched with the pain of the pins and needles. Her feet felt no better and she was miserable as she gently unwound her thick shawl from about her head and shoulders. It had offered little protection against the biting cold and already she was dreading the next morning when she would start the whole process of job-hunting again.

However, her sad mood didn't last too long when Sadie fetched her a steaming mug of tea and told her, 'There's a letter come for you today, lass. It's on the mantelshelf, look. I bet it's from yer mam.'

Amber snatched it down eagerly and after removing a load of dirty clothes from the fireside chair she sank into it and split the envelope open.

Her throat tightened with tears as she saw her mother's familiar handwriting and she began to read.

Dear Amber,

I hope this letter finds yer well and settled in with Mrs Grimshaw. Do give her my best wishes. Have yer managed to find a new job yet? I am settling very happily at your uncle's and at present Martha (Mrs Carter) and me are busily planning the wedding. It's only going to be a quiet affair at the end of June but both she and your uncle would love you to be there to share the happy day with them. I do 'ope you'll be able to make it. They seem so suited and I'm sure they'll be very happy together. I just wish they'd realised they were right for each other years ago. So much wasted time! Still, better late than never, eh?

I've started taking little Fancy for a walk each evening to give them some time alone together and have to say I've really bonded with the little dog; she has such a sweet nature and so does Biddy. I'm going to start work in the shop next week, just part-time to give your uncle and Martha a bit more space, and your uncle has bought me some lovely new clothes to wear there. I must say I feel very posh in them. I'm going to have a new outfit for the wedding too! So all in all things are working out for me far better than I had hoped, although of course I miss you all something terrible.

Anyway, my lass, I'll go now as it's almost dinner time and whatever Martha is cooking smells very nice!

Take care,

Love yer,

Mam xxxx

'All right, is she, lass?'

'Yes, thank you, she sounds fine,' Amber replied as she carefully folded the letter and placed it back in the envelope. 'She's settling well.'

'Hm, but you're missin' her, ain't you?'

The kindly voice brought tears to Amber's eyes as she nodded but then the door suddenly burst open, bringing in a gust of icy air, and Nancy hurried in.

'Brrr, it's enough to freeze the 'air's off a brass monkey out there,' she declared as she hastily slammed the door shut.

'An' what brings you 'ere at this time o' day, lass? You ain't got the sack have yer?' her mother asked with a worried frown.

'No, I ain't, Mam, don't worry.' Nancy chuckled as she hurried towards the fire nudging the children out of the way

237

as she went. 'I've been sent wi' a message for Amber as it happens, so I can't stay long. Mrs Boswell is watchin' the babies. I've got time fer a cuppa, though, if there's one goin'.'

'A message for me?' Amber raised her eyebrow. 'Who from?'

'From the master,' Nancy told her. 'I were just takin' the bottles up to the nursery when he stopped me in the hall to ask if I'd come an' ask if you'd go to see him at the house at ten o'clock tomorrow mornin'.'

'What would he want to see me for?' Amber snapped suspiciously. Just the mention of that loathsome man could put her hackles up.

Nancy shrugged. 'Don't ask me, lass. I'm only the monkey not the organ grinder!'

'Sorry, Nance.' Amber looked repentant. 'I didn't mean to snap at you.'

'S'all right,' Nancy answered as her mother placed a mug of stewed tea in her cold hands.

Amber's first instinct was to ask Nancy to tell him to go to hell, but then she bit her tongue. What if he needed to speak to her about her daughter? Could it be that something bad had happened to her? Was she ill?

'So what'll I tell him then?'

Amber took a deep breath. 'Tell him I'll think about it,' she said eventually.

'An' how are you copin' lookin' after them two babies?' Mrs Grimshaw asked.

'I'm copin' fine,' she told her, looking sad. 'Though I'll be glad when Mr Greenacre employs a new nanny. I'd sooner do me proper job. Charlotte is a little beauty, good as the day is long, but little David . . . well, he's a different kettle o' fish altogether. He ain't thrivin' at all an' the doctor is really worried about him. In fact, things ain't good up at the house at all at the minute what wi' the mistress bein' so poorly an' all. Mrs Ruffin looks shattered but she insists on carin' for the mistress herself an' won't hear o' the master bringin' a nurse in. Poor sod, from what I've heard whispered she ain't long fer this world.'

'That's awful.' Mrs Grimshaw shook her head, setting her double chin wobbling. 'An' her were such a bonny young woman an' all.'

Amber told Nancy about the letter she'd received from her mother then and they chatted for another few minutes before Nancy set off back to Greenacres leaving Amber to suffer another evening of noise and mayhem at her mother's.

As the children snored around her that night, Amber lay awake into the early hours of the morning trying to decide what she should do, but when she eventually fell into an exhausted sleep she was no nearer to reaching a decision. The next morning, she was up with the lark and after helping Mrs Grimshaw to feed and dress all the children she set off again in her quest for a job, although she was fast losing heart now.

And then just before ten o'clock in the morning she found herself standing in front of the gates that led to Greenacres just as she had known she would deep down. She hated the thought of having to be in Barnaby Greenwood's presence again but her need to have information about her child overcame her hatred and she set off down the drive.

When the house came into view she hesitated. Should she take the servants' entrance at the back of the house? Her chin rose defiantly. Why should she? It was the master who'd requested she should call so she would enter by the front doors for the first time. She had no doubt it would set the staff gossiping but she was beyond worrying about that. She climbed the steps to the door, pausing to self-consciously smooth the material of the warm cape her uncle had bought her, glad that she was dressed in her decent clothes, before pulling on the bell that hung to one side of the doors.

It was Mrs Boswell who answered and when she saw Amber, she looked surprised to say the least.

'Hello, Mrs Boswell. I have an appointment wi' Mr Greenwood at ten o'clock. He wished to see me,' Amber informed her grandly and just for a moment the woman's jaw dropped open.

'Then you'd best step inside and I'll inform him that you're here.'

While Mrs Boswell scuttled away to find the master, Amber looked around her with awe. She'd rarely been into this part of the house before and hadn't realised how luxurious it was. She didn't have long to admire it, however, before Mrs Boswell came back. 'Mr Greenwood will see you now, Amber. Would you come this way?'

Amber followed her along a corridor until they came to the door that she guessed must be the master's study.

When Mrs Boswell held it open for her, Amber stepped past her to see Barnaby Greenwood seated in a high-backed leather chair behind a large mahogany desk.

He rose instantly and gestured towards a chair in front of his desk. 'Ah, Miss Ainsley. I'm so glad you came,' he greeted her, for all the world as if she was one of his wife's well-to-do friends. 'Do sit down.'

'I'm quite all right standin' if it's all the same to you.' Her voice was so sharp that it could have sliced butter and she saw him cringe. 'So what did you want me for?'

He gave a nervous cough as he ran his hand through his thatch of blond curly hair. 'Actually, I have a position vacant here that I hope you'll be interested in.'

She narrowed her eyes as she stared at him. 'Oh, so you're offerin' me me old job in the laundry back, are you?' she said scathingly. She would have welcomed the position of laundry maid anywhere else but she had no intention of ever being his lackey again.

'Oh no, no!' He shook his head and after taking a deep breath he went on, 'As you may be aware our nanny left recently and Nancy has been caring for my twins. But that was only on a temporary basis and I've asked you here to offer you the position of nanny full-time.'

Amber was so shocked that now she did drop heavily onto the seat he had formerly offered. '*What?* you want *me* to care for your babies?'

When he nodded, she laughed mirthlessly. 'Well, that's a turn up for the books, ain't it? You do realise I ain't had no trainin' in that department, don't you, apart from carin' for the two Temple lads for a short time? An' why didn't you come an' offer the job to me at Mrs Grimshaw's instead o' gettin' me to come here?'

'I didn't want to make you feel uncomfortable,' he explained. 'People might have wondered why I was seeking you out and offering the post to you when so many others are seeking jobs.'

241

'How *very* thoughtful of you!' Her voice dripped sarcasm and again she saw him flinch. This was clearly as hard for him as it was for her.

But then she forced herself to ask, 'An' what about . . . about *my* daughter? Is she safe an' well?' There was a catch in her voice that she couldn't control and it was not lost on him.

'She is thriving.' Although his voice was steady when he answered he could feel her pain and he bowed his head in shame as he asked, 'So will you consider the post, Miss Ainsley? The wage would be twenty-five pounds a year plus you would be entitled to every Sunday afternoon off, of course.'

She stared at him uncertainly. It was more than she had ever been offered in her life and she would have somewhere to live into the bargain, yet the thought of being so close to him and having to see him often turned her stomach.

'Per'aps if I could meet the babies before I make me mind up?' she suggested cautiously and he nodded enthusiastically.

'Why, yes . . . yes, of course you can. I shall take you up to the nursery myself.'

He hurried from behind his desk and held the door open for her and when they saw Mrs Boswell in the hall he asked, 'Would you mind taking Miss Ainsley's cloak please, Mrs Boswell? I'm taking her up to the nursery to meet the twins.'

It was hard for Amber not to smile as she handed the woman her cloak, and Mrs Boswell's eyes were like saucers as she watched the master of the house escort the former laundry maid up the sweeping staircase as if she was visiting royalty.

'You could have knocked me down with a feather,' she confided to the cook when she returned to the kitchen, and

242

they both shook their heads, wondering what the hell was going on.

Once they reached the nursery floor, Barnaby again held the door open for Amber to pass through ahead of him, and the first thing she saw was Nancy with young David on her lap as she tried to tempt him to take his milk.

'Amber!' Nancy's face broke into a broad smile at sight of her friend but spotting the master behind her she quickly looked down at her young charge again.

'So how is our young man doing today, Nancy?' Barnaby asked, injecting some cheerfulness into his voice.

'Not too bad, sir, though he still won't take much milk. Cook even tried puttin' a bit o' honey in it to try an' tempt him but he just falls asleep on it.'

As Amber stared down at the drowsy baby, her face softened. His hair was the exact same colour as his father's but his face was pale and he was so small that he looked almost new born.

'He's lovely,' she said softly and Barnaby nodded in agreement.

'Yes, he is, isn't he? And this is his sister over here.'

There were two cribs set to either side of a blazing fire and approaching the one that Barnaby had pointed to she found herself staring down at a baby girl.

'This is little Charlotte,' Barnaby told Amber and although she hated this man with a vengeance, she could hear the love in his voice for his children.

This child had hair much like the colour of her own, she found herself thinking, and her long dark eyelashes were curled on her peaches-and-cream cheeks. Her limbs were plump and Amber thought she was easily the most beautiful baby she had ever seen. It would be a pleasure to care for these two cherubs, she thought, if only it didn't mean being in such close proximity to their father.

After a nod to Nancy, Barnaby led her from the room and once back in his study he asked hopefully, 'So, is it a position you would consider, Miss Ainsley?'

She stared back at him, torn in two directions: her heart told her she could be very happy in this job, but common sense told her that she would be putting herself too close to his attentions again.

'Only if you can swear on your babies' lives that you'll keep your filthy hands to yourself,' she spat eventually. 'Cos as sure as eggs is eggs I'll tell you now if you ever so much as try to touch me again I'll shout it from the rooftops an' sod what happens to me!'

He bowed his head. 'You have my word as a gentleman, Miss Ainsley!'

'Huh! Well, you'd have had to be a gentleman in the first place for that to mean owt,' she retaliated and again he looked ashamed.

'Then yes, I will swear on the babies' lives that I will never force you to do anything you don't wish to do,' he said solemnly, and as much as she despised him, she felt that he was telling the truth. Perhaps his wife's illness had finally brought him to his senses? And then she flushed with guilt as she thought back to their time together. In truth the blame for their affair didn't lie entirely with him. She had worshipped the ground he walked on and lived for the times they were together. But then he had betrayed her when she

244

had needed him the most and she knew that she could never forgive him for that.

'All right . . . in that case we'll give it a try,' she told him, still not completely sure that she was doing the right thing. But, she asked herself, what other option did she have? She'd nearly worn her boots out over the last few days traipsing from door to door looking for work. And at least here at Greenacres she knew everyone, although what they would think of the master offering her such a prestigious position after her being the laundry maid there she couldn't imagine. *Still*, she thought, *that's his problem to sort out.* 'So when do you want me to start?' she asked.

Chapter Twenty-Five

'Ooh, I'm so pleased to see you?' Nancy said happily when Amber arrived two days later carrying her small bundle of clothes. 'I've loved lookin' after the little 'uns but I prefer me job downstairs. It can get a bit lonely up here wi' only the two babies to keep you company. Your room is through there, by the way. I've taken my things out an' changed the bed for you.' She pointed to a door leading off the main nursery.

Entering it, Amber found herself in a very comfortable bedroom with a double bed in the centre of one wall, drawers to either side of it and pretty flowered curtains hanging at the window. A wardrobe took up most of the space on the other wall and next to that was a marble-topped washstand on which stood a large jug and bowl. A small table and chair were placed in the window from which there were lovely views of the grounds, and after spending time at Nancy's mother's cottage Amber thought it was quite luxurious – it would certainly be nice to be able to stretch out in bed after sharing with Nancy's little sisters. They seemed to be all bony elbows and knees and she was surprised she wasn't bruised.

'The master says I'm to stay up here wi' you for the day to show you the ropes,' Nancy went on, coming to stand beside her.

'Hm, and how often does he show his face?' Amber couldn't keep the loathing she felt for him from her voice and Nancy was quick to pick up on it.

'At least three or four times a day,' she admitted. 'But don't get worryin' about it. He's completely besotted wi' the babies an' he wouldn't dare to try an' lay a hand on you up here. To be honest, it's a good job he does bother with 'em. The mistress has never shown a scrap of interest in 'em, in fact I reckon I could count on one hand how many times she's seen 'em since they were born, and they're nearly five months old now, poor little sods. Although in fairness to her she is very poorly now. Poor old Ruffy looks worn out, but she won't hear o' Mr Greenwood gettin' a nurse in. An' the rows! Phew, she lays into the master as soon as he sets foot in her room, an' it makes me wonder why he bothers. But then, she is still is his wife, ain't she?'

'And where do I eat?' Amber asked. 'Do I go down to the kitchen an' eat wi' the staff like I used to?'

Nancy looked away, clearly uncomfortable. 'Well, I dare say you could if the babies were asleep. But it's only fair to tell you that some of 'em ain't too happy about you gettin' this post. They're askin' why the master should favour you when you were just the laundry maid before. Still, I wouldn't let it worry you. If you don't feel comfortable down there, I'll bring your meals up on a tray.'

'I think I might just let you do that,' Amber said with a worried frown. 'At least until I know what sort of reception I'm goin' to get. But now tell me about the babies' routines. I can put this stuff away later.' And after throwing her bundle onto the bed she returned to the nursery with Nancy.

Over the next hour Nancy showed her the small stove where she could warm the milk for the little ones' bottles, and also where the water closet was out on the landing. Amber was quite taken with that; it would certainly beat having to go outside to use the toilet in the freezing cold.

'All the dirty washin', yours included, will be collected each mornin',' Nancy went on. 'An' when it's been washed an' ironed it will be brought back to you.' Next she showed Amber where the babies' clothes and toiletries were kept and when the twins started to stir she showed her friend how to make their bottles.

'I should have a go at feedin' David first,' Nancy suggested. 'He's the hardest to care for. Charlotte will eat till the cows come home, bless 'er, an' she's as good as gold, but he's a whinger cos he ain't well most o' the time.'

Amber gently lifted the little boy from his crib and when he opened his eyes he stopped crying momentarily to stare up at her curiously.

'Oh dear, he's as light as a feather,' Amber said in dismay and Nancy nodded in agreement.

'I know, but it ain't for the wants o' me not tryin' to fatten him up.' She shook her head. 'Between you an' me I don't reckon the doctor thinks much of his chances. There's been talk of there bein' somethin' wrong wi' his little heart. I don't reckon he'll be for this world for much longer.'

Once the milk had been warmed to the right temperature, Amber lifted David from his cot, shocked again to feel how light he was. There wasn't an ounce of fat on him and his little face was gaunt.

'Poor little thing,' she muttered as she tried to gently push the teat of the bottle between his lips. 'He's so painfully thin! All skin and bone.'

'Unlike this one.' Nancy chuckled as Charlotte slurped greedily at her milk. Within no time at all her bottle was empty but David hadn't even managed an ounce. Eventually Amber gave up trying to tempt him to take any more and she awkwardly changed his binding, realising that it was going to take a bit of practice before she got it right – it wasn't as easy as it looked – while Nancy changed Charlotte's

The little girl gurgled and cooed with her chubby little legs kicking whilst David just lay there.

Almost two hours later they heard footsteps on the nursery stairs and when the door opened Barnaby stepped into the room.

'Ah, so you arrived,' he said rather unnecessarily and Amber nodded, avoiding his eyes. She was wearing the plain dress her uncle had bought her for working in the shop in Scarborough and with her hair neatly pinned up and in her best boots, he noted that she looked very neat and tidy – pretty in fact.

Barnaby instantly crossed to Charlotte and the second she saw him the little girl gurgled with delight and he lifted her into his arms.

'And how is my special girl today, eh?' Barnaby crooned and seeing how gentle he was with her, Amber was shocked. He clearly loved his children so perhaps he wasn't all bad after all. Next he went to lift David into his other arm and nudging Amber, Nancy suggested, 'Shall we take these pots down to the kitchen?'

Amber was only too happy to oblige and after loading them onto a tray they set off, giving Barnaby some time alone with the infants.

They had just reached the first-floor landing when Mrs Ruffin appeared from the mistress's bedroom looking flustered and seeing them, she smiled weakly. 'She's having a bad day,' she confided, cocking her head back towards the room. And nodding down at her apron, which was stained with tea, she added, 'She didn't want her tea so she threw it at me.' She shook her head. 'But how am I supposed to get her to build her strength up if she won't even try to eat and drink? It's almost as if she's given up.'

Both Amber and Nancy felt sorry for her. It was no secret that the mistress was gravely ill and they could only imagine how upsetting it must be for Mrs Ruffin, who loved her like a daughter. They continued down the next flight of stairs together and had almost reached the bottom when Mrs Ruffin told them, 'I've sent for the doctor to call in and have a look at her again. He should be here anytime now. Do you want me to ask him to pop up to the nursery and have a look at David while he's here?'

'I don't suppose it would hurt,' Nancy answered. 'Though he's no worse. Sayin' that he's no better either an' we still can't get him to eat or drink much.'

Mrs Boswell appeared and eyed Amber's dress curiously. She had only ever seen her in the old clothes she used to wear in the laundry and she was surprised to see how different she looked dressed in smarter clothes.

'Are you settling in?'

Amber noted a tone of disapproval in her voice but she answered calmly, 'Yes, thank you, Mrs Boswell.'

'Good.' The woman looked at Nancy. 'You can report back to your normal duties first thing in the morning, Nancy.'

'Yes, missus.' Nancy bobbed her knee and when the housekeeper disappeared off into the drawing room to check that the maid had done a proper job of the dusting and polishing, Nancy and Amber moved on to the green baize door at the end of the hallway that led into the kitchen. One of the grooms, a gardener and the parlourmaid were sitting at the table drinking tea when Amber followed Nancy in, and the second she entered they fell silent. Noting the suddenly frosty atmosphere, Amber felt so embarrassed that she wished the ground would open up and swallow her.

'So . . . you're back?' The cook was rolling pastry on the large, scrubbed pine table but paused to stare at Amber who inclined her head.

'Hm, you've done all right for yerself, girl, haven't you? It's quite a step from being a laundry maid to a nanny, ain't it? I wonder what you did to deserve it?'

Amber was only too aware of what she was insinuating and knowing that she had to stand her ground, she retorted, 'Mr Greenwood must have thought I'd be suitable, mustn't he?'

The cook grinned. 'Aye, he must, although he's turned a fair few others away over the last couple o' weeks who would have been an' all. We hear he got you a nice little cushy job in London wi' the Temples over Christmas as well.'

Amber grit her teeth to stop herself retaliating. Surprisingly it was Mrs Ruffin, who had followed them in, who told the cook tartly, 'Perhaps Mr Greenwood thought that Amber would do well at the job. She certainly never shirked in her other one from what I could see of it.'

The cook positively bristled, although she clamped her mouth shut and said nothing more and Amber deposited the tray on the end of the long wooden draining board by the sink and fled the room.

Outside in the hallway she paused to blink the tears from her eyes before lifting her skirts and racing back up the stairs.

Barnaby Greenwood was cradling David on his lap when Amber entered the nursery and looking up he said, 'Ah, Miss Ainsley . . . or may I call you Amber? I'm glad of this moment alone with you as there's something I'd . . .' His voice trailed away as Nancy appeared in the doorway and Amber frowned.

'Yes, what is it?' she asked.

'Oh, er . . . it's nothing that won't wait,' he assured her, standing up and placing his son in her arms and without another word he was gone, leaving Nancy to scratch her head.

'An' what were all that about?'

'I've no idea,' Amber admitted. 'But if it's anythin' important I've no doubt he'll tell me in his own good time.'

Later in the afternoon the doctor called and after examining little David he shook his head. 'Still refusing his feeds, is he?' He addressed the question to Nancy who he knew had been caring for them.

Nancy nodded and he sighed. 'Ah well, you can only do your best, my dear.' And snapping his bag shut he quietly left the room.

Nancy and Amber ate their meal in the nursery together that evening but soon it was time for Nancy to return to the servants' quarters and once she was gone Amber knew a moment of panic. She didn't really know anything about caring for babies, after all, and suddenly the responsibility weighed heavily on her.

When their next bottles were due, she warmed the milk on the little stove and lifted Charlotte who was already awake and getting impatient. She really was the most beautiful child and as she nestled against Amber clutching her bottle with her chubby little hands, she stared up at her new nanny and Amber couldn't help but admire her.

Within minutes the bottle was drained and laying her on a blanket on the floor, Amber began to undress her to change her into her nightclothes. The child gurgled contentedly as Amber took the pins from her binding, crooning reassuringly to her all the time. Within no time at all the child lay there completely naked and it was then that Amber's hands flew to her throat and she began to keen softly in her throat as the midwife's words at the birth of her child sounded in her head. *And look, they call this an angel's kiss.*

Amber's head wagged from side to side in denial as she stared down at the tiny heart-shaped birthmark on the baby's thigh, but before she could digest what she was seeing a voice from behind her made her swing around.

'Ah, you've realised then? I was hoping to be able to talk to you before you did.' It was Barnaby who looked fraught as he stood there wringing his hands.

'I . . . I don't understand!' Amber's voice came out as a squeak. 'The . . . the midwife who delivered my baby said *she* had an angel's kiss too. Or is she . . .'

He nodded. 'Yes.' There was no point in lying. He'd known she'd find out. He only regretted that he hadn't made the admission sooner. 'Charlotte is your baby, Amber, but please let me explain . . .'

'I think you'd better!' she snapped as her whole world tipped upside down yet again.

Chapter Twenty-Six

They stared at each other for a moment as the fire crackled and threw shadows across the wall until finally Barnaby said, 'I know I promised you I would find her a good home and I fully intended to do it, I *swear* it. But then I got an urgent message saying you'd delivered a girl and I was to fetch her straightaway. Louisa was already in labour with David and so I fetched Charlotte to Louisa's parents' cottage. I had to tell Mrs Ruffin who she was, of course, and needless to say she wasn't best pleased with me. But Louisa was in a bad way – a very bad way, actually. In fact, at one point, we didn't think she was going to survive the birth. By the time David was delivered, she was almost unconscious and unaware of anything going on around her and it was then that I put the idea to Mrs Ruffin that we could tell people she had had twins. Already I couldn't bear the thought of giving Charlotte away, you see? After all, she's as much my child as David is, isn't she? And once I'd clapped eyes on her . . .'

When Amber continued to stare at him in a stony silence, he licked his suddenly dry lips and went on in a quavering voice, 'Only Mrs Ruffin and the midwife who delivered my son know of this and I bought the midwife's silence. And that is why I thought you might like this job. Forgive me if I've done wrong and now that you know I will quite understand if you decide to leave. I just wanted to give you the opportunity of caring for our daughter if you so wished.'

A whirl of emotions rushed through Amber. If she were to walk away now, she could pursue her life with no ties as she'd intended. And yet as she looked back down at Charlotte her heart filled with love and she knew that if she were to go now, she might well regret it forever.

'If you *do* decide to stay, which I hope you will, no one will ever be any the wiser, I promise you,' he rushed on, sensing her indecision. 'And who better to look after her than her own mother?'

'I think I need some time to take all this in and make my mind up,' Amber told him in a wobbly voice. Strangely, although she still loathed him and wouldn't trust him as far as she could throw him, she believed him when he promised that he would never lay a hand on her again.

'I've also decided to get another girl in from the village to act as your nursemaid,' he went on. 'I realise that it's a lot for anyone to care for two young babies, especially when one of them is as sick as David is.' His hand unconsciously reached into the infant's crib and gently stroked his hair, and Amber knew that he genuinely did care for both children, even though they were from different mothers. 'Once you have help you can have more time off,' he went on persuasively. 'So will you just consider staying?'

Unable to look at him she nodded and without a word he quietly left the room as she scooped Charlotte up into her arms and studied her tiny face. This was *her* baby, her own flesh and blood and she knew already that no matter what happened now she would never be parted from her again.

It was Nancy who brought her breakfast tray up the next morning and staring into Amber's face she said anxiously, 'You know then?'

Amber nodded. 'Yes – but why didn't you tell me?'

Nancy shrugged. 'I didn't feel it were my place to, but I told Mrs Ruffin you'd guess in no time. It were her that told me. She'll never breathe a word to anybody else an' neither will I so you need have no fear that it'll ever come out.'

'I'm surprised Mrs Ruffin will even speak to me,' Amber said in a small voice.

'Oh, you needn't have no worries on that score neither,' Nancy reassured her. 'She knows the master took advantage of you an' why you didn't say anythin'. At least he were honest an' told her the truth an' she'll say nowt cos of upsettin' the mistress. But what will you do now?'

'I'm not sure.' Amber sighed. 'All I do know is that if I do go, I'll shame the devil an' take Charlotte and blow the consequences.'

'But how would you explain her?' Nancy looked worried. 'Me mam told me there's enough talk down in the town already about you bein' offered this job wi'out you clearin' off wi' the baby. It wouldn't take long for everyone to put two an' two together an' then you'd be classed as a fallen woman. What bloke would want you then?'

257

Amber snorted, her nostrils flaring. 'As if that would worry me! I'll never get married now after the way he let me down. It's put me off men for life!'

'Hm, then you'd best tell Bertie Preston that. He's still goin' round spoutin' off that he's gonna wed you. In fact, me mam said he had a fight wi' Ronnie Orwell t'other day cos Ronnie made some sarky comment about you landin' this cushy job!'

'Huh! I wouldn't marry Bertie Preston if he were the last man on earth,' Amber told her. 'And I've told him so, so why he won't accept it, I don't know.'

'Just thought I'd warn you,' Nancy said, holding her hands up as if she were warding off a blow. 'But I'd best get back now. Mrs Boswell is on the warpath an' she'll be on me tail if I'm much longer. Ta-ra fer now.'

With a sigh, Amber turned back to her daughter and gave her a big cuddle.

Two days later Barnaby came to the nursery mid-morning with a young girl in tow. She was very small and Amber reckoned she couldn't be more than eleven or twelve years old but she had a ready smile.

'Miss Ainsley, this is Becky,' he told her. 'She's going to do a trial with you as a nursery-maid, if that meets with your approval.'

Amber eyed the girl, wondering if she would be strong enough to cart the babies about each day. She was so slight that she looked as if one good puff of wind would blow her away but she was an attractive little soul with fair curling hair tied in the nape of her neck and big blue eyes that almost looked too big for her small face.

As if the girl could read her mind, she said quickly, 'I'm good wi' babies, miss. I've got eight younger brothers an' sisters at home an' I've always helped me mam to look after 'em.' She chewed on her lip then with her small hands clasped in front of her, and realising how much the job must mean to her, Amber nodded.

'Very well, I don't see why we shouldn't give it a try.'

The girl positively sighed with relief and Barnaby told her, 'In that case, you may go and fetch your clothes and things, Becky. I see no reason why you can't start straightaway.'

The girl dipped her knee and backed towards the door and once she had gone, Barnaby lifted David from his crib. 'I know she doesn't look that strong but she assures me she's used to children and I, er . . .' He coughed to clear his throat. 'Her father and uncle died on *The Neptune* and I believe her mother is struggling to bring the family up alone without their wages coming in. Becky is the only one anywhere near old enough to get a job yet and I thought . . .'

At the mention of the fateful ship that had cost her own father and two brothers their lives, Amber's eyes watered and she angrily swiped the tears away with the back of her hand. Their deaths were still very raw for her too and she could understand how Becky and her family must feel.

'I'm sure she'll be fine,' she said coldly and he nodded as he placed a gentle kiss on David's head and laid him back in the crib. They had come to an unspoken kind of truce where they rarely spoke to each other when he visited the nursery, apart from him asking after the children, and Amber found that she could cope with that.

Once he'd left the room and both infants were sleeping peacefully, Amber crossed to the window and gazed down at the town far below. Not so long ago the little cottage in Argument's Yard had been the only home she had ever known but now it hit her that she didn't really have any-where to call home anymore, and all the people she loved, or those that were left, were scattered far and wide. Her brothers were off somewhere working on the railways and her mother was hopefully still settling happily into her new life in Scarborough. But then her eyes settled on Charlotte and a soft smile played about her lips. Not quite everyone she loved was gone from her life, she thought, because now she had a beautiful daughter.

Half an hour later Becky returned, escorted by Mrs Boswell and clutching a small bundle of clothes in an old pillow case, and Amber was pleased to see her – it would be nice to have someone to talk to apart from the babies.

'I've told Becky that she may prepare the room next to yours to sleep in, if you'd be so kind as to show her where the clean bedding is kept, Amber. And I've also sent a mes-sage to the mistress's dressmaker to call and measure you both up for new uniforms.'

Becky's eyes lit up. 'What? A brand-new one?' she asked excitedly. She'd never owned a single new garment in the whole of her life and the ill-fitting gown she was wearing was so darned and faded that it was impossible to imagine what colour it might once have been. 'What colour will it be?'

'It will be a soft grey, much like the one Amber is wear-ing now,' the housekeeper informed her and Becky clapped her hands with glee, causing David to start in his crib and Amber to glare at her.

'Sorry,' the girl muttered repentantly.

'Hm, well I suggest you go and get your room ready then report back here to help the nanny,' Mrs Boswell told her, and only too keen to please, Becky dipped her knee and hurried away to do as she was told.

'Just inform me if the girl doesn't prove to be suitable,' Mrs Boswell told Amber primly before leaving the room.

As it happened, Becky proved to be like a ray of sunshine on a dark day and by the end of the afternoon Amber had taken to her and was surprised to see just how good she was with the children. She did everything Amber asked her to do with good grace and a smile on her face and Amber noted that she was better at changing their bindings than she was. She was a lot stronger than she looked too.

'I've always helped me mam do it,' Becky explained and as she began to chatter on about her younger siblings Amber could see that she had come from a very close-knit family. 'It were hard to lose me dad an' me uncle though.' Her face became solemn and Amber could feel her pain.

'I know, I lost my dad and two of my brothers too.'

The door opened at that point and Barnaby appeared so the conversation stopped and Becky hastily stood up and bobbed her knee.

'Afternoon, Mr Greenwood, or is it evenin' yet?'

He smiled, clearly far more at ease with Becky than he was with Amber. 'It's almost evening,' he replied. 'And I thought I'd just pop up to see how you've done on your first day before I go in to dinner.' He glanced over at Amber and she nodded.

'She's been a very good help, actually, and she's a natural with the children.'

'Good, good.'

Although David was asleep, as usual, Charlotte was whining at the sight of him and laughing now he swung her into his arms making her giggle. 'And how have you behaved today, you little monkey?'

She cooed with delight as she buried her chubby little hands in his hair and it was clear to see how much they loved each other. In fact, Amber thought as a little pang of jealousy fired through her, she seemed to be far closer to her father than she was to her. But she supposed that was to be expected. He had been in her life since the day she had been born whereas she herself was merely a newcomer.

Once he had gone, Becky helped Amber to bathe both the infants and finally, they were both fast asleep in their cribs and Amber could relax a little.

'What do you usually do of an evenin'?' Becky asked.

Amber shrugged. 'Oh, I just read usually, but why don't you go down to the kitchen for a while and make the most of it while it's quiet?'

Becky frowned. 'Why don't you come down as well?'

'I'm quite happy up here,' Amber answered a little too quickly. She rarely ventured below stairs apart from when she had to and Nancy now delivered all her meals and the babies' meals to the nursery. It was easier that way as at least then she didn't have to face the awful silences that settled on the room when she entered. Even Jimmy, the young groom who had once had a soft spot for her, was reluctant to meet her eyes and she knew she was the subject of much gossip.

Becky shrugged. 'All right, if you're sure you can manage. I might be able to cadge another slice o' that lovely cake they brought up fer us at teatime.'

Amber smiled. Becky seemed to be constantly hungry, which probably accounted for how small she was, and the girl tripped away.

She returned almost an hour later and looking up from the newspaper she was reading, Amber greeted her with a smile.

'Nancy said to tell you she'd pop in to see you afore she goes to bed,' Becky informed her, stifling a yawn.

'Reet, well seeing as the little ones are settled per'aps you'd like to turn in an' get an early night? I can manage if they wake up.'

'Are you sure?' Becky didn't want to look as if she was shirking, especially on her first day, although she was longing to snuggle down on the feather mattress in the room that was to be all hers. At home she had shared a bed with three of her little sisters so having a bed all to herself was going to be a luxury indeed.

When Amber nodded she left hurriedly before she changed her mind and it was only then that Amber realised it was almost Sunday and she would be entitled to a whole afternoon off. But where could she go? she wondered. There was no family left there for her to go and see anymore and it was still far too cold to just go walking about.

Nancy solved that problem when she dropped in to see her just before bedtime and told her, 'Me mam says you're to come home for tea wi' me on Sunday. Now that Becky's here to mind the bairns we can have the same afternoon off together – if you think she'll cope, that is?'

'I'm sure she will and I'd like that.' And so it was agreed.

Chapter Twenty-Seven

In the early hours of Monday morning there was a tap on Barnaby's bedroom door and he opened his eyes blearily to see Mrs Ruffin standing there in her night attire.

'I think you'd better come, sir,' she told him. 'The mistress is in a lot of pain and no amount of laudanum seems to be helping.' She then quietly closed the door and hurried back to her mistress as Barnaby dragged his robe on and headed along the landing in his house slippers.

Louisa was rolling around the bed clutching her stomach but the second he entered the room her eyes narrowed to slits.

'Come to see what you've brought me to, have you?' Her voice dripped hate. 'Well, I hope you're happy now!'

He wrung his hands together feeling helpless as he looked at the pitiful wreck she had become. Her face was ravaged with pain and there was no longer any trace of the beauty she had once been. Her face seemed to have shrunk and there were huge purple circles beneath her eyes. Even her hair, which had once been her crowning glory, was now limp and sparse.

'I'll send for the doctor,' he told her but she growled deep in her throat.

'And what good can he do? No, what I want you to do is send for my mother and father. I want them both here.'

Barnaby dreaded another visit from his in-laws, especially so soon after the last one, but he didn't hesitate. 'Of course, I'll write to them first thing in the morning.'

'*No!*' Her voice cracked like a whip. 'I want you to send someone to fetch them or go yourself. *Now!*'

'But my dear. It isn't even light yet. Can't I set off later?'

'No, I want them here *now!*'

With a sigh, he glanced towards Ruffy, who was standing silently with tears glistening on her lashes and then nodded. 'Very well, I'll go and get ready immediately.'

Mrs Ruffin followed him out onto the landing and once the door of the bedroom had closed behind them, she confided, 'I fear she doesn't have much longer. She's eating practically nothing now and the pain is constant, poor lamb.'

'I see.' He swiped a lock of dishevelled blond hair from his forehead and nodded. 'Very well, I'll do as she asks and return with her parents as soon as I'm able to.'

When he entered the stables dressed in his jodhpurs and a warm overcoat, he found them in darkness and most of the horses asleep in their stalls. The grooms were clearly all in bed and rather than disturb them Barnaby saddled his stallion himself. He was aware that it would be a treacherous journey in the dark across the moors but what choice did he have?

Eventually he was ready and swinging himself up onto the saddle he clicked his tongue to encourage Star, his pure black thoroughbred, across the cobbled yard, then once they were clear of it and on the drive, he urged him into a gallop and they were off.

'Eeh, yer should 'ear the poor mistress howlin',' Becky told Amber the next morning after taking the breakfast tray down to the kitchen. 'The staff are creepin' about the house like ghosts an' yer can 'ear her in every room apart from up 'ere. They're whisperin' downstairs that they reckon she's on 'er last legs.'

'How awful.' Amber felt sorry for her, she was still only a very young woman after all.

'The doctor's just arrived,' Becky went on. 'They're sayin' the master left word fer someone to fetch him first thing. He went off in the middle o' the night to fetch her parents, apparently. Rather 'im than me, venturin' across the moors in the dark.'

Amber shrugged. She didn't much care what happened to the master if truth be told, but she did feel sorry for the mistress.

It was early evening when the master arrived home looking weary, and after leaping lithely down from the saddle, he threw Star's reins to the groom in the yard and told him, 'Be sure to give him a good rub down, he's worn out.'

The groom didn't need to be told that. The horse's head was drooping and steam was rising from his flanks in the bitterly cold air as he led him away, muttering soothing words.

Barnaby meanwhile strode into the house and without stopping to remove his muddy riding boots, much to the maid's disgust, he took the stairs two at a time.

'How has she been?' he asked Mrs Ruffin the instant he entered Louisa's room.

Before she could answer, his wife barked, 'You can address your questions to me, you know! I'm not quite dead yet, although it's no thanks to you! And where are my parents?'

'They're following on in their carriage,' he answered. Then his expression softened as he asked, 'Would you like me to have the babies brought down for you? It might cheer you up.'

'That's about the last thing I need,' she retorted as she waved her hand dismissively and with a sigh he turned and left to ask the maids to prepare a room for his in-laws.

It was very late that evening by the time they arrived and they were both tired and irritable after the long journey. Some of the staff had already retired to their beds but Nancy had volunteered to wait up to greet them and get them anything they might need.

'Tea, as quick as you please, girl,' Margaret Hamilton-Tate told Nancy rudely as she flung her hat and cape towards her in the hall. 'And something to eat to tide us over until break-fast wouldn't go amiss either!'

'Yes, ma'am.' Nancy quickly hung the cape up and while Mrs Hamilton-Tate went straight upstairs to her daughter's room, her husband made for the drawing room. Thankfully Nancy had thought to go in and make the fire up so it was warm and cosy as he crossed to a cut-glass decanter and poured himself a generous shot of whisky. He felt he needed it after the journey they had just endured being jostled about on the rough roads across the moors.

Having found her daughter sleeping, his wife joined him a short time later and soon after Nancy brought them a pot of tea and some slices of cold meat pie left over from dinner. She'd waited up long enough now and was ready for her bed so if they needed anything else they could damn well get it themselves, she decided as she stamped away up the bare wooden stairs that led to the servants' quarters.

Shut away in the nursery, the next few days passed much as they always did for Amber and Becky, apart from two short visits from Margaret Hamilton-Tate who came to briefly visit her grandchildren.

'She's a cold fish, ain't she?' Becky snorted with disgust after one such visit. 'She won't even pick the babbys up fer fear o' creasin' her posh gowns. Still, it's her loss, ain't it? I reckon they're both little crackers.' As usual she was cradling baby David, who she had taken a great shine to. She had endless patience with him but despite all her best efforts, even she had got little response from him.

'An' I know the mistress is poorly but she ain't asked to see 'em either, not once since I've been 'ere. It seems that the only one who gives a stuff about 'em is Mr Greenwood.'

Amber was secretly pleased that the mistress didn't show a great interest in the children. She could only imagine how hard it would have been to see Louisa playing mother to her own daughter. She also felt a little resentful that it was the master and mistress who had chosen her child's name, although begrudgingly she did have to admit that it suited her and she did like it, so she supposed she should at least be grateful of that.

By the time Sunday rolled around Amber was more than ready for a little time out of the house, although she quaked inside at the thought of leaving Charlotte. Not that she didn't trust Becky with her or David. The girl had turned out to be a little star with the children and she was good company too, and often made Amber laugh with her tales of some of the things she and her siblings had got up to when she had lived at home. 'Me mam were allus threatening to bang our bloody 'eads together, or skelp our arses when we got caught out for some mischief or another,' Becky would chortle. 'But 'er bark were allus worse than her bite an' we knew 'ow to get round 'er.'

Amber was brushing her hair and Becky watched enviously. As the nursery nurse she was only allowed one Sunday afternoon off a month, whereas Amber was allowed every Sunday afternoon, apart from the one when Becky wasn't there when she happily took charge of the two babies by herself. As the nanny, Amber was allowed privileges that the rest of the staff were not, which she was well aware was just another bone of contention with them.

'Just think, by the next Sunday I get to go 'ome I'll 'ave one o' me new gowns to wear,' Becky said dreamily as she scrubbed her hands in a bowl of water and Amber smiled at her indulgently as Nancy came in dressed in her Sunday best dress and bonnet.

'Ready fer the off, are you?'

Amber nodded as she lifted the warm cloak her uncle had bought her. The wind was blowing up a storm outside and it was still bitterly cold so she knew she'd be glad of it.

'Now are you quite sure you can manage? The babies won't be due another feed till mid-afternoon now and they should have a nap then. I shall be back for six o'clock sharp to help with their baths.'

'I'll be right as ninepence,' Becky assured her and so she and Nancy set off.

'Ooh, it ain't the best o' weather, is it?' Nancy said as they shivered their way down the drive. It had started to rain and the drops on their face felt like little icicles. 'But never mind, we'll soon be out of it an' hopefully me mam will have the kettle on.'

Heads bent they hurried on and soon the town came into view below them. Beyond the harbour the sea was choppy and the girls felt sorry for the fishermen who would be out on it. They had a living to make regardless of the weather and went out in atrocious conditions at times. There were very few people about, most preferring to stay in the warm, but as they passed the town hall, Amber's stomach did an uncomfortable flip when she saw Bertie Preston coming towards them with another young chap.

The last time he had seen her he had been scathing but from the gossip she had heard he'd had a change of heart again and was keen to woo her once more as his first words proved.

'Ah, Amber, I were hopin' to see yer,' he said pleasantly as he strolled towards her. His top hat was set at a jaunty angle and he was wearing a pin-striped suit and a gaudy waistcoat topped off with an old silk cravat that looked totally unsuitable for such cold weather.

'Were you? I don't know why. I thought we'd said all we had to say to one another,' Amber responded with her nose in the air.

'Now, don't be like that.' He extended his hand but she ignored it. 'Yer know deep down that you an' me are goin' to end up together one day; it were written in the stars. An' you gettin' a fancy job up at the big 'ouse shouldn't change that. I'm prepared to forget the way you've treated me an' what people are sayin' about yer an' we can go on from 'ere.'

Amber stared at him coolly. 'That's very kind of you, Bertie. But when are you goin' to get it into your head that I don't *want* to be your girl? I ain't now an' I never will be! An' it's nothin' to do wi' me new job!'

She saw angry colour flame into his cheeks as Nancy looked on with her mouth gaping open. Bertie had a reputation for being violent at times and she wondered how Amber dared to speak to him that way, especially in front of his smirking friend, who was clearly enjoying the spectacle.

'Fair enough.' His eye was twitching and his hands were clenched into fists as he stared back at her. 'But you're gonna regret this day, you just mark my words. Yer think yer too good fer the likes of us now yer Greenwood's whore, don't yer?'

The colour drained from Amber's cheeks. 'I am *not* Mr Greenwood's whore,' she responded heatedly.

'No? Well, it's funny how you got the job o' carin' fer his brats when 'alf the women in the village would 'ave snapped 'is 'and off to get the position, ain't it?'

They were almost nose to nose now and it would have been difficult to know which of them was angrier but thankfully Nancy defused the situation by grabbing Amber's arm and yanking her aside saying, 'Clear off, Bertie. Amber's told yer she ain't interested, so go an' find another girl who is!'

'Oh, I will, don't you worry!' He bared his teeth at her and without another word turned and stormed away.

'Well, I reckon he got the message this time,' Nancy said in a small voice as Amber sagged back against the wall. 'An' I also reckon it's safe to say that yer just made yerself an enemy there, lass. Bertie Preston is a bad 'un to cross so just watch yer back, eh?' Taking Amber's elbow she hurried her on to her mother's house.

'Good grief,' Mrs Grimshaw exclaimed when the girls spilled through the kitchen door a few moments later. 'Why, yer look like a pair of drowned rats ... an' Amber, yer as white as a sheet. What's wrong, lass?'

'We just had a run-in wi' Bertie Preston, Mam,' Nancy informed her as she ushered Amber towards the fire. 'An' he weren't too nice to her!'

'Hm, he's a bad 'un he is,' Mrs Grimshaw said. 'An' you'd do well to give 'im a wide berth. But what were it about?'

'He said ... well, he were rude an' reckoned that somethin' were goin' on between Amber and Mr Greenwood,' Nancy answered in a lowered voice so that her siblings, who were scattered about the room, wouldn't hear her.

Mrs Grimshaw nodded. 'There's a few hereabouts sayin' the same, if truth be told,' the woman answered – there was no point in lying. 'Did yer turn him down or something?'

When Amber nodded, Mrs Grimshaw sighed. 'Us as know yer know it ain't true,' she said soothingly. 'But I suppose yer can understand why they're thinkin' it, can't yer? I mean, that were a good job to land up at the house an' he has been showin' yer preferential treatment. All you can do, lass, is take it in yer stride an' in no time at all they'll be talkin' about some other poor devil.'

Amber supposed she was right and for the first time she wondered if she shouldn't have taken her uncle up on his offer of going to live with him. But then she thought of Charlotte and she knew that she could never leave her now.

The afternoon passed all too quickly and before they knew it it was time to set off back to the house.

'Our Nancy won't be gettin' another afternoon off fer three weeks now but you're welcome to come every week,' Mrs Grimshaw told Amber as the girls lifted their still damp outer clothes from the clotheshorse where they had been steaming in front of the fire.

'Thank you, Mrs Grimshaw, I appreciate the offer.' Amber gave her a peck on the cheek and she and Nancy went out into the fast-darkening afternoon to begin the long climb back up the hill. Thankfully there was no sign of Bertie Preston, although Amber kept a cautious eye out for him the whole way.

'Crikey, ain't that the doctor's carriage outside again?' Nancy asked as they reached the end of the drive leading to Greenacres.

'Looks like it, the mistress must be took bad again.'

They hurried inside and whilst Nancy took the servants stairs to her room, Amber walked up the elegant sweeping staircase that led to the first floor before beginning the climb up to the nursery floor.

Both the babies were dozing in their cribs when Amber entered the nursery and Becky was sitting at the table trying to make sense of the words in the newspaper.

'Hello, I were just wishin' I could read an' write,' she said wistfully. 'All these squiggles are double Dutch to me. Me mam could never afford to send us to school, see?'

'So why don't I try to teach you?' Amber slipped her cloak and bonnet off and hung them up on the back of the door before going to check on the babies.

273

'What? Yer'd do that fer me?' Becky's mouth gaped.

'Why not? It's really not that hard once you've learnt your alphabet. We'll start this evening after the babies are settled in bed, eh? And do you know why the doctor's here again? Is it the mistress poorly? I was worried it might be David.'

'Must be,' Becky answered with a shrug. 'David's fine, or at least he's no worse than he always is. He wouldn't touch his pobs or his milk again.'

They began to boil the water for the infants' baths and later that evening as Amber gave Becky her first lesson, Nancy sidled into the room to bring them their supper.

'The missus is in a really bad way,' she confided. 'An' there's all 'ell breakin' loose downstairs. The master an' Mr Hamilton-Tate are goin' at it hammer an' tongs in the study by the sound of it. I heard 'em as I was carryin' this up. Yer couldn't be off it really, they must be able to 'ear 'em all over the bloody 'ouse!'

'Nice to work somewhere so peaceful, ain't it?' Becky said, tongue in cheek, and they all laughed.

Chapter Twenty-Eight

A thin, mewling cry coming from the nursery next door woke Amber in the middle of the night. She was out of bed in a second and after hastily lighting a candle she hurried in to see who was crying. She saw immediately that Charlotte was sleeping peacefully so she turned to David's crib. Gently lifting him into her arms she crossed to the chair at the side of the fire and stroked his hair as she sat and rocked him to and fro. He didn't appear to have a temperature or be in any pain so eventually, when his eyelids drooped again, she planted a kiss on his cheek, laid him carefully back in his cot, tucked his covers about him, and with a yawn went back to her own bed.

As usual Charlotte was the first to wake the next morning ready for her breakfast and Amber chuckled as she lifted her into her arms, enjoying the clean baby smell of her. Seconds later, Becky appeared knuckling the sleep from her eyes.

'Morning,' she said blearily as she went to heat the milk for the babies' bottles and make the porridge that they could now eat. Once that was done, she crossed to David's crib and as she leant over him her hand flew to her mouth and she gasped.

'I-I think there's sommat wrong wi' David,' she said tremulously.

Instantly Amber was on her feet and hurrying over with Charlotte still in her arms. She thrust the child at Becky who took her automatically and bending she lifted David from his cot. He was limp and his skin looked pale.

'Run down for Mr Greenwood,' she ordered with a note of panic in her voice. 'I don't think he's breathin'.'

Becky dumped Charlotte, who was protesting loudly, back into her crib and was off like a March hare.

Minutes later Barnaby Greenwood burst in with Becky close behind him, his face a mask of concern.

'What's wrong?' He snatched his son from Amber's arms but the child was like a little rag doll and Barnaby began to keen. 'Oh, my dear God . . . Becky, run to the stables and get one of the grooms to go for the doctor. Tell him it's urgent and *hurry*!' He turned to Amber, and still cradling his son he asked, 'What happened?'

'I-I don't know.' Amber was devastated. 'He woke in the night and I got up and rocked him back to sleep and then when I got up he was like this . . .'

At that moment Margaret Hamilton-Tate swept into the room and taking in the pitiful sight in front of her she rasped, 'What's going on here? What's all the fuss about? The nursery-maid just raced past me and almost knocked me over in the hallway saying something about a problem with one of the babies!'

'It's David. I've sent for the doctor.' Barnaby's eyes never left his son's face and crossing to him Margaret took his wrist and felt for a pulse.

'Hm, well I'm afraid there is nothing he will be able to do,' she said quietly. 'This child is dead. Has been for a few hours, I should say. He's stone cold.' Turning to Amber, she demanded, 'Where were you?'

'I-I was right there in the next room and I always leave the door open. I didn't hear a thing after he woke once in the night. He seemed perfectly all right when I left him.'

'But he clearly wasn't,' the woman snapped disparagingly and Amber felt tears of regret start to her eyes. Was this her fault? she wondered. Why hadn't she noticed that something was seriously wrong?

The doctor arrived within half an hour and it was all he could do to prise the child from his father's arms. Barnaby hadn't said a single word since he'd told Margaret that he'd sent for the doctor and it was clear that he was deeply in shock.

'It looks like his little heart gave out,' the doctor said when he had gently examined the little boy. 'I'm so sorry, Barnaby, but to be honest I'm surprised he lived as long as he did.'

'Is it my fault?' Amber asked in a small voice as tears rolled down her cheeks.

The doctor shook his head. 'Absolutely not, lass. This could have happened at any time.'

This at least made her feel a little better but only marginally.

The doctor laid David back in his crib and gently pulled a blanket over his ashen little face. 'I'll call in to the undertaker's on my way home and get him to fetch him.'

'No!' Barnaby's head snapped up. 'He can lie here in the drawing room until the funeral.'

'Very well, in that case the undertaker can come and measure him for a coffin.' The doctor laid his hand on Barnaby's arm. 'I'm so sorry,' he said once more and with a shake of his head he lifted his bag and left.

Barnaby sat staring into space, lost in his grief, until Charlotte's disgruntled whimpers turned to angry wails and it seemed to snap him out of his spell.

'I think she wants feeding,' he said quietly and rising, he left the room.

The day of David's funeral dawned exactly one week later and as the horse-drawn hearse drew up outside, Amber and Becky watched from the window of the nursery with tears rolling down their cheeks. Two men dressed in black tail-coats and wearing tall silk top hats bore his tiny coffin from the house and gently placed it inside the hearse.

Another carriage drew up behind it and Barnaby and his in-laws climbed inside. Mrs Greenwood was far too ill to attend and Amber and Becky watched as the sad procession disappeared off down the drive. It was a cold, rainy and overcast day and Amber was glad. It wouldn't have seemed right to lay David to rest on a bright sunny day somehow. Downstairs was pandemonium as the maids raced about preparing the dining room for the buffet Cook had made for the mourners when they returned.

'I reckon they're plannin' on feedin' the five thousand,' Becky told Amber after venturing down to the kitchen. 'I ain't never seen so much food all in one place in me whole life. Goodness knows 'ow many people they're expectin'.'

'I shall just be glad when it's all over,' Amber muttered miserably as she cuddled Charlotte. 'I still can't help but think there might have been somethin' I could do.'

'Yer can stop wi' that silly nonsense straightaway,' Becky scolded. 'Didn't the doctor 'imself tell yer there wasn't?'

It was almost an hour and a half later when Mr Greenwood and the rest of the mourners began to arrive home and soon Becky and Amber could hear the murmur of voices from downstairs.

'Crikey, look at the amount o' carriages outside.' Becky was standing in the window, amazed at how many people were turning up, and still they kept coming. It was raining heavily by then and the wind was shaking the glass in the nursery window. Around mid-afternoon the nursery door creaked open and Margaret Hamilton-Tate appeared dressed in a severe black bombazine gown edged with black velvet ribbon that rustled as she walked. Mr Greenwood was close behind her and one glance at his red eyes confirmed to the girls that he had been crying. It was funny, Amber thought as she jiggled Charlotte on her knee, after the callous way he had treated her, she had imagined he didn't have any finer feelings, but the death of his son had clearly affected him badly.

'There you are, Barnaby. Didn't I tell you that the girl would be quite all right?' the woman snapped unfeelingly. 'I really don't know why you feel that you must check on her all the time. She has two people here to see to her needs and she has always been so much more robust than David was.'

She didn't even glance in the two girl's direction. Both Amber and Becky had soon realised that the woman considered speaking to servants was far beneath her except when absolutely necessary.

But despite his mother-in-law's words Barnaby crossed to the child and as soon as he drew near, Charlotte gave him a big grin and lifted her chubby arms to him.

'I know you're probably quite right,' he told his mother-in-law wearily. 'But David's passing is still very raw and I feel better when I'm with her.'

'Hmph! She'll be ruined rotten at this rate!' The woman tossed her head and bounced out of the room and as they heard her clattering down the wooden staircase that led from the nursery, Barnaby seemed to relax a little, although both Amber and Becky suddenly felt as if they were in the way.

'I'm sorry if I'm breaking her routine.' His voice was so full of pain that even Amber almost felt sorry for him for a moment.

'It's all right. She ain't due to go down fer her nap fer another half hour or so.' It was Becky who answered him while Amber busied herself putting the baby's freshly laundered clothes away. She only ever spoke to Barnaby when she had to and he was getting used to it now.

He stayed for another ten minutes then with a sigh he handed Charlotte back to Amber. saying, 'I suppose I'd better get downstairs to the visitors.'

She inclined her head and as he left the room Charlotte began to wail. She always did when her father left her and it disturbed Amber. She'd hoped that very soon Charlotte would be closer to her than Barnaby but it was crystal clear that the little girl adored him, and more surprisingly still, that he adored her.

'Shush then,' she soothed, rocking the baby to and fro. 'He'll be back before you know it.'

Charlotte stared up at her from eyes that were the exact same colour as her own and after jamming her thumb in her mouth her eyelids began to droop and she finally slept.

'Right, while she's havin' a nap, let's get this crib out of 'ere an' into the next room,' Becky suggested, pointing at David's cot. 'I can see it upsets the master every time he comes in an' I can't say as it makes me feel very nice either. I think of 'im every time I look at it, the poor little mite. We should sort all his clothes out an' all, an' ask the master what he wants done wi' 'em. There's plenty down in the town who'd be grateful for 'em.'

Amber nodded in agreement and so, after tucking Charlotte into her crib, they set about manhandling the other one into the next room and sorting David's clothes into a pile.

It was very late in the afternoon by the time the last mourner left and within minutes of them leaving Barnaby was back again. He had been the same ever since David had died. It was almost as if he was afraid that something was going to happen to Charlotte too. But the second he entered the room he stopped and stared at the space where David's crib had stood before asking, 'Where is it?'

It was Becky who answered nervously, 'We, er . . . moved it into the next room, sir. We thought it might be too upset-tin' for yer to have to see it every time yer came in. An' we've sorted all his clothes out as well. What would yer like us to do wi' 'em?'

A muscle twitched in his cheek and his eyes grew bright as he answered, 'You'll do nothing with them for now. I don't want a single thing of his to go out of the house, do you understand me?'

Looking suitably chastened, Becky nodded.

Feeling she had to defend the girl, Amber piped up, 'We were only tryin' to help. It can't have been easy for you seeing his empty cradle every time you came in!'

Hands clenched, he stared at her for a moment before turning and slamming from the room.

'Oh dear, here we were thinkin' we were helpin' an' it looks like we've only made things worse!' Becky chewed on her lip for a moment before asking tentatively, 'What is it between you an' the master anyway? I've noticed you only speak to each other when yer have to.'

Felling embarrassed, Amber shrugged. 'I suppose I just don't care for him,' she mumbled and Becky frowned.

'But why not? He's a good enough boss, ain't he? An' they said downstairs yer worked in the laundry afore you came up here. That's a big step up, surely. I'd 'ave thought yer'd be pleased about it.'

'A job is a job.' Keen to change the subject, Amber nodded towards the water jug. 'But now get some water on to warm an' make yourself useful. It'll be time for this little 'un's bath soon.'

Sensing that enough had been said on the subject, although she had no idea why, Becky went to do as she was told. Deep down she was already worrying that as there was only one baby left to care for now it might be decided that she was no longer needed, but she prayed that this wouldn't be the case. It was the best job she had ever had. She had a warm bed all to herself, as much good food as she could eat and spare money to give to her mam to help feed her siblings back at home. But then what would be would be.

Chapter Twenty-Nine

April, 1846

'Look at the pretty flowers, darling.' Amber turned the perambulator Mr Greenwood had bought for Charlotte towards the copse of trees and the sweet little girl sucked on her thumb as she stared in awe at the sea of bluebells beneath the tender green leaves. It had been a long hard winter and now Amber was loving being able to take the child out into the fresh air, although she still had to be careful because the April showers could come from nowhere and she didn't want the baby to get wet and catch a chill. Charlotte was now seven months old and the apple of Amber's eye, and now when she looked at her she wondered how she could ever have thought of giving her away.

However, over the last few weeks Amber had become increasingly unsettled and more and more she thought of how wonderful it would be if she were to have her own little home where she could have Charlotte all to herself. She was painfully aware that Mr Greenwood had only given her the position of Charlotte's nanny because of guilt but she hated to feel indebted to him. And so for the last few weeks she had spent her Sunday afternoons searching for a position that provided accommodation where she could take her baby to work with her – after all, she had reasoned, lots of other mothers worked. But it was proving to be far harder than she had thought it would be and up to now she'd had no luck at all.

She knew deep down that Barnaby Greenwood would be devastated if she were to take the baby away, for since losing David, he had grown even closer to the child, but the way she saw it, she had every right to. Charlotte was her daughter too and she doubted he would cause a fuss in case she was to tell everyone how the child had come about. In addition, his wife was now holding on to life by a thread, if the rumours that Becky brought back to the nursery from below stairs were anything to go by, and she doubted he would want anything to upset her to the point that it would speed her end. And so Amber felt quite within her rights to claim the child and as far as she was concerned, he would just have to get used to it. After all, had she done as he had ordered her to, Charlotte would never have been born.

She spent the next hour happily wheeling Charlotte about the manicured lawns pointing out things of interest to the child until the sun suddenly went in and the sky became leaden, so she hurried inside before the rain came.

When she got back to the nursery it was to find that Becky had just brought their lunch up on a tray, so after settling Charlotte to play with her gaily painted wooden bricks on the hearthrug, she settled down to enjoy her soup and the crusty bread fresh from the oven.

Becky was a little chatterbox and as she rattled on Amber glanced over at her and smiled. She had perfected the art of letting half the chatter go in one ear and out of the other. The girl had changed almost beyond recognition from the skinny

284

waif she had been when she first arrived. Her once gaunt face was now rounded and her hair shone and Amber's one regret was that once she took Charlotte away, poor Becky would be out of a job. But then something she said made Amber's ears prick up.

'What was that you just said?'

Becky swallowed a mouthful of soup and swiped the back of her hand across her mouth. 'I said me mam went fer a job at Barstow's farm last week. It's about two miles inland, but after meetin' the farmer an' his wife she said she wouldn't 'ave taken it even if they'd offered her double. They never keep staff fer long apparently cos of how they treat 'em. Mam said the farmer's wife 'as got a tongue on her that's sharp enough to cut glass an' he's a dirty old sod apparently who can't keep 'is hands to 'imself, if yer get me meanin'? They've got two son's an' all an' they ain't much better from what I've 'eard. It would 'ave been too much of a trek fer 'er all that way there an' back every day anyroad. They're lookin' fer someone to live in. I feel sorry fer whoever they get. They reckon they're right slave drivers.'

Amber said nothing but her mind was working overtime as she wondered if it would be worth trying for the position herself. She had no doubt she could give the farmer's wife as good as she got, and if the old man or his sons tried it on with her, she'd soon put them in their place. And it would be a roof over hers and Charlotte's heads so surely it would be worth paying them a visit.

And so, the following Sunday afternoon, after making sure that Charlotte had everything she needed, she left her in Becky's capable care and set off. She had a vague idea where the farm was and it was such a beautiful day, she quite enjoyed the walk. On the edge of the arable fields she passed, there was a profusion of wild flowers – the common fumitory, black medick, buttercups and bird's-foot trefoil – with multi-coloured butterflies flitting among them. She recognised the small tortoiseshells and meadow browns that her father had once pointed out to her on a walk in happier days, and thoughts of him brought a lump to her throat and slowed her steps as she almost allowed herself to be lost in memories. But then she raised her chin and after removing her bonnet she walked on swinging it by its ribbons.

Today she had worn the summer dress her uncle had bought for her and could she have known it, she made a pretty picture as she made her way across the meadows. At last, as sweat stood out on her brow, she saw the farm below her in a hollow and began to make her way down to it. A large sheepdog on a chain began to bark as she came to the gate that led into the farmyard and seconds later a frowning young man holding a pitchfork appeared from a large barn and looked her up and down. She noticed immediately that he had a bad limp, his hair was wild and unkempt and he looked as if he hadn't shaved for weeks. 'An' what can we be doin' fer you, me little maid? Lost are you?' he asked gruffly.

'Oh no, no,' Amber assured him. 'Actually, I heard that there was a job goin' here an' I wondered if you'd found anyone for it yet?'

'It's me mam you'll be wantin' to see then.' Suddenly he was all smiles as he threw the pitchfork down and limped towards her to swing the wide farm gate open. Chickens scattered, squawking indignantly, and Amber screwed up her nose as the smell of the place hit her nostrils. The farm-house windows were grimy and the yard was covered in chicken droppings. Lifting her skirt she picked her away across them and followed him to the open door where he shouted, 'MAM! Someone 'ere to see yer.'

She peered past him into the gloomy room, which looked no cleaner than the outside, and soon a door close to the sink opened and a small woman appeared. She was almost as far around as she was high, which caused her to waddle rather than walk, and like the young man, she looked none too clean. A shabby shawl was tied across her chest and her thinning grey hair was pulled into an untidy bun on the back of her head. As she came closer, Amber saw that there were hairs growing on her chin and many of her teeth were miss-ing. Those that were left were brown and rotting and Amber stifled a shudder as she thought of the witches she had seen in story books when she was a little girl.

'So what was it yer were wantin'?' the old woman asked suspiciously. 'If yer've come fer donations fer the church or sommat we ain't got no money to spare.'

'Oh no, it's nothing like that,' Amber quickly assured her. 'I've come because I heard there were a job goin'?'

'Oh arr!' The woman narrowed her eyes and folding her plump arms she hitched her enormous breasts up. 'An' 'ave you done farm work afore?'

'Well, no I haven't,' Amber admitted. 'But I'm a very quick learner an' I ain't afraid o' hard work.'

'Hm.' The woman stared at her doubtfully. 'An' if I were to take yer on trial, an' I do say *if*, when could yer start.'

'As soon as you like,' Amber gushed. 'And I wouldn't mind what I had to do. But there is just one thing . . .' She twisted the thin gold band that her mother had bought her to wear in Scarborough around on her finger, glad that she'd remembered to put it on. 'I'm a widow, you see? And I have a baby daughter . . . But that wouldn't stop me doing any job you wanted me to,' she rushed on when she saw Mrs Barstow frown.

'Mm, well now that puts a different slant on things,' the woman observed. 'How are yer supposed to work wi' a baby hangin' round yer neck an' that means I'd 'ave to be feedin' an' housin' the two o' yer so there wouldn't be a lot left in wages.'

'I wouldn't need much,' Amber assured her as she held her breath. 'And Charlotte would be no trouble at all, she's very good and I'd just strap her to me.'

'So what do yer think, son?' Mrs Barstow asked the young man Amber had met on arrival.

He shrugged indifferently. 'Do wharrever you want, Mam. But if she's a widow, then I'm the bloody Prince o' Wales.'

The woman frowned at him. Her poor lad had been born a cripple and none o' the lasses thereabouts would give him the time o' day, so he shouldn't be so sniffy. Cos a little maid like this with a bastard to care for might be the best he could do.

She stared at Amber for another few moments – she was sure she'd seen her somewhere before, but then she said, 'All right, I'll give yer a trial. But that's all it'll be, mind. If yer don't come up to muster after a month, yer out, right?'

Amber nodded.

'Come on Sunday an' I'll show yer where you an' the lit-tle 'un will be sleepin'.' And with that the woman turned and shuffled back to wherever she had come from, telling Amber that the interview was at an end.

Turning about, Amber lifted her skirts again and made her way back across the farmyard with the young man closely following. When they reached the gate, he opened it for her.

'See yer Sunday then!' He was openly leering at her and Amber felt awkward.

'Yes.' Amber nodded and hurried on her way, wondering if she would live to regret what she had just arranged.

Becky was surprised when Amber arrived home early. 'I weren't expectin' you just yet,' she remarked cheerfully. 'I thought you'd gone to see Mrs Grimshaw.'

'I just fancied a walk.' Amber hated lying to her and as she went to check on Charlotte, who was fast asleep in her crib, she wondered again if she was doing the right thing. Barnaby Greenwood would obviously be very distressed when he knew that she'd taken their daughter. But given that his reputation and marriage was at stake, would he dare to search for her? It remained to be seen.

The following morning Amber saw Mrs Ruffin coming out of the mistress's room and after glancing about to make sure they couldn't be overheard she drew her to one side and whispered, 'Mrs Ruffin, I have to speak to you.'

The woman frowned as Amber went on, 'I'm so sorry but I can't stay here anymore. Every time I see Mr Greenwood I . . .'

As her voice trailed away Mrs Ruffin patted her arm sympathetically.

'But the thing is . . . I'm taking Charlotte with me.'

The woman sucked in her breath and shook her head, feeling torn. After the way Barnaby had treated Amber she could easily understand how she must feel every time he visited the nursery, and yet she also knew that after losing David, he doted on the little girl more than ever. He rarely visited Louisa now because every time he set foot through the door she became distraught and blamed him for the position she was in. Having his interfering in-laws there didn't help either, so he now spent most of his time out at the shipyard or supervising the cargo that came in on one or another of his ships.

'Do you think he'll try to find us? An' how do you think this might affect the mistress? I know she's really poorly an' I wouldn't want to make things worse for her,' Amber said in a hushed voice.

Again the woman shook her head. 'I'm not so sure that he will come looking but it will be bad news for you if he does because if word gets out that she's your daughter too, your name will be mud, lass. As for Louisa, well in truth, she's never shown a scrap of interest in either of the babies since they were born. All I can advise is that you must do what you feel is right for you and the child now.'

'Thanks for understandin',' Amber said in a choked voice. 'I'll be goin' on Sunday. I've found a position that'll allow me to take Charlotte wi' me.'

'In that case, good luck and may God go with you.' The woman gently squeezed Amber's arm and went on her way with tears in her eyes. This house had seen so much heartbreak over the last few months and now it looked like it was going to see some more.

Chapter Thirty

In the early hours of the following Sunday morning, when the dawn was just streaking the sky, Amber rose and began to pack two carpetbags for herself and Charlotte. She took only the essentials, for she knew that she wouldn't be able to carry any more with Charlotte to carry as well. Thankfully there was no chance of Becky appearing before seven o'clock at the earliest and so when she was quite sure that she had everything they needed, she sat down and began to pen a letter to Barnaby – she supposed she owed him that much at least.

For a moment she stared at the blank page, wondering what she should write, then after dipping her pen nib into the ink well she began.

Dear Mr Greenwood,
  By the time you read this letter you'll have discovered that me and Charlotte have gone. I'm sorry to do this to you but she is mine as well and I find it very hard to be in the same house as you so I've found me a job where I can take Charlotte with me. I hope you'll understand and not try to find us. I promise she'll be loved and cared for always.
  Amber Ainsley

She was aware that it was very short but under the circumstances she felt the note said all that needed to be said, so after sealing it in an envelope and writing his name on it, she propped it up on the mantelpiece and went to wake Charlotte for an early breakfast.

Unusually the infant whinged and complained, almost as if she sensed what Amber was about to do, but Amber was determined and after wrapping the baby in as many layers of clothes as she could fit on her, Amber tied her shawl about her shoulders and strapped Charlotte into it so that she nestled against her chest. She then lifted the carpetbags and after glancing about one last time she slipped from the room and tiptoed down the stairs like a thief in the night, praying all the time that Charlotte wouldn't cry and waken anyone.

She didn't breathe freely until she had turned out of Greenacres' gates on to the road. Charlotte had slipped into an uneasy doze with her head lolling against her mother's chest so after glancing behind to make sure that they weren't being followed, Amber set off on the long walk to Barstow's farm.

Today she found the going much harder than she had the first time she had gone there, for before long the weight of the bags and Charlotte was making her huff and puff and she had to stop frequently to rest her arms and rub her back. Above her seagulls were squawking and wheeling in the sky and once in the distance she spotted old Trampy Ned heading into town, but apart from them Amber felt she and her baby might be the only living things for miles around. It didn't help that it was not yet fully light so she frequently slipped and slid as her feet caught in potholes. At last, after what seemed like hours, she came to the top of a hill and there was the farm nestled down below her. Negotiating the steep bank was no easy task for the grass was still wet with dew but finally she made it to the farm gate where she dropped her bags and leant heavily against it as she fought to catch her breath. The farm dog instantly appeared from his kennels and his bark was enough to waken the dead – it certainly woke Charlotte who began to wail miserably as Amber jiggled her up and down and tried to comfort her.

'It's all right, me little lass,' she crooned. 'We're here now an' you an' me are goin' to be as happy as can be, you just see if we ain't.'

Mrs Barstow's son burst out of the kitchen door, adjusting the braces that were dangling about his knees, and wielding a lethal looking shotgun.

'Oh . . . it's you!' Much to Amber's relief he lowered the barrel and snapped his braces up over his shoulder. He was wearing a dirty grey vest and he looked even worse than Amber remembered from her last visit. 'You'd best come on in, an' can't yer shut that bairn up?'

He opened the gate for her but made no effort to retrieve her bags so Amber wearily lifted them up again and followed him into the kitchen. There she saw Mrs Barstow and two men sitting at a dirty table eating breakfast. There was an older man who Amber assumed was the farmer and another younger one who closely resembled the young man who had just shown her in.

'So you've come then.' Mrs Barstow lifted a chipped mug and slurped at her tea as she stared at Amber from narrowed eyes. 'What do yer think of 'er, Herbert?'

The older man looked Amber up and down and shrugged. He was shovelling food into his mouth as if he hadn't eaten for a month and as egg yolk dripped down his chin, Amber felt slightly nauseous. He would certainly never win any awards for table manners.

'Looks a bit on the skinny side to me. I hope as her can pull 'er weight.'

'Oh she will, I'll see to that,' his wife promised him. Then pointing to a small ladder that stretched up to a hatch in the ceiling in the corner of the room she told Amber, 'You an' the babby'll be sleepin' up in the loft. Tek yer things up then get down 'ere an get some work done.'

Amber's lips set in a straight line; she'd expected to be offered a cup of tea at least, but she snatched up the bags again and went towards the ladder, which she noticed was rather rickety. It wasn't easy getting them up into the loft one at a time but neither of the men offered to help so Amber had no choice but to take them up herself, which was no easy feat. At the top of the ladder, she stopped to throw her bags through the hatch, then with Charlotte still whimpering against her chest, she stared around the gloomy room in horror. When she'd managed to clamber in, she stood up carefully, keeping her head low to avoid banging it on the sloped ceiling, and took a couple of steps, shuddering as her feet crunched over droppings. Pushed right to the back beneath the sloping eaves was a filthy straw mattress and she poked a toe against it in disgust. Surely they can't expect me and Charlotte to sleep on that filthy thing? she thought angrily, brushing a cobweb from her face.

Clutching Charlotte to her, she clambered back down the ladder. 'You can't expect me to sleep up there. Its rat-infested an' *filthy!* There must be somewhere else?'

'I s'ppose she could 'ave that little room that's empty next to the laundry,' one of the men suggested.

Mrs Barstow sighed. 'Eeh, you ain't been 'ere two minutes an' yer causin' problems a'ready,' she moaned.

But on this Amber was prepared to stand her ground. 'Well, I'm sure anywhere will be better than up there,' she snapped.

'In that case, yer'd better tek her out to see it, Melvin,' the old woman instructed her son. 'But I'll warn yer now, it'll be full o' junk an' it ain't been used for years.'

'In that case I shall get it emptied out, clean it and *then* I'll start whatever you want me to do,' Amber responded, and with a toss of her chin she followed Melvin back out into the nippy morning air.

When he threw the door to the room in question open, Amber couldn't stop herself from sighing with dismay. 'You wouldn't put a dog in here!' she exclaimed as she stared at the heaps of rusty tools and rubbish piled up higgledy-piggledy inside it.

Melvin grinned as he picked a piece of bacon from between his stained teeth with a grubby fingernail and spat it into the yard where a passing chicken quickly pecked it up.

'You could always sleep in the pigsty,' he mocked, raking her with a contemptuous glance. 'Reckon you'd be right a' home wi' them.'

Amber felt her temper flare. What gave this revolting man the right to judge her? 'I suppose I'll have to take the

295

loft in that case,' she said with an angry huff. From what she could see of it, even if this room was cleaned out there was hardly enough room in it to swing a cat around and no way of heating it either. Although it was spring the nights still tended to be nippy and she didn't want to risk Charlotte catching a chill.

'Suit yersen.'

Amber followed him back to the kitchen where she found the old woman still sitting where she had left her.

'I've decided to stay in the loft. So where can I get the cleanin' things I'll need to clear it out?'

'Mop an' buckets over there an' there's rags an' a bowl under the sink,' Mrs Barstow told her as she started to pack the bowl of a clay pipe with tobacco. She was clearly in no rush to begin the housework, although the kitchen looked barely cleaner than Amber thought the pig sties would.

'Reet, I'll go an' get changed an' then I'll get crackin',' Amber told her and once again she toted Charlotte up the ladder, thinking that by the time she'd got them somewhere at least clean to sleep she'd be worn out.

As Amber quickly changed her dress for her oldest blouse and skirt, Charlotte sat rubbing at her eyes and whinging again, which was quite unlike her because she was usually such a sunny-natured child. But Amber supposed it was to be expected and she felt guilty. She had taken her away from everyone and everything that was familiar so it was no wonder that the poor little mite was so miserable.

Once she'd carried her back downstairs, she placed her on the grubby hearthrug in front of the fire, grateful that there was a steel fireguard about it, and after heating some water in the sooty-bottomed kettle on the fire she filled the bucket.

'Will she be all right there just while I get the loft clean?' she questioned the old lady.

Mrs Barstow snorted. 'Aye, as long as yer don't expect me to pander to 'er. I ain't her nanny yer know!'

With some trepidation, Amber glanced at the baby who was playing with her rag doll, the only toy Amber had brought for her, and then she hefted the heavy bucket up into the loft before coming back down for a broom and some cleaning rags.

As she busily swept and mopped, she constantly kept going to the loft hatch to check on Charlotte, who was grizzling again now. She felt torn in two. Half of her wanted to get downstairs to her baby but the other half knew that the loft had to be cleaned to make it anywhere near habitable.

'I shall need some clean straw for the mattress,' she informed Mrs Barstow when she came down to fill the bucket with clean water for the third time. By then she was filthy, her hair was full of dust and cobwebs and her hands, which were unused to manual work now, were red and sore.

'So fetch some from the barn,' Mrs Barstow said unhelpfully. 'I ain't took you on to work fer you!'

After three trips to the barn, Amber had managed to restuff the mattress with clean straw, although she had a horrible feeling it wasn't going to be any too comfortable to sleep on. Still, she consoled herself, at least it was clean. Every time she appeared, Charlotte cried harder to be picked up and it was breaking Amber's heart but there was nothing she could do about it.

By mid-morning she had made the loft as clean as she could and after carrying the cleaning things back down the stairs she told her new mistress, 'I need to give Charlotte some pobs now. Could you tell me where to find the bread and milk?'

The old woman was still sitting in the same place and she waved an arm towards a bucket on the draining board. 'You'll find fresh milk in there. The old man brings us a fresh bucketful in every mornin'. Bread's in the pantry but you'll need to bake a fresh batch this afternoon. It's time yer were thinkin' o' gettin' the dinner on an' all. There's a shin o' beef and plenty o' fresh vegetables so yer can make a stew. I take it yer can cook?'

'I can as long as yer don't expect anythin' fancy,' Amber retorted as she heated up some milk in a pan on the range cooker. That too needed a good scrub and the wooden draining board next to the deep stone sink was piled high with dirty pots and pans. Once she'd made the baby's meal, she tried to feed her, but Charlotte slapped the food away every time she offered her a spoonful. Her little eyes were red from crying and Amber felt like crying too as she thought of the cosy nursery back at Greenacres. But it was too late for regrets now. She was just going to have to make the best of things and hope that Charlotte got used to her new way of life.

'Leave 'er be,' the old woman scolded after twenty minutes when Amber was still trying unsuccessfully to get Charlotte to eat something. 'Strikes me that one 'as been spoilt! She'll eat when she's 'ungry enough.' She narrowed her eyes then and commented, 'Them's mighty fine clothes the little 'un is wearin'. Were yer husband a rich man?'

Avoiding having to answer Amber rose and fetched a grubby cushion from an old sofa to one side of the fireplace. Charlotte was rubbing her eyes now and clearly ready for her morning nap and once Amber had laid her down, she drifted off to sleep.

'So what would you like me to do first?'

The old woman snorted as she took a sip of what Amber suspected was gin from an old cracked mug. 'Use yer eyes, lass! I can't do a lot what wi' me rheumatics. I'm a slave to 'em. That's why you're 'ere.'

Amber boiled some water and washed the pile of filthy pots in the sink first, which was no easy task as they had stood so long that the grime was caked to them. She then set to and prepared a large dish of stew and once it was simmering gently, she tackled the tiny lead-paned windows. The room looked so much lighter once she could see through them again and she rightly guessed that they hadn't been cleaned for years. The only trouble was that now it was so much easier to see how filthy everything else in the room was.

Next to be tackled was the floor and after the second mopping Amber was shocked to discover that there were quarry tiles on it. The curtains that hung at the windows were so filthy that it was impossible to see what colour they might be so she hooked them all down and left them to soak in a boiler in the outside laundry room – she would wash them tonight and hang them out to dry in the yard when Charlotte was safely asleep that night.

The men appeared from working in the fields three hours later and without taking their boots off, they trampled all over the clean floor and sat down at the table without even bothering to wash their filthy hands.

'You could at least have taken your boots off; I've scrubbed the floor,' Amber told them angrily and they laughed.

'Ooh, 'ark at 'er ladyship,' Harold, the older of the sons mocked with a wink at his brother, Melvin. 'Yer'd think we were in some fancy 'otel!'

Amber slapped a bowl of stew in front of each of them and a loaf of bread and they fell on the food like animals as she went to fetch the pot of tea she'd made. It was then that Charlotte woke up and instantly started to grizzle, and after a moment the old farmer placed his hands over his ears and pulled a face. 'Can't yer shut that brat up?' he shouted to make himself heard above the baby's cries. 'That racket is enough to deafen yer!'

'It's because everything is strange to her,' Amber said defensively as she lifted Charlotte into her arms and began to rock her. She felt quite hot and Amber prayed that it was only because she was teething and not because she had caught some terrible disease in this filthy hovel. With the baby on her hip she spooned a small amount of stew into a bowl and after mashing it down she tried to feed her again but once more Charlotte turned her head away and refused to take so much as a bite.

'Oh, just give 'er a crust spread wi' some butter to chew on,' Mrs Barstow snapped eventually. 'If she's teethin' it'll 'elp 'er gums.'

But once again, Charlotte slapped the food away, and Amber blinked back tears.

Once the men had eaten their fill they left again for their afternoon's work and Amber set to as well.

By bedtime she was almost dropping with exhaustion. Even the work she had once done in the laundry at Green-acres had been easier than this, and the fact that Charlotte was clearly so unhappy didn't help matters. Nor did the fact that the family had almost completely ignored her. Melvin had made no secret that he thought she was the lowest of the low, but as for the other two men, they barely even looked in her direction. Still, she supposed that was better than the alternative, so she shouldn't complain.

Upstairs in the loft, she put some clean clothes over one side of the mattress for Charlotte to lie on so she would be more comfortable, and once she had rocked her off to sleep she tucked her beneath the blankets and wearily tipped water into the bowl to wash in by the light of the oil lamp. Then, lying down Amber took Charlotte into her arms and let the tears that had been threatening all day roll down her cheeks. Despite the fact that she disliked Barnaby Green-wood with a vengeance, she couldn't help but wonder how he might be feeling. He had behaved shamefully towards her but she was forced to admit that he had appeared to adore his children – both Charlotte and David. He had been devastated when David had died and she had no doubt he would be devastated now that Charlotte was gone too. But her need to have Charlotte to herself and to bring her up the way she saw fit had been overpowering. Now all she could do was pray that she had done the right thing, for both hers and Charlotte's sakes. Only time would tell.

Chapter Thirty-One

Earlier that morning, as he always did after breakfasting with his in-laws, Barnaby had made his way to the nursery to see his daughter before he left to visit his shipyard. He was not in the best frame of mind as his father-in-law's interest in the business was becoming annoying. Many years ago, just before Barnaby's marriage to Louisa, Robert had invested a substantial amount of money in Barnaby's business in exchange for a majority share in both the shipyard and the fishing trawlers, and he had also bought her Greenacres, the beautiful house they lived in, as a wedding present. It hadn't overly concerned Barnaby as in law what was the wife's automatically became the husband's and ever since he had worked tirelessly to build the business up to the thriving concern it was today, so there was no reason now for his father-in-law's interference.

Still, he thought as he took the nursery stairs two at a time, as Margaret spent most of every day with Louisa in the sickroom, Robert was probably poring over the books and poking his nose in just to pass the time.

By the time he pushed the door to the nursery open, he was smiling again at the prospect of spending a little time with his baby daughter. His heart still ached from the loss of his son and his wife now had no room in her life for him, but Charlotte could always make him smile. However, the second he entered the room the smile slid from his face as he saw Becky sitting there with tears streaking down her face.

'What's wrong?' He glanced about noting the empty crib. 'And where are Charlotte and Amber?'

'Please, sir, I don't know.' Becky sniffed and swiped at her tears. 'But I found this on the mantelpiece. It's fer you.'

He was across the room in three long strides and almost ripped the envelope from her hand as a sense of impending doom settled over him like a big black cloud. He tore the envelope open and as he read what was written on the sheet of paper inside his face paled to the colour of parchment.

'They've gone!'

'Well, she never said nowt to me about goin'! Where've they gone?' Becky asked falteringly.

'Oh, er . . .' Barnaby had to think quickly. He had dreaded something like this happening. 'It's nothing to worry about. Amber has had to go away for a while so she's taken Charlotte with her but they're both quite safe.'

'But what about *me*?' Becky said plaintively. 'What am I supposed to do till they get back?'

He knew that Becky's family relied on her wages so he answered dully, 'Don't worry, I'm sure Mrs Boswell can find you plenty to do downstairs. Your job is quite safe, Becky.'

'Thank yer, sir.'

The relief on her face was evident and without another word Barnaby turned and made for the privacy of his room – he had some serious thinking to do. Once his bedroom door had closed behind him, he leant heavily on a chest of drawers and lowered his head as a lump formed in his throat. What was he to do? If he reported Amber to the police for taking his child and they found her she was bound to tell them why, and what would that do to his wife? She was dying bit by bit, and it wouldn't be fair to embroil her in such a scandal – it could even speed her demise. He doubted she'd care that he'd strayed, but the humiliation of everyone knowing that he had tried to foist the laundry maid's daughter on her . . . He shook his head. No, he couldn't do that to her when she was so ill. And anyway, didn't he deserve all that he had coming to him? He had hoped that giving the post of nanny to Amber and allowing her to be close to her child would be enough for her, but it clearly hadn't been. She had never made a secret of the fact that she detested him and he supposed he couldn't blame her when he thought back to how shamelessly he had treated her.

But to lose Charlotte . . . As the image of her chubby little face floated in front of his eyes a tear ran unheeded down his cheek. No, he couldn't have Amber hounded for taking what was, after all, her child, and so somehow he would have to stick to the story he had told Becky – at least until after Louisa had . . . He couldn't bring himself to think of her dying, but it was inevitable and it struck him that once she was gone he would have no one. It was a daunting thought.

Once he had managed to compose himself, he went downstairs to tell Mrs Boswell that Miss Ainsley had been called away unexpectedly to visit a sick relative and he had given permission for her to take Charlotte with her.

'Really? This is the first I knew of it,' the woman said doubtfully. 'And how long are they expected to be gone?'

'Well, with my wife being so poorly, I told her to take as long as she needed,' he lied. 'And so it will be for an indefinite period. Meanwhile, I would be grateful if you could employ Becky below stairs until Miss Ainsley and Charlotte return.'

'Oh, I can do that easily enough now that we have Mr and Mrs Hamilton-Tate staying,' she assured him. 'Was there anything else, sir?'

'No, that will be all, thank you, Mrs Boswell.'

She bobbed her knee and went on her way as Barnaby went to the stables to have his horse saddled. Perhaps he would go into town before he went to work. It wouldn't hurt to make a few discreet enquiries as to where Amber might have gone, and if he could only find her, he might be able to persuade her to bring Charlotte back.

However, when he rode into town a short time later, looking as if he had the worries of the world resting on his shoulders, he found the whole place swarming with police.

'What's going on here?' he enquired of a sailor with a kit-bag on his back who was heading for the docks.

'Somebody broke into the post office durin' the night be all accounts.' The man spat out the mouthful of tobacco he had been chewing. 'Trouble was, the postmistress heard him an' when she come down to see what were goin' on they clubbed her to death. Poor old sod, she were a good woman were Mrs Tilsley.'

'Good grief! Do they have any idea who it was?'

The man shrugged. 'Rumour has it that that young Bertie Preston an' his cronies had a hand in it,' the sailor said in a whisper. 'The coppers are lookin' fer 'em now but they've all gone to ground, the buggers! There's been a few shop break-ins durin' the last few weeks an' Bertie an' his gang have been in the frame every time but they ain't managed to pin owt on 'em as yet. But anyway, I'd best get on, I don't want to miss me ship sailin'. Ta-ra.'

The man went on his way and Barnaby walked his horse on to the market square. It was certainly turning out to be an eventful day one way or another.

Back at the house Mrs Ruffin was tending to Louisa who was now so weak that she was reliant on her maid for everything.

'That's it, my love. Just raise yourself a tiny bit more,' she encouraged as she slid a clean nightdress over Louisa's head. She had just gently washed her from head to toe, as she did each morning, but it seemed that no amount of washing could erase the smell of death that hung in the air now. 'I'm sure your mother will be in to read to you soon, you'll like that, won't you?'

As she laid the young woman back on the lace-trimmed pillows, Louisa caught her arm. She was burning hot and her eyes were feverishly bright as she clutched at her swollen stomach with her other hand. 'Yes, yes, I will, but before she comes in I need to speak to you, Ruffy. I . . . I know that I haven't got long left,' she said. 'And truthfully, I shall welcome death; the pain is just so awful, even the medicine isn't helping for long.'

'That's quite enough of that silly talk, my girl,' Ruffy scolded. 'Somehow we're going to get you well.'

Louisa shook her head. 'No, my dear Ruffy, you know that isn't true . . . and so if you truly love me as you say you do, will you do something for me?'

'Of course . . . anything, you should know that.' The lump in Mrs Ruffin's throat was so large that it was threatening to choke her. 'What is it you want, just name it.'

'I want . . .' Every word was an effort now. 'I want you to end it for me.'

'*What!*' Mrs Ruffin was so horrified that she snatched her arm away.

'I wouldn't ask if there was any chance of me getting better,' Louisa told her. 'But all I have left to look forward to is pain for however long I have left and you could end that pain for me.'

Mrs Ruffin's head bounced from side to side as she reached for the bottle of laudanum the doctor had left. 'Look, have a drink of this, you'll feel differently when it starts to work.' With shaking hands, she tipped a few drops into a glass of water but when she raised it to Louisa's lips, Louisa shook her head.

'No Ruffy, that's only a *temporary* release, and after what the reverend told me when he came to see me the other day, I know I have something so much more to look forward to. When I go to heaven, I'll never be in pain again and I'll be an angel.'

'You already *are* an angel,' Mrs Ruffin muttered with a crack in her voice.

Thankfully the painful conversation was brought to an abrupt end when the door opened and Louisa's mother appeared.

'I'll leave you two to it for a time while I take these dirty clothes to the laundry,' Mrs Ruffin said hurriedly, snatching up the laundry and marching from the room.

Once on the landing she took a deep breath and leant heavily against the wall as her shoulders sagged. Never in her life had she denied Louisa anything, but was she strong enough to do what she had asked of her today? Deep down she knew that death would be a blessed release for the poor soul, for it tore her heart in two watching her suffer. From the time she had taken over the care of her when Louisa was just a tiny baby, she had loved her as her own and now she couldn't imagine life without her. With a sigh she pulled herself together and wearily went down the stairs.

'So why have you allowed the nanny to take Charlotte away?' Margaret asked Barnaby at dinner that evening.

News of her going had spread through the house and caused more than a little gossip. After all, everyone was saying, the child could quite easily have stayed with Becky, who was more than capable of looking after her. Barnaby was aware the excuse he had given would only ring true for so long but he would worry about that when questions started to be asked about why Amber and Charlotte hadn't come back. Neither his wife nor Charlotte's grandparents had ever shown much interest in her after all, so none of them were going to miss her.

Robert didn't even look up or show any interest in his wife's question. He was too busy concentrating on the delightful Queen of Puddings in front of him. Barnaby wondered how he had any room left for it after he had helped himself to two portions of the rack of lamb, and before that he'd eaten a large dish of broccoli and stilton soup.

Now he dabbed at his lips before replying calmly, 'I thought it might be a good idea to get her away from the house while Louisa is so ill. The servants are creeping about like ghosts and I believe that children can pick up on things like that so it I think it's best she's in a happier environment for a time.'

'Mm, I suppose you have a point. Now, if you gentlemen will excuse, I'm going to go up and see how she is. She's had a particularly bad day today.'

Both men rose from the table as she left the room, and once she was gone they retired to Barnaby's study for a glass of port and one of the excellent cigars Barnaby had shipped in from Cuba.

At last Barnaby's father-in-law retired and Barnaby could make his way to his own room. Once there he sat on the end of his bed and dropped his head into his hands as he tried to envisage life without either of his children. Louisa would not be here much longer, David was dead and now he had lost Charlotte too, the one person who had made his life worth living. Already he missed her smile, the way her face would light up the moment she saw him, and the sweet baby smell of her. At that moment, he wasn't even sure if he wanted to go on, but one thing he was sure of: this was God's way of repaying him for the wrong he had done to Amber and now he would never have the chance to put things right. Stifling his sobs with his fist he finally allowed his tears to fall.

Chapter Thirty-Two

As the cock crowed in the farmyard, Amber rolled herself to the edge of the straw mattress and began to fumble about for her clothes. Each morning she was expected to be up to make sure the fires were lit and start the men's breakfasts before they rose. Thankfully, Charlotte was still asleep with her thumb jammed in her mouth. That was one blessing at least, for with every day that passed the child was becoming more fractious. Added to that she had now discovered that she could roll about the floor, so Amber had no doubt that soon she would be crawling and getting herself into all sorts of danger.

The old lady had taken to having a lie-in each morning, claiming that her arthritis was playing her up, and Amber had now just about taken over all the household cleaning and cooking, which wasn't easy when she had to keep one eye constantly on her baby. Melvin was also proving to be a problem as he seemed to take delight in goading and insulting her. She had no idea why he'd taken such dislike to her, and she did her best to stay out of his way.

Once she was dressed and had checked that Charlotte was still fast asleep she climbed down the ladder and began the task of lighting the fires as quietly as she could.

The only good thing about living there was that there was never a shortage of food. Pigs provided pork and bacon, the chickens laid an abundance of eggs, there was fresh milk each morning from the cows and the vegetable garden and orchard supplied more produce than one family could ever eat. What they didn't need was taken to market and sold each week, which was the one thing that Amber had refused to do. She had no wish to be seen there and so the old lady had taken to going with the farmer, which suited Amber.

There was bacon sizzling in the old cast-iron frying pan and the tea was mashing when the menfolk appeared, scratching their bellies and yawning with their braces dangling about their knees. Amber hadn't seen any of them even attempt to have a wash since she'd been there and as they entered the room the smell of stale sweat came with them. She hurriedly fried the eggs and slapped their breakfasts down on the table in front of them, then hearing Charlotte start to whimper she wiped her hands down the front of her apron and started to climb the ladder to the loft with the men's complaints ringing in her ears.

'I ain't never knowed a bairn cry as much as that 'un. It's enough to drive yer barmy!' This was from the old farmer and she cursed under her breath although she knew deep down that it must be trying. Charlotte was no longer the happy child who had arrived there just one week ago and she still wasn't eating properly despite Amber's best attempts to tempt her, which was worrying her no end.

Once the child was dressed, she carried her downstairs and offered her some of the porridge that had been gently simmering on the range all night, but Charlotte turned her head away and in the end Amber gave up.

Thankfully the men left shortly after to begin their jobs so she settled the child down with a saucepan and a wooden spoon to play with while she cleared the breakfast pots from the table. The room looked very different now to when she had first arrived, for during the time she'd been there Amber had scrubbed and polished everything in sight – not that any of the family seemed to appreciate it. They seemed quite happy living in squalor so long as their meals were on the table, but at least Amber had the satisfaction of knowing that Charlotte was sitting on a clean floor now.

By the time the old lady appeared, her wispy grey hair standing about her head in a halo and still in her grubby nightgown, the pots were all washed and dried.

'So what do you want me to do today?' Amber asked as she poured her a cup of tea from the large brown earthenware teapot. It was quite stewed by then but Mrs Barstow didn't seem to mind as she slurped at it.

'Yer can try yer 'and in the dairy,' she told her. 'We could do wi' some cheese to tek to market on Thursday.'

Amber's heart sank as she glanced at Charlotte who was sitting like a little statue staring into space. There was no way she could take the baby in there with her, but as if she had read what she was thinking Mrs Barstow piped up, 'I'll keep me ear open fer the bairn.'

'Thank you.' Amber bent to drop a kiss on Charlotte's springy curls. 'I'll be back mid-morning to give her some milk. Are you sure you'll manage?'

'I 'ad three o' me own, didn't I? Though there's only two of 'em survived,' Mrs Barstow said as she began to lavishly butter a slice of toast. So with some trepidation Amber set off for the dairy.

As promised, when she judged it to be mid-morning, she scurried back to the kitchen only to stop dead in her tracks when there was no sign of Charlotte.

'Where is she?' she demanded. But before Mrs Barstow could answer she heard a sound coming from the small cupboard where the men kept their coats and boots and flying over to it she flung the door wide to see Charlotte sitting on the floor in the darkness sobbing her little heart out. Amber snatched the quivering little body into her arms and turned on the old woman. 'What the *hell* did you lock her in there for?' Her voice shook with fury as she rocked Charlotte up and down.

'She wouldn't stop whingin' so I thought I'd teach 'er a lesson. You're too soft wi' that bairn, that's the problem!'

'How *dare* you!' Amber had never been so angry in her life. 'If you ever . . . *ever* do that to her again I'll be out of here like a shot, I promise you that!'

'Oh, keep yer 'air on. She's all right, ain't she?'

Amber slammed over to the range to warm some milk for the infant but she was shaking with rage. Thankfully Charlotte's crying had stopped and before the milk was warm she had fallen asleep on her mother's shoulder, worn out with fear and crying.

'It's all right my little lass,' she whispered to her. 'That'll never happen again, I promise.' She sat for a good half an hour holding the child and if the old woman didn't like it then Amber decided she could lump it.

On Thursday the farmer and his wife set off for market and Amber sighed with relief when the little pony and cart pulled out of the farmyard. Had Melvin and Harold gone with them it would have been better still, but unfortunately they stayed behind to continue with their chores, although thankfully Amber didn't see much of them apart from when they came in for their meals and she was heartened to find that as the day progressed Charlotte seemed to be a little more alert.

It was early evening when the farmer got back and both he and his wife were pleased as they'd sold all of their produce.

'They still ain't caught the buggers who done fer the old postmistress,' Mrs Barstow told her over dinner. 'But Bertie Preston an' 'is cronies are nowhere to be found. That tells yer somethin', don't it? They're the prime suspects be all accounts an' the police are offerin' a reward if anyone can tell 'em where they are.'

Amber kept her eyes on her plate. She saw no reason to tell them that Bertie had once wanted to marry her and that they'd been brought up in the same yard.

'Some o' the women that came to the stall was on about the young mistress up at Greenacres an' all.' Mrs Barstow went on as she loaded her fork and rammed the food into her mouth. 'They reckon the poor young bugger is on 'er last legs now. The reverend were called out to see 'er yesterday, apparently, so I doubt it'll be long now.' Food was spraying all over the table and Amber averted her eyes, revolted. She was sure the pigs in the sties had better table manners than this family did.

Amber glanced at Charlotte, who was lying quietly on the hearthrug in front of the fire. For some reason over the last few days she had stopped crying. In fact, she seemed to have stopped doing everything and she was worried that

314

she might be sickening for something. She just lay there hour after hour like a little rag doll with a glazed look in her eyes. Amber almost preferred the crying; this wasn't like Charlotte at all.

'Do you think I should call the doctor in to take a look at her?' she'd asked Mrs Barstow before she left for market and after quickly feeling the baby's forehead the old woman shook her head.

'Ner, she ain't 'ot. She's probably just realised that 'er cryin' won't get 'er anywhere.'

And so Amber had reluctantly taken her advice, but she had hardly taken her eyes off Charlotte all day.

Once dinner was over and she had washed and dried all the pots, Mrs Barstow, who had resumed her favourite position in the fireside chair smoking her clay pipe, pointed to the bucket of pig swill by the door.

'Pop that over to the pigs would yer?'

Amber frowned. 'But I was just about to give Charlotte some milk. Couldn't one of the men do it?'

'They've been graftin' all day,' Mrs Barstow remarked, as if Amber hadn't. 'An' I'll give the little 'un her milk. Pass it over 'ere!'

Reluctantly Amber handed it over and once she had placed Charlotte on the old woman's lap, she lifted the bucket and set off across the yard to the pigsties where she quickly emptied the food into the long metal trough. Instantly the enormous pigs came snuffling towards it and she leant on the wall surrounding the sty, watching them with a smile. She couldn't deny that the animals were cared for and that was something at least.

It was a beautiful evening and she suddenly wished that she could go for a walk to Whitby Abbey and watch the sea from the clifftop. But that was out of the question. The fewer people who knew where she was the better so it was for the best if she didn't venture far from the farm. She had written to her mother to tell her where she was and had received a letter in reply in which her mother urged her to take Charlotte to Scarborough where she and the baby would be welcome, but Amber didn't want to do that. Her uncle and Mrs Carter would be getting married very soon and they had already been kind enough to offer her mother a home when she was widowed so Amber didn't want to be a further burden on them, as tempting as the offer was. But overriding this, she was far more afraid that her uncle's would be one of the first places Barnaby might go to look for her and she shuddered at the thought of losing Charlotte again.

She was so lost in thought that she didn't hear someone come up behind her until an arm snaked about her waist. She started and pulled away. She knew who it was before she even turned around by the smell of him: it was Melvin and his expression was ugly.

'So I were right about you.' He grinned nastily. 'Accordin' to me mam, yer the subject o' much gossip down in the town an' if what they're sayin' is true your nowt but a filthy liar!' He gestured towards the wedding ring on her hand.

'What do you mean?' Amber stepped away from him with her hands on her hips but her heart was thumping so loudly she feared it was going to jump out of her chest.

'Well, it appears you ain't been entirely honest wi' us, 'ave yer?' He plucked a piece of straw and began to chew on it as he leant lazily against the wall, obviously enjoying her discomfort.

'Word 'as it that the Greenwoods' nanny 'as took off wi' his baby daughter who just 'appens to be called Charlotte. Coincidence, eh? An' stranger still is the fact that he ain't got the law out lookin' fer 'em. Folks are sayin' that's because she's *their* babby, his an' the kid's nanny.'

'I-I don't know what you're talkin' about,' Amber flustered but he was like a dog with a bone and not ready to give up on the gossip just yet.

'I wonder 'ow much Greenwood'd pay to get his precious babby back, eh?'

'He wouldn't pay anything,' Amber snapped, although fear was crawling along her spine. 'Cos she ain't got nothin' to do with him.' She tried to pass him and head back to the kitchen. But he wasn't done with her yet and he caught her wrist.

'You don't fool me, girl! That kid is 'is, all right.'

'Let me tell you now, Melvin Barstow, Charlotte is *mine*! And if you *dare* try to take her away from me, your ugly face an' your crippled leg'll be the least of your problems, cos I'd get the police to lock you up and make sure they throw away the key!' Amber yanked her wrist from his grip and with her eyes flashing fire she walked towards the kitchen, although inside she was quaking. She'd hoped that if she had settled far enough out of the town it would be a case of out of sight out of mind but it seemed the townspeople were beginning to put and two together and if Melvin did send word to Barnaby, and he came looking for her . . . She shuddered. *She* might be the one to find herself in prison.

Charlotte was just finishing her milk when she re-entered the kitchen and once again Amber saw that the infant's eyes were growing heavy so, lifting her from Mrs Barstow's lap, she carried her up to her loft room to wash her and settle her into bed before she had to set about preparing supper for the menfolk. Even though they had only just eaten the huge steak and kidney pie she'd baked that afternoon, as well as a pile of potatoes and vegetables, she knew they'd be hungry again soon. She sometimes wondered if they had hollow legs.

When she arrived back downstairs, Melvin was back sitting at the table but thankfully he didn't mention the altercation they'd had and she was grateful for that at least.

It was late by the time she wearily climbed the stairs to her room. She started work early each morning and didn't retire until late each night and now all the hard work was catching up with her and she was realising just how easy a life she'd had back at Greenacres where all she'd had to do was care for Charlotte and all her meals were delivered to her. Her laundry was done for her too, but now her hands were red raw, her ankles were swollen from the many hours she was on her feet and there were dark bags beneath her eyes from the hours she lay awake at night feeling guilty and worrying about how unhappy Charlotte seemed to be.

Although Amber hated to admit it and tried to convince herself that things would get easier, she knew deep down that Charlotte was like a different child now. She never lifted her arms to Amber as she had to her father and her face never lit up when Amber entered a room as it had when the child saw him. Now, as she cuddled her baby's warm little body close to her, tears slid down her cheeks. *Perhaps it's time I started to look for another position*, she told herself, but even that would prove to be easier said than done. She was given no time off and she could hardly cart Charlotte for miles searching for work. And even if she did, would she find another post now that the people in the town were questioning Charlotte's true parentage? Eventually she dropped into an uneasy doze and the tears dried on her cheeks.

Chapter Thirty-Three

The following day, however, the decision was made for her. Every morning, once breakfast was finished and the men left to work about the farm, Amber went to collect the eggs from the hen coop and the barn where the chickens had a tendency to lay. Some time ago, Mrs Barstow had volunteered to give Charlotte her morning bottle of milk while Amber got on with the job, and hoping that this would help to endear the child to her Amber had readily agreed to allow it. On this particular morning, Amber was halfway through the task when she cursed softly as the handle on the wicker basket that she put the eggs in broke and some of the eggs spilled across the floor.

'Damn,' she muttered as she hurriedly placed them back in the basket before any more got broken. There were far too many eggs to put in her pockets so she lifted the basket gingerly with two hands and carried it back to the kitchen.

As she entered the kitchen, she saw that Charlotte was just finishing her milk and she crossed to take the empty bottle from Mrs Barstow.

'I need another basket,' she told the woman as she carried the glass bottle to the sink. 'The handle just broke on the other one.'

Whilst she was there, she decided she may as well put the bottle into soak until she had time to clean it but as she peeled off the rubber teat the strangest smell wafted up to her and she frowned as she lifted the bottle to her nose. When she realised what it was, she gasped in disbelief and horror and spun about to look at the table next to where Mrs Barstow sat. On it was a small bottle of laudanum and a bottle of gin.

'You . . . you've been *drugging* my baby,' she said with a wobble in her voice, wondering how anyone could be so cruel. 'How *dare* you! No wonder the poor little mite has been sleepin' all the time. You could have killed 'er!'

'Oh, stop bein' so sensitive,' the woman responded nonchalantly. 'It's shut the brat up, ain't it? She were near drivin' us all mad wi' 'er grizzlin' an' wailin' all the time. An' all mine were brought up on a drop o' gin an' it never 'urt them.

Slowly Amber's disbelief turned to rage and after throwing the bottle into the sink she snatched the baby from the old woman's arms. 'Well, I'll not give you the chance to do it again!' she stormed and turning about she raced to the stairs that led to the loft. Already Charlotte's head was nodding as the mixture she had been given took effect, so after laying her on the mattress, Amber began to throw their things into the bags she had brought with them. It took no time at all to pack their few clothes and she threw them down the ladder where they landed with a resounding thud in the kitchen. Next, she strapped Charlotte to her in her shawl and followed the bags down only to find Mrs Barstow waiting for her at the bottom.

'Just what do yer think yer doin'?' she demanded in a panic. She had never given Amber so much as one kind word or a single word of praise since she had been there but she was no fool and had quickly realised that Amber was a hard worker. She had totally transformed the farmhouse and had worked from dawn to dusk, unlike most of the idle so-and-sos she'd employed in the past. The old lady had had it easy since Amber's arrival and now she was reluctant to let her go. 'I'll not give yer a penny o' yer wages if you just up an' go an' leave me in the lurch!' she threatened, but Amber tossed her head and snorted as she snatched up a bag in each hand.

'You can *stick* the wages where the sun don't shine.' She elbowed the old woman out of the way and the next minute she was striding across the farmyard.

Melvin was just coming out of the barn and seeing her with her bags and the baby tied to her he limped across to the gate. 'An' where are you goin' in such a hurry?' he asked.

Amber glared at him as she dropped one of the bags just long enough to open the gate. 'Just as far away from this dump an' you lot as I can get,' she ground out.

'B-but yer can't just up an' leave,' he whined.

'Just watch me and go to *hell*.' And with that Amber moved on as fast as her legs would take her.

It wasn't until she came within sight of Greenacres that she finally paused to rest and the tears came. Her arms felt as if they had been pulled out of their sockets and she was sweating as she stared down at Charlotte whose little head was lolling to one side. *How could I not have seen what the wicked old woman was doing to her?* she asked herself. But this was not the time for guilt; she finally had to face the fact that Charlotte had missed her father and she had been wrong to take her away from him in the first place. She didn't even know what sort of reception she was going to get when she reached the house or if Barnaby Greenwood had reported her to the police for kidnapping his daughter. He could well send for them and have her arrested, but there could be no going back now and as long as Charlotte was happy again, she didn't much care what happened to herself. So after taking a deep breath she moved on and despite the fact that she was in her oldest work clothes, she held her head high as she climbed the steps to the front door and rang the bell.

Seconds later, Nancy answered it and her face lit up like a ray of sunshine at sight of her friend. 'Amber! Eeh lass, we've been so worried about yer.' Ignoring the bags on the step she took Amber's elbow and drew her into the hallway just as Barnaby Greenwood appeared from his study. Amber was shocked at the sight of him. His shoulders were stooped as if he had the worries of the world resting on them and he seemed to have aged ten years since the last time she had seen him. He stared at her for a moment as if he couldn't quite believe what he was seeing, then suddenly he sprang forward and as he laid his hand gently on Charlotte's head, she was shocked to see that there were tears in his eyes.

'Let me carry her up to the nursery for you,' he said gently, for all the world as if he were speaking to his equal, and Amber quietly undid the shawl that bound the child to her and watched as he took the infant from her and cradled her against his chest.

'Nancy, see that some refreshments are sent up to the nursery,' he told the girl and with a bob of her knee and a broad smile on her face Nancy rushed off to do as she was told.

They didn't speak again until they reached the privacy of the nursery and Amber stood there not sure what she should do. She had expected him to rant and rave at her but instead he eventually dragged his eyes away from Charlotte's face to say softly, 'I didn't think I was ever going to see her again. Why did you bring her back?'

Amber gulped. 'Because she was un'appy an' because . . . she were missin' you.'

His eyes returned to his daughter's face as if he couldn't get enough of her and raising his head, he said gently, 'Thank you.'

'What? You mean I ain't in trouble? Ain't you got the police lookin' for me?'

He shook his head. 'How could I report you for anything after the way I treated you? And anyway, I don't think they'd have been too interested when they found out that you'd taken your own daughter.'

She lowered her eyes, feeling ashamed. When it came to his children, Barnaby wasn't nearly as bad as she had painted him in her mind. 'So what do you want me to do now? Shall I go?'

'Go?' He raised his eyebrows. 'Why would you do that? Who else could I get to care for Charlotte better than her own mother? No, please stay. I told the servants and anyone who asked that you'd gone to care for a sick relative and that you could be gone some time. There's no need for them to know otherwise, although . . .' His mouth twitched and the shadow of a smile appeared. 'It might be a good idea to get changed out of those clothes before you see any of them.'

She too smiled as she gazed down at her shabby work boots, and darned skirt and blouse, but then Charlotte stirred and slowly opened her eyes and as she looked up into her father's face the most wondrous smile stretched from ear to ear and she gave a little crow of delight as her arms crept about his neck.

'I'll . . . go and get changed then.' Amber felt as if she had a lump the size of a house brick in her throat and she had the sensation of choking as she fled into her old room, holding back a sob. It was the first time Charlotte had smiled – *really* smiled – since they'd left and Amber's heart felt as if it was breaking. The child had never smiled at her like that.

Half an hour later she presented herself back in the nursery. She had washed and changed and fixed her hair into a neat bun but there was nothing she could do about the state of her work-worn hands. Only time would heal them.

The door opened and Barnaby's mother-in-law appeared to stare disdainfully at Amber. 'Ah, the servants said you were back.' She turned her attention to Barnaby and told him, 'Don't you think you should go and spend some time with your wife? She isn't long for this life, as you well know.'

Amber was aware that she barely glanced at Charlotte, and she wondered if Margaret Hamilton-Tate knew the child wasn't even her blood relation. Or perhaps she sensed it and that was why she showed no interest in her?

Barnaby was well aware that Louisa really didn't care if he was there or not. She was in so much pain now that she was only semi-conscious for much of the time. Over the last few days, she had seen everyone she wished to see, the reverend and her solicitor and now it felt as if they were all just waiting for the inevitable end. Even so he nodded and reluctantly passed Charlotte back to Amber, saying, 'I'll send Becky back up.'

Amber nodded and once he'd left the room, she set about bathing and changing Charlotte. The child seemed happy to be back in familiar surroundings and as the day wore on, she became more alert and much more her cheerful little self.

In the afternoon, Amber and Becky took her out into the garden and after laying a blanket on the grass they let her roll about in the sunshine.

'It's good to 'ave you back; I missed you both,' Becky said with sincerity and Amber smiled. Her plans to have Charlotte all to herself and live independently had gone seriously awry but at least she could still care for her, which meant the world.

Throughout the day Louisa deteriorated and as evening drew in, her mother retired leaving strict instructions with Mrs Ruffin to fetch her should her daughter get any worse.

Mrs Ruffin seriously doubted that this was possible and as she gently bathed the young woman's head with cool water she felt as if her heart were breaking. From the second she had taken over the care of Louisa when she was just a tiny baby her whole life had been devoted to her, and now she couldn't bear to think about being without her – she was her reason for being.

'There, my brave lass,' she crooned and Louisa's eyes blinked open as her hand sought Ruffy's.

'R-Ruffy, please . . . I *beg* you; the pain is so terrible.' As she drew her legs upwards, she gasped and grimaced with pain. '*P-please*, help me. I can't bear it anymore. Please, if you love me . . . put me out of my misery . . .'

Mrs Ruffin swallowed, and in that moment she knew that her beloved girl had had enough. Her eyes locked with Louisa's and very slowly she nodded as she gently eased the pillow from beneath her head.

'I love you, my lass. You'll never know how much,' she said brokenly, and as she saw the gratitude in Louisa's eyes, she placed a kiss on her forehead and gently placed the pillow across her face and pressed down hard. Louisa was too weak to fight even if she had wanted to and within an amazingly short space of time Mrs Ruffin sensed that she was gone from her.

As she lifted the pillow, she saw that the pain was gone from Louisa's face and she looked at peace. She gently lifted her head and replaced the pillow.

'Sleep tight, my precious lass,' she muttered and turning about blindly she stumbled across the room to swish aside the curtains and open the window so that her beloved girl's soul could fly free. At last Louisa was free of pain but Mrs Ruffin knew that hers was only just beginning.

Beyond the window the wise old owl sat hooting in his favourite tree and a silver moon hung suspended in a black velvet sky. Everything looked exactly as it had the night before but Mrs Ruffin was painfully aware that nothing would ever be the same again.

Crossing back to the bed she bent to place one last kiss on Louisa's pale cheek before fetching her cape and walking woodenly out of the house. She had nothing and no one to live for anymore. She had no idea where she was going, but eventually, she found herself at the harbour. It was deserted and there was nothing to be heard but the sound of the waves slapping against the quay. A number of boats were anchored there and as she stared past them to the sea beyond, she felt bereft. Only once before in her life had she felt such grief when, as a young mother-to-be, the mine owner from the pit where her husband worked had come cap in hand to tell her that her darling husband had been killed in a fall below ground. Her grief had been so intense that only days later the child she had been carrying had been born too soon. It was a little girl and Maude Ruffin had felt that her life was over.

The months that followed had passed in a blur of heartbreak until the small amount of savings they'd had was almost gone and she applied for the post of nanny to the Hamilton-Tates' new baby daughter. She was accepted for the job and the minute she held Louisa in her arms she had begun to heal and in her heart, Louisa had become the daughter she had always longed for.

She stared despairingly down into the murky depths. She was on the very edge of the quay, just one more step and she could disappear beneath the dark water and be with her precious girl forever, but did she have the courage to take that step? she asked herself. And then suddenly Louisa's beautiful face appeared floating beneath the turquoise depths. She looked like a mermaid with her lovely hair floating about her and she was smiling as she held her arms up towards her.

'I'm coming, my love,' Maude Ruffin murmured, her heart soaring and, just for a moment before she plummeted into the cold water, she had the sensation of flying. Louisa seemed to be waiting for her and after wrapping her arms about her beloved Ruffy she drew her down and down and as she sank there was a gentle smile on Ruffy's face.

Chapter Thirty-Four

Early the next morning Margaret Hamilton-Tate entered her daughter's room to find her cold and dead, and her screams echoed along the landing. Even Becky and Amber heard her up in the nursery and Becky stared at Amber. 'What do you think's 'appened?'

Amber shook her head sadly. 'I can only think it's the mistress passed away. But we'll know soon enough.'

Nancy arrived shortly after with their breakfasts on a tray and confirmed what Amber had feared. 'Apparently the poor bugger were stiff as a board when 'er mother went into her room this mornin', but the strangest thing is, Mrs Ruffin never fetched anyone an' they can't find 'er!'

Amber frowned. They all knew how devoted Mrs Ruffin was to her young mistress and she couldn't imagine her leaving her. 'What do you mean, they can't find her?'

'Just what I say. She's gone an' the master's got the grooms an' the gardeners out lookin' for 'er now!'

'Poor thing, she'll be heartbroken,' Amber said compassionately. 'Perhaps she just needed to get out for some fresh air? It's funny that she didn't tell anyone that the mistress had passed though, ain't it?'

Shortly after, Barnaby appeared to visit Charlotte, his face pale and strained. 'I suppose you've heard by now that my wife has passed away?' he said quietly as Becky discreetly slipped out of the room with her arms full of dirty laundry.

Amber nodded solemnly. 'Er, yes . . . I'm sorry for your loss,' she said stiffly, for despite her more charitable thoughts towards him the day before, she still couldn't forgive him for what he had done to her and she doubted she would ever feel completely at ease in his presence.

With his arms clasped behind his back he crossed to the window and stared sightlessly out across the lawns. 'Her parents have informed me that they wish to take her body home to be buried in their family plot in Pickering.'

'Oh . . . I see. And have you agreed to that?' Amber didn't quite know what to say.

'Yes. I think it's what Louisa would have wanted. She was never really happy here,' he said regretfully.

'Then I can only repeat, I'm sorry for your loss.'

He shrugged. 'If truth be told I lost Louisa years ago – that's if I ever really had her. I couldn't make her happy, you see? Immediately after the funeral I shall return and Louisa's solicitor will meet me here the following day to read her will, although I envisage everything being fairly straightforward. But anyway, that's quite enough of my troubles, how is Charlotte this morning?' He crossed to the crib where the baby was just stirring and gently ran his finger down her cheek. 'She gets to look more and more like you,' he remarked softly and Amber felt herself flush.

They heard the sound of a carriage pulling down the drive then and crossing to the window Barnaby saw it was the undertaker who had come to measure Louisa for her coffin. 'If you'll excuse me, I have business to attend to,' he told her with a nod. At the door, he suddenly paused. 'I shall be attending the funeral so I shall be away for a few days. You will . . . you will still be here when I get back, won't you?'

Hearing the fear in his voice she drew herself up to her full height and clasping her hands tightly into her waist she assured him. 'Yes, I'll still be here. I won't try to take Charlotte away from you again, if that's what you're worried about, on that you have my word.'

'Thank you.' Their eyes met just for the briefest of moments then he was gone, closing the door gently behind him.

Amber let out a deep sigh of relief. She was sorry his wife had died, it was such a shame for one so young to be afflicted with such a terrible illness, and yet selfishly she was glad that she wouldn't have to see him for a while.

Nancy informed her later that day that Louisa's body was to be taken to her parents' home in two days' time. Meantime she would lie in her coffin in the drawing room at Greenacres where friends who couldn't travel to Pickering would be able to call and pay their respects.

'And is there any news of Mrs Ruffin yet?' Amber enquired anxiously. She had grown fond of the woman.

Nancy shook her head. 'Not a peep so far but they're still out lookin' for 'er and she can't have gone far.'

As was the custom following a bereavement, every curtain in the house was tightly drawn and would not be opened again until Louisa had been laid to rest. It made the nursery gloomy and so as soon as it was warm enough Amber got Charlotte ready to go outside and get some fresh air. She lay a blanket on the grass and sat her down in the middle of it and Charlotte suddenly surprised her when she rolled on to all fours and crawled off in the direction of the copse nearby.

'Eeh, Mr Greenwood will be tickled pink when he sees her do that,' Becky commented as she chased after her. When she was tired of that they took her into the copse and Charlotte oohed and ahed at the beautiful sight of the carpet of bluebells spreading as far as the eye could see.

They didn't return to the house until it was time for lunch and Amber was delighted when Charlotte ate everything that was offered to her. It was very clear that she, at least, was happy to be home again and the fresh air had clearly done her good. Or was it because she was with her father again? Amber wondered.

It was mid-afternoon by the time Barnaby made another appearance but Charlotte was having an afternoon nap so he didn't wish to disturb her.

'I'll call back after dinner,' he told Amber. Then taking a deep breath he said, 'I'm afraid the constable from the village has just called to say that they have recovered a woman's body from the harbour. The description he gave sounds suspiciously like Mrs Ruffin and I have to go and identify it.'

'Oh no!' Becky started to cry softly.

'How awful,' Amber said sadly and then she shocked herself when she volunteered, 'Would you rather I did it?'

Without even having to think about it he nodded vigorously. 'I would be extremely grateful if you would. I'll accompany you in the carriage, of course, but I'm afraid I'm not very good at this sort of thing. Could you be ready in half an hour?'

Amber nodded. 'Yes, I'll wait for you down in the hall.'

After he'd left, Becky frowned at her. 'Are you sure you want to do this? I mean . . . it ain't goin' to be very nice, especially if it is Mrs Ruffin.'

Amber shrugged. 'It's the least I can do for her, she was always very kind to me.' But deep down she was hoping that it wouldn't be Mrs Ruffin.

As promised, she was downstairs waiting for Mr Greenwood at the agreed time, very conscious of the fact that she didn't have a black gown to wear – her grey one would just have to do.

'May I ask where she is?' she asked when he had followed her into the carriage and they were on their way into town.

'She's in the morgue at the undertaker's.' Barnaby shook his head as if he couldn't take it in. 'I know she adored Louisa but surely her death wouldn't make Mrs Ruffin take her own life?'

'Perhaps she didn't take her own life,' Amber pointed out. 'Perhaps she was so upset that she slipped into the water.'

He nodded. 'It is possible, I suppose. But we'll never know, will we? Unless foul play is suspected of course.'

They travelled the rest of the way in silence and once they reached the market square where J. Hackett, the undertaker's, was situated, Amber climbed down from the carriage telling him, 'Stay there if you want. I'll be fine on my own.'

In honesty her heart was pounding and she was beginning to regret making the offer, but Amber was one for keeping her word so she strode purposefully to the door of the funeral parlour and entered. Heavy purple velvet curtains hung at the window and the heady scent of lilies met her as the bell tinkled. Mr Hackett appeared in a starched white

333

shirt, a black cravat and a black suit with tails on the jacket. He was a tiny little man with sparse white hair and a pair of gold pince-nez glasses perched on the end of his nose.

He smiled at her. 'And how may I help you, my dear? Have you suffered a bereavement?'

'Not personally, Mr Hackett,' Amber told him quickly. 'But my employer, Mr Greenwood from Greenacres, has asked me to come an' identify the body of a woman you have here. We fear it might be the nurse of his late wife.'

'Ah yes, of course. Well, she's outside in the morgue. Would you follow me please?'

Amber gulped before following him through the door at the back of the parlour and yet another door that led out into a yard.

'That door there leads to the chapel of rest.' He pointed to the first door and moved on. 'And this is the morgue. But are you sure you are up to this, my dear? You're not going to faint on me, are you? You wouldn't be the first.'

'I shall be quite all right, thank you,' Amber told him with her head held high and so, after extracting a key from his pocket, he unlocked the door and ushered her into a large gloomy, windowless room.

'I'll just light the lamp,' he told her as he hurried over to an oil lamp that was standing next to a long trolley on which lay a body covered in a crisp white sheet. Amber supressed a shudder.

'So are you ready?'

She gulped again and nodded, praying once more that this would not be Mrs Ruffin, and very gently he peeled the sheet back from the corpse's face.

Amber's breath caught in her throat as she stared down at the serene face of Mrs Ruffin. She looked so peaceful that Amber could almost imagine she was simply asleep and would wake up at any moment, although of course she knew this wasn't so.

'Y-yes, that's Mrs Ruffin,' she said in a choked voice as a tear slid down her cheek.

Nodding gravely, Mr Hackett quickly pulled the sheet up again. 'Then could you ask Mr Greenwood what he wishes me to do with the body? Would you happen to know if Mrs Ruffin had any next of kin that I could inform?'

'I'm afraid I don't know,' Amber admitted as she turned and stumbled towards the door. 'But I'll go an' ask him now.'

Once she was outside one look at Amber's face told Barnaby all that he needed to know and he sighed as he swiped the hair from his forehead.

'Mr Hackett wants to know what you want him to do wi' her body,' she told him and after standing and thinking about it for a few moments he nodded and strode into the parlour, leaving Amber to clamber back into the carriage.

'I'm going to ask Louisa's parents if she might be buried as close to Louisa as possible in Pickering,' he told her when he came back out. 'I think it's what both Louisa and herself would have wanted. She was more like a mother to her than a nanny and a maid. But I shall have to speak to them first before I can give Mr Hackett the decision.'

Amber thought that would be the right thing to do, although she didn't feel that it was her place to comment and so the journey back to Greenacres was made in silence.

'Er . . . thank you for doing that for me,' he said awkwardly when they entered the house again and with a stiff nod Amber hurried back to the nursery.

Later that afternoon, Mr Hackett delivered the young mistress's coffin and she was transferred from her bedroom down to the drawing room where friends could come and say their last goodbyes to her before she started her final journey to Pickering the next day.

'The Hamilton-Tates have agreed to take Tumble, Louisa's dog, to end his days wi' them, an' they've also agreed that Ruffy can be buried close by to the mistress in the churchyard where they 'ave their family plot,' Nancy informed them when she popped up to the nursery after finishing her jobs that day. 'They weren't too keen on the idea from what we can all gather but the master put 'is foot down apparently an' told 'em it would 'ave been what the mistress wanted. Mr Hackett is takin' 'er to Pickerin'. It's funny, though . . . the way Ruffy died, I mean. What would she 'ave been doin' down at the 'arbour in the middle o' the night, eh?'

'We'll never know,' Amber said stoically and the subject was dropped, although speculation on what had happened would provide a source of gossip in the town for many months to come.

The following morning the Hamilton-Tates and Barnaby set off, with Louisa's body following in a hearse close behind them, but not before Barnaby had been to see Charlotte to say his goodbyes.

'Daddy will be back very soon,' he promised as he cuddled her to him and once again Amber almost felt sorry for him, although she was careful not to show it.

'So 'ow long do you think he'll be gone?' Becky said as they watched the sad procession wend its way down the drive.

'I've no idea.' Amber shrugged. She certainly wouldn't miss him but she had no doubt that Charlotte would. She was blossoming again since they had come home.

Four days later, Mrs Boswell received a letter saying that Louisa's funeral would be taking place the following morning and to expect the master back by nightfall.

'So I wonder what'll 'appen 'ere now?' Becky mused worriedly.

'I should imagine that things will go on much as they did before,' Amber said.

'Hm, well let's just 'ope you're reet! I can't afford to lose this job, not when they're so 'ard to come by.'

'I shouldn't think there's much chance o' that happening,' Amber comforted her. If only she could have known how wrong she could be.

Chapter Thirty-Five

'The master's back,' Nancy told them the following evening when she brought their supper up to them.

'He'll be out of luck if he's hopin' to see Charlotte,' Amber commented as she finished putting the infant's clean clothes away. 'She's been fast asleep for the past hour now.'

'I doubt that'll stop 'im comin',' Nancy answered.

She was proved right when shortly after the nursery door opened and Barnaby appeared. Becky had retired to bed by that time and as always, Amber felt uncomfortable being alone with him.

'So, er . . . did the funeral go all right?' She felt as if she should say something as he crept over to the crib to peep at his daughter.

'As well as these affairs can go,' he answered shortly. 'Has she been all right?'

'Charlotte? Yes o' course she has.' She didn't bother to tell him that the child's eyes had strayed hopefully towards the door every time it had been opened, only for her to be disappointed when she saw that it wasn't him.

'Very well. I'll wish you goodnight and I'll be back to see her first thing in the morning before Louisa's solicitor arrives.'

Amber continued with what she was doing and breathed a sigh of relief when the door closed behind him.

Charlotte gurgled with delight when she laid eyes on him the next day and again Amber felt envious of their closeness. The child was crawling everywhere now and even trying to pull herself up on the furniture and Amber had an idea that it wouldn't be long before she took her first steps.

'So why don't you like the master?' Becky asked when Barnaby had gone to keep his appointment. 'You're always as jumpy as a kitten when 'e's about an' you never say a word to 'im unless you 'ave to.'

Amber shrugged. 'I'm not paid to talk to him, I'm paid to look after Charlotte,' she retorted shortly.

Realising she'd clearly said something to upset her Becky wisely let the subject drop.

Downstairs, the solicitor was arriving and after showing him into the master's study Nancy went to fetch Barnaby.

'Good morning, Mr Dickenson,' Barnaby greeted him when he entered the room. 'May I get you anything? Tea, coffee?'

'No, no thank you.' The portly gentleman with the handlebar moustache removed his hat and ran his finger around the inside of his shirt collar as if it was suddenly too tight for him. He wasn't looking forward to what he had to do one little bit and the sooner it was done and he could get away the better it would be as far as he was concerned.

Slowly he withdrew Louisa's will and said tentatively, 'Before we begin may I offer my condolences for your loss.'

He shook his head. 'It's so sad to see one so very young pass away. And also, may I add that I believe there will be things in here you will not be happy about. Louisa and her father made considerable changes to her will on the day she summoned me here and unfortunately, as she was my client, I had no choice but to do as she instructed.'

'What are you talking about, man? Just get on with it,' Barnaby said irritably, and so the solicitor did as he was asked.

When he had finished, he glanced up to see Barnaby staring at him, his face chalk white, as if he couldn't believe what he had heard.

'B-but there must be some mistake? My father-in-law invested in *my* business in exchange for a majority share. As for the house, he gave that to his daughter – *my wife* – so surely it now belongs to me?'

'That isn't *quite* correct,' Mr Dickenson answered. 'He actually gifted his *daughter* the money for a majority share in the business as a dowry, so technically most of the business has always belonged to her. But what he failed to tell you was that he encouraged her to add a clause to her will which stated that should both you and your father-in-law outlive your wife, both the house and her dowry share in the business would revert to him.'

Barnaby bounced out of his chair and began to pace up and down the room like a caged animal. 'So tell me in layman's terms what this means exactly and what I can do about it!'

'Well, you will be allowed to keep any of the money you made prior to your marriage, and your share of the profits

340

that have been made since then, and of course the two ships that were already yours before you met your wife. He has also agreed to you keeping the smallest of the warehouses on the harbour that I believe you purchased with the money he gave you, but as of today this house and most of the business now belong to Louisa's father. As regards what you can do about it . . .' He shook his head. 'We *could* try contesting the will but I doubt there is a court in the land who would go against your wife's wishes. She was ill, admittedly, but she was of sound mind and so I fear there is very little you can do but accept the situation.'

'So where am I supposed to go?' Barnaby felt as if he was wading through sludge as the full implications of what the solicitor was telling him struck home.

'As I said, you do still have money so I would suggest that you could afford to buy another, humbler property for you and your young daughter to live in. It wouldn't be as salubrious as Greenacres, of course, but at least you won't have to be homeless. And Mr Hamilton-Tate has given you four weeks to vacate the premises. The contents of the house will then be auctioned and I have been instructed to put the house up for sale.'

'He never said a word about this while I was in Pickering,' Barnaby said bitterly. 'And what about the shipyard? It will fold without someone to keep an eye on things and run it.'

Again the solicitor avoided his eye as he shuffled his papers about. 'Your father-in-law has instructed a manager to move in and take control of the business on his behalf forthwith. And he will be changing the name, but he did work out how much you are owed during his stay here.'

Now Barnaby understood why Robert Hamilton-Tate had taken such a great interest in the ledgers while he had been there.

'This is what he has agreed to you keeping.' Mr Dickenson handed Barnaby a sheet of paper with a sizeable amount written down on it, although he knew that once he had purchased a home suitable for his daughter to live in it would eat in to it considerably. 'And are there any provisions made for Charlotte?'

When the solicitor shook his head, Barnaby felt a pang of guilt. Could it be that his in-laws had suspected that the child had no blood ties to them or did they simply not want anything to do with her? Whatever the reason he would be solely responsible for her from now on.

'And what about the staff here?' he asked, his mind reeling.

Mr Dickenson shrugged. 'I suggest you call a staff meeting and inform them that they would be well advised to search for other posts. Like yourself they will need to vacate the premises within one month. Mr Hamilton-Tate has assured me that he will pay their wages until then. I'm so sorry, Mr Greenwood,' he said as he hastily stood up. He had done as instructed and he had never felt so wretched in his career. 'It only remains for me to wish you good luck for the future. If you should decide that you wish to contest the will, I will of course help all I can, but—'

'I won't be doing that,' Barnaby interrupted him. There was no way he would give his father-in-law the chance to humiliate him more than he already had done.

'In that case, good day, Mr Greenwood.'

The two men shook hands and once he was alone Barnaby sank onto the nearest chair and dropped his head into his hands. He was right back where he had started, a little better off admittedly, but now he had a daughter who was dependant on him and he would have to begin all over again.

It was some time before he managed to pull himself together enough to leave his office and when he did he immediately went in search of Mrs Boswell to ask her if she could arrange for the staff to gather in the hallway that evening at six o'clock.

And so at six o'clock sharp, everyone from the laundry maid to the gardeners were gathered together, all looking slightly apprehensive as they sensed they were about to hear something they were not going to like. The only person absent was Amber, who had sent Becky to hear what was going on as Charlotte could not be left alone.

After looking around at their solemn faces, Barnaby took a deep breath and told them in as few words as he could what had transpired, and before he had finished many of the female members of staff were weeping.

'But what'll we do, where will we go?' some of them wailed and Barnaby felt wretched, but what choice did he have?

'I am so sorry,' he told them with a break in his voice. 'And rest assured that you will all find a small bonus in your wages.' Then he turned about and went and closeted himself in his study where he poured himself a stiff whisky. He had never been more in need of one.

Becky, meanwhile, had returned to the nursery looking stricken and the moment she entered the room, Amber asked, 'Whatever's the matter, lass? You're as white as a ghost.'

Once Becky had told her, she too looked worried. What would Barnaby do now and would this mean that she could no longer care for her daughter? She couldn't bear the thought of being separated from her and for the first time she watched the nursery door impatiently waiting for him to appear.

It was almost two hours later before he came, by which time Charlotte was fast asleep. Becky had cried non-stop ever since hearing the devastating news and Amber had sent her off to her room for an early night.

'So what's going to happen now?' Amber said the second he set foot in the room. 'To Charlotte, I mean?'

He crossed to a chair and sank heavily into it. 'I've been trying to think of that,' he said wearily. 'And I do have a proposition to put to you but you may not be agreeable to it.'

'Oh?' Amber raised her eyebrow.

'I shall be buying another property,' he told her. 'It will be nothing as grand as this one, of course. I shall start to look around for somewhere suitable immediately. And I thought . . . Well, I hoped that you might come to live there with us so that you could continue to care for Charlotte because I will have to work. The only trouble is you will be laying yourself wide open to yet more gossip. It's bad enough as it is but imagine what people will say if they know you are living unchaperoned with me.'

'People can say what they like about me,' Amber said heatedly. 'Just so long as I can be with my girl.'

Barnaby nodded before going on, 'The other thing is I won't be able to take on any staff. Not until I get another business properly up and running that is. So it would mean—'

'It would mean I'd have to be head cook an' bottle washer into the bargain,' she finished for him. 'But that's all reet. I ain't afraid o' hard work.'

'Even so, I'd like you to think about it before you make a final decision,' he encouraged, before leaving the room, closing the door softly behind him.

Early the next morning Barnaby set off on his house-hunt but everything he looked at was either too expensive or so rundown that it was almost derelict.

'Did you find anywhere suitable?' Amber asked when he visited the nursery that evening and he shook his head.

'No luck at all, I'm afraid. But never fear, it's early days,' he told her with far more optimism than he was feeling. It had been hard to accept that he was no longer the owner of Greenacres and the shipyard and when he thought of how tirelessly he had worked to build the business up he felt angry and heartbroken, but there was nothing he could do about it and so he was just going to have to get on with things. 'Did you give some thought to what I said?' he asked and Amber nodded without hesitation.

'Yes an' the answer is still the same. Me name is mud down in the town so we may as well give 'em somethin' else to talk about. I don't much care what they say so long as I can be with Charlotte.'

With a brisk nod, he left the room. Amber knew she was doing the right thing, but it didn't mean she wasn't nervous about living in a small house with a man she didn't like. Still, if she wanted to be with her daughter, what other choice did she have? She'd tried supporting her on her own and it had been a disaster, so she would just have to make the best of it. And if she was completely honest with herself, the fact that Barnaby hadn't blamed her, nor tried to call the police on her when she'd taken Charlotte, showed that perhaps he really was sorry for the way he had treated her. And if that was the case, she supposed she should try to put her resentment aside and at least be friendly towards him – for Charlotte's sake. But then she shook her head. No. No doubt he'd had his own selfish reasons for not reporting her, so even though she couldn't help feeling a little sorry for him after everything that had happened, she still didn't trust him. And she wasn't sure if she ever would.

The atmosphere was grim over the following week as some of the staff began to drift away. The cook was the first to go when she left to live with her daughter in Goathland, a pretty village out on the moors.

'I were thinkin' o' retirin' soon anyway,' she told the master, which eased his conscience a little as far as she was concerned, at least. Next, Nancy informed Amber that she'd been taken on as a barmaid at an inn in the town.

'It'll be totally different to what I've been doin' 'ere,' she told Amber sadly. 'But at least I'll be bringin' a bit o' money in an' I can live back at 'ome wi' me mam again. But what are you goin' to do?'

Amber took a deep breath. 'I'm goin' to live wi' Mr Greenwood when he finds a suitable house so I can carry on lookin' after Charlotte.'

Nancy's eyes stretched wide as she whistled through her teeth. 'Crikey, lass, are you sure that's a good idea? I mean, there's enough gossip flyin' around about you two as it is. If you move in wi' 'im you'll be branded a scarlet woman.'

Amber shrugged. 'So be it! I don't care so long as I get to be wi' me baby.' She cuddled Charlotte to her and they sat silent for a time wondering what the future had in store for them all.

Chapter Thirty-Six

A week later on a beautiful day in May, Barnaby went to the nursery to tell Amber, 'I think I've found a house that may be suitable for us but I'd like you to come and see it before I make a final decision. You may know the property in question. It's an old sea captain's house on the headland about half a mile from Whitby Abbey.'

'I know the one you mean, but ain't that been empty for a long time?'

He nodded. 'Yes it has, and it'll need a lot of work to bring it back to how it should be. But I think it would be worth it. What do you think?'

'It's worth a look,' she agreed.

So early the next morning after collecting the keys from the estate agent in town, they set off with Charlotte in the carriage to view it.

As they drew near, Amber noted that some of the tiles were missing from the roof and what should have been the front garden was so overgrown that it looked like a jungle. The front of the house was surrounded by a picket fence in desperate need of painting and the gate was hanging off its hinges.

'I know it looks a little daunting,' Barnaby told her. 'But I can afford to get men in to repair the roof and do some of the work and it is a sizable property. It stands in half an acre of garden which would be enough for us to have our own small vegetable plot and perhaps keep a few chickens. I believe there's an orchard as well, so we wouldn't be short of fruit and veg.'

When the carriage drew to a halt Barnaby alighted and reached in to take Charlotte as Amber clambered down after him.

As they battled through the overgrown weeds to the front door, Amber noticed that a lot of the glass in the little leaded windows had been broken, probably by children or vandals. Even so, as he had said, it was a large building and the views of the sea on one side and the moors stretching away into the distance on the other were breathtaking.

Barnaby had to give the front door a good shove to get it to open and it creaked alarmingly as he pushed it wider for them to enter. They stepped into a good-sized hallway with black-and-white tiles on the floor and panelled walls. A staircase with beautifully carved bannisters led up from one side of it and Amber could hardly wait to explore the upstairs, but first she would concentrate on the ground floor.

The first door leading off the hallway led into the kitchen, which, although furnished, was under such thick layers of dust that it was impossible to see if any of it would be salvageable. A large range cooker stood against one wall and next to that was an inglenook fireplace with a bread oven set into the wall on one side of it. There was a deep stone sink with a pump attached, which told them there must be a well somewhere, and a long wooden draining board. Cobwebs hung like festoons of delicate lace from the rafters and the moths had been feasting on the curtains. But as Amber looked about, she didn't see the work that needed doing. In her mind's eye she could see it as it could be and she smiled before tripping away to examine the rooms that led off it while Barnaby looked after Charlotte.

Across the hallway another door led into a sizable parlour with a deep fireplace and she could picture it at Christmas with a tree to the side of it and a lovely log fire roaring up the chimney. This room, too, was furnished but again it was impossible to see what sort of state the furniture was in. Back in the kitchen, the next door she opened led into what she supposed was the laundry room-cum-dairy. There was a big copper for heating water in one corner next to another large stone sink. There was also a mangle and a dolly tub and a big tin bath hanging on the wall, so she guessed that this must also have been where the previous tenants had bathed. A door to the far side of it led out into the back garden, which was very sizable indeed. This too was overgrown but she knew it could be lovely with some hard work. An outside toilet was attached to the house and across the yard was a large wooden outbuilding, which, she judged could easily house a horse and carriage should Barnaby wish to keep one. They also located the well and after hoisting a bucket of water up from it they were delighted to see that it was crystal clear.

Back inside she climbed the sturdy wooden staircase to find herself on a landing with three good-sized bedrooms leading off it, the largest of which overlooked the sea. Again, each room was fully furnished but it remained to be seen if any of it was useable.

'So what do you think?' Barnaby asked tentatively when she joined him in the kitchen, and for the first time since he had sent her packing after discovering that Charlotte was on the way, she gave him a beaming smile, quite forgetting for the moment that she was supposed to detest him.

'I think with some tender loving care this could make a beautiful home for Charlotte,' she said with hesitation. 'But why has it been left empty for so long?'

'Apparently the sea captain that owned it left it to his nephew when he died. He wanted to come and live in it but his wife didn't, so in the end he gave up trying to persuade her and decided he might as well sell it. The house is called "The Crow's Nest" by the way. I think it's been empty for at least four or five years now and it smells very damp and musty, doesn't it?'

'It just needs a good airin' and a good clean, but you would have to get the windows and the roof repaired before anything else,' she told him sensibly. 'And it's not too far from Whitby either, I could walk there to do the shopping.'

A ray of sunshine was doing its best to pierce through the grimy windows and as it shone on her hair it reminded him of spun gold. Charlotte's was exactly the same colour and in that moment he realised just how much she looked like her mother.

'Another urgent job would be to get the fencing all around the garden repaired,' he said thoughtfully as he stared back at his little daughter. 'One side of the garden is quite close to the cliffs and we don't want any accidents with this little madam here. She'll be walking before we know it, the way she's going on. So, does the house meet with your approval?'

Again, she smiled and her eyes shone as she looked about the room, imagining how it would look when it was all clean and shining with pretty curtains hanging at the windows and rugs on the tiled floor. 'Yes, it does,' she said softly. The only down side to living there would be the fact that she would have to share it with him.

After a quick tour of the garden, they set off back to the town where Barnaby paid a deposit on their new home.

'It's a very straightforward sale,' the elderly solicitor who was handling the house informed him. 'I can have the deeds signed over to you within a couple of days if you'd care to return with the balance.'

And so it was agreed and as they returned to Greenacres, Amber hoped that she had made the right decision.

Nancy and Becky listened to her avidly as she told them all about it that evening.

'I just 'ope you're doin' the right thing,' Nancy whispered when Becky went down to the kitchen to fetch their dinner tray up. Mrs Boswell had temporarily taken over the cooking duties since the cook had left and it was beginning to look like she didn't know how to cook anything but porridge and stew.

'I don't really have much choice if I want to be wi' me baby, do I?'

'No, I suppose you don't,' Nancy agreed glumly. 'But be prepared, the townsfolk are goin' to call you to hell an' back when word gets out.'

Two days later, Barnaby got the keys to the house and by the end of the week he had men in repairing the windows and the roof. Others were sent to scythe down the worst of the weeds in the gardens. Finally, he sent in a sweep to sweep all the chimneys and at last it was time for Amber to put her stamp on it. Becky was left to care for Charlotte while the groom took Nancy, Amber and all the cleaning materials they might need to make a start on the inside.

'Blimey, this is some place, ain't it?' Nancy said wonderingly as Amber showed her around. 'An' it's so big!'

'I know,' Amber said happily. 'But now we'd better make a start. Goodness knows how long it's goin' to take to make the place liveable.'

Crossing to the window she tore down the curtains making dust fly into the room, then she flung all the doors open to get some air in. Meanwhile Nancy lit the fire so they could boil some water and looked about, wondering where they should start. They were certainly going to be busy, that was for sure!

'Let's wash all the furniture down and see what's worth salvagin' first, shall we?' Amber suggested. 'An' what ain't any good we can drag outside an' have a bonfire.'

Two hours later they stopped to make a cup of tea as they sat staring at what they'd uncovered. There was a solid oak dresser that Amber thought would look lovely with plates and china on, and the large table that took up the centre of the room was fine and sturdy, although the seats of the chairs would need re-covering as the moths had feasted on them. There were two leather wing chairs either side of the fireplace and after washing the many layers of dust off them they, too, were found to be in remarkably good condition.

'Ooh, I can just picture you sittin' 'ere in front o' the inglenook on a cold winter night,' Nancy said enviously and Amber snorted.

'Don't go gettin' carried away,' she said wryly. 'Just remember I'm only goin' to be here for Charlotte. I can't ever see me an' the master sittin' enjoyin' each other's company. I wouldn't spit on him if he were on fire.'

Nancy glanced at her with a curious expression on her face before suggesting tentatively, 'Don't you reckon you're bein' a bit 'ard on 'im? What I mean is, I know what he did to you was despicable but I think he's tried to make amends one way or another an' he has got a lot on 'is plate at the minute, what wi' losin' little David an' 'is missus, then losin' the house an' 'is business an' all! Most men would 'ave turned tail an' run after what he's 'ad to put up wi' lately but he won't do that cos he thinks too much o' little Charlotte.'

Amber tossed her head as she threw an old cushion out for the bonfire. 'Aye, he does love her, admittedly,' she said begrudgingly. 'But I still can't forgive him for lyin' to me, an' abandonin' me when I needed 'im most. He might be sorry for it now, and he might love Charlotte, but I'll *never* forgive him, an' I can't trust him!' Though, deep in her heart, she wondered whether this was still completely true.

'In that case, I can't see there bein' much 'appiness in this 'ouse,' Nancy said quietly and she returned to what she had been doing while Amber stared at her thoughtfully. As much as she hated to admit it, she supposed Nancy was right about certain things. Back at the house it was easy to avoid Barnaby apart from when he visited the nursery, but here they would be living in very close proximity to each other so she supposed she ought to at least try to be civil to him, for Charlotte's sake if nothing else.

The carriage arrived at six o'clock that evening to take them back to the house and as Jimmy, the young groom, helped Nancy into the carriage, Amber noticed the way their eyes locked and how he held her hand for just a little longer than was necessary.

'Would I be right in thinkin' that you an' Jimmy are becomin' a little bit more than friends?' Amber teased as, exhausted from a hard day's work, they settled back against the leather squabs.

Nancy blushed prettily. 'He's asked me if I'd like to walk out wi' 'im on me days off,' Nancy admitted. 'An' I've said yes.'

'But what will happen if he has to move away when his job at Greenacres finishes?'

Nancy smiled. 'That's all sorted. Mr Greenwood is givin' 'im a job in his warehouse.'

'Then I hope everythin' goes well for you,' Amber said sincerely. Nancy had been a true friend and had stood by her through the most difficult of times so it would be nice if she could find a little happiness; she deserved it.

They met Barnaby just coming out of the nursery when they arrived back at Greenacres and the hint of a smile twitched at the corner of his lips as he noted the state of them. Amber had a dirty smear across her nose and their clothes were filthy.

'How did it go?' he asked and still unable to look him in the eye Amber paused and nodded as Nancy went ahead of her.

'We've got the kitchen and the parlour clean an' we've been able to save almost all o' the furniture, although all the curtains an' soft furnishin's were beyond repair. We're goin' to tackle the hallway an' the stairs tomorrer an' make a start on the bedrooms, though I'm guessin' we'll need all new bed linen. We'll need new curtains for each room an' all.'

'Could some of the ones we have here be cut down to size?' he asked.

Amber nodded. 'Yes, they could an' they'd look lovely in the house. Me an' Nancy could alter 'em.'

'Then take whatever you like. The same goes for bed linen or whatever else you might need. I dare say if the house is to be sold my in-laws won't miss them.'

There was a note of bitterness in his voice and again Amber almost felt sorry for him. As Nancy had pointed out, after what had happened to him, most men would have turned tail and run as far away as they could get but he was still here, trying to do right by as many people as he could.

He smiled again as he nodded down at her old soiled skirt. 'I won't keep you any longer. I've no doubt you'll be longing to get washed and changed and have something to eat. I'll see that Mrs Boswell sends you both something up, although I believe it's stew again. She's an excellent housekeeper but I'm afraid her abilities as a cook are rather limited. Oh, and er . . . thanks for what you're doing, Amber.'

It was on the tip of her tongue to tell him abruptly that she wasn't doing it for him, she was doing it for Charlotte, but she bit back the words and merely nodded.

Later that evening, when Charlotte was sleeping, Amber left her in Becky's care, and she and Nancy wandered about the house collecting curtains, bed linen, cushions and anything else they thought would help to make the house comfortable.

356

They had quite a pile of things by the time they had finished and Nancy giggled as she fingered a pair of soft, deep-crimson velvet curtains. 'These'll look grand in the parlour,' she said. 'It's goin' to be quite a place by the time we've finished. An' some o' that furniture an' the framed maps o' the world we found there are superb. They'll look grand on the walls once we've given 'em a good polish. There is just one thing that occurred to me though . . . somethin' you may not 'ave thought about. What'll 'appen if you meet someone an' want to get wed? I mean, I can't ever see the master lettin' little Charlotte go.'

'Huh! There's no chance o' that happenin', not in a million years,' Amber snorted. 'After what he did to me, I wouldn't ever trust a bloke again as far as I could throw him!'

'All right then . . . what if it's the master who meets some-one? Where will that leave you?'

Amber frowned; that was something she hadn't thought of either. He was undeniably a good-looking man after all, and still relatively well-off, so no doubt there'd be a number of women setting their caps at him now that he was widowed.

'I suppose that's somethin' I'd have to face if an' when I came to it,' she admitted as she stifled a yawn. 'But now I don't know about you but I ache in every bone in me body an' we've only tickled the surface o' what needs doin' at the house as yet, so I suggest we both go an' try an' get a good night's sleep, eh?'

Nancy nodded in agreement and after wishing her good-night, she trotted off to her room leaving Amber to check on Charlotte before she too tumbled into her bed, exhausted. It had been a long hard day and there were many more of them ahead before they'd manage to put the house to rights.

Chapter Thirty-Seven

By the end of the first week the downstairs of the old sea captain's house and everything in it was gleaming like a new pin. Men were now busily working outside erecting a sturdy fence around the garden to keep Charlotte safely away from the cliff edge and Amber was delighted when one of them informed her that there was actually a path at the end of the garden that led down to their own little private beach – she could just imagine how much Charlotte would love playing on the sand and paddling in the blue sea.

Each night she and Nancy had sat altering the curtains from the enormous windows at Greenacres to fit the windows in the new house, and the material they cut off had been used to stitch pretty cushions for the chairs and the wooden settle. Now every downstairs room looked cosy. Throughout the house they had found framed maps, pictures and ornaments from every part of the globe, no doubt fetched back by the captain and they had all been lovingly cleaned and placed about the house. The furniture they had salvaged had been polished until they could see their faces in it and they had begun to bring pots and pans from Greenacres for the kitchen. The large gardens had been scythed and although they would still need a lot of work, they would be manageable now and somewhere safe for Charlotte to play in.

'I almost envy you movin' in 'ere,' Nancy said dreamily as they waited for Jimmy to come and fetch them early one evening in late May, just days before Amber and Barnaby were due to move in.

Back at Greenacres the majority of the staff had left and it felt strangely empty.

'I would be lookin' forward to livin' here too,' Amber admitted as she brushed a stray curl from her damp forehead, leaving a smear of dirt over her face. 'If it weren't for . . . you know?'

'Aye, I know, lass. But that's a small price to pay for bein' able to bring up your daughter an' I've no doubt you'll rub along all right. Though I should warn you, when I went to see me mam on Sunday she said the gossip 'as already started in the town. I'm afraid once yer do move in yer name is goin' to be muck.'

Amber shrugged. 'There's nowt I can do about that, is there?'

They heard the sound of the carriage then so after putting away their cleaning things they hurried out, glad of the chance for a rest.

When they arrived back at The Crow's Nest early the next morning, the first sign they had that anything was amiss was the sight of the front door swinging open in the early sea breeze.

'Are you sure you shut the front door last night, Nancy?' Amber asked anxiously.

'Quite sure. I'd not be so daft as to leave it open,' Nancy responded indignantly.

Jimmy had spotted it too. 'You two had best wait 'ere while I go an' check there's no one inside,' he said, hopping down from the carriage and tethering the horse to the picket fence.

As Amber and Nancy climbed down, he disappeared inside only to return a few minutes later with a grave face.

'Someone's been in, all reet!' he told them angrily. 'An' you're not gonna like what they've done, the rotten buggers!'

With her heart in her mouth Amber followed him back up the path and when she entered the kitchen her hand flew to her mouth. The lovely curtains they had sat and sewn so painstakingly had been yanked from the poles and the china Amber had selected so carefully for the dresser was smashed and strewn about the floor. But it was the wall against the fireplace that stabbed at her heart the most, for across it someone had written, *Whore!* in big, bold letters.

'Eeh, who'd do such a thing? An' after all our 'ard work!' Nancy wailed.

Amber blinked back the tears that were burning behind her eyes and climbed the stairs to find the same chaos up there. The bedding had been ripped from the beds and trampled with dirty boots before being strewn about and some of the old sea captain's beautiful maps had been callously smashed.

'Whoever did this should be bloody *'orsewhipped*!' Nancy cried indignantly. 'The lousy swines!'

Jimmy, who had been having a good look around downstairs, joined them then, and hoping to ease the situation he said, 'Look, things ain't quite as bad as they look. For a start off whoever wrote that on the wall in the kitchen wrote it in soot an' ashes from the fire so it should wash off fairly easily. An' the curtains ain't damaged, I just 'ad a good look at 'em. I'm gonna get one o' the men workin' on the fence to come in an' put the poles back up for you an' they'll be good as new.'

True to his word, he left them and soon returned with one of the men, who immediately began to rehang the curtain poles that had been wrenched from the walls.

'Look, I 'ave to go,' Jimmy told them reluctantly. 'The master'll be waitin' down at the warehouse for me. He's busy gettin' it ready for 'is new venture an' I'm givin' him a hand. But should you 'ave any trouble durin' the day just shout from the door an' one o' the men outside will come runnin'.'

The two young women nodded and when he had left, they began to collect all the dirty bedding together. As Jimmy had pointed out, it was dirty but thankfully a good wash would put everything to rights, although they could well have done without all the extra work.

Just over an hour later, as Amber was sweeping up all the broken glass from the smashed picture frames and Nancy was washing off the awful word scribbled on the wall, Barnaby appeared in the doorway, his face a mask of rage as he looked at the wanton destruction the intruder had caused.

'Do either of you have any idea who might have done this?'

The two girls shook their heads and he proceeded to stride from room to room. 'I think it would be wise if we had one of the men stay here each night until we move in, just in case whoever did this decides to come back,' he said. 'And I'm so sorry for all the extra work it has caused you both.'

''T'ain't your fault,' Nancy answered matter-of-factly. 'But I'd love to get me 'ands on the lousy bastards!'

Amber as yet hadn't even acknowledged his presence but he came over to her and gently took a framed map from her hands.

'Luckily the map and the frame aren't damaged,' he said quietly as he studied it. 'I'll get a new piece of glass cut for it.'

'An' what about all the lovely china?' Nancy motioned towards the broken crockery she had swept into a pile.

'Just take some more from the house,' he instructed, his mouth set in a grim line. 'There's so much there no one will even notice it's gone.'

He stared at Amber for a moment but when she still didn't even look at him, he left.

Nancy watched him jump into his saddle and said sadly, 'I can't 'elp but feel a bit sorry for 'im! I mean, he's 'ad a lot o' trouble lately, ain't he?'

'I dare say he has, but he's still a lot better off than most people in the town,' Amber said bitterly. 'He's still got this house, two ships an' a warehouse.'

'That's true,' Nancy admitted. 'But it ain't a fraction o' what he 'ad, is it? I 'eard 'em say down in the kitchen last night that 'e's goin' to use one o' the ships for transportin' goods abroad an' the other for fishin'. That's what him an' Jimmy are gettin' the warehouse ready for.'

Amber shrugged. 'I dare say he'll make a go of it,' she said ruthlessly. 'After all, he didn't have much when he met the mistress, by all accounts, but he worked to build the shipyard up thinkin' it was his!'

'Well, I reckon it were a dirty trick of 'is father-in-law's,' Nancy responded. 'All them years the master worked on what were never goin' to be 'is business if the mistress passed afore 'im an' he never even knew it.'

Amber shrugged again as she looked around to see what needed doing next. She still found it very difficult to muster up any sympathy for Barnaby. 'What's done is done an' now we've all just got to try an' make the best of it,' she said stoically and side by side they carried on working.

The following morning, just as they were about to set off to the house, a letter arrived at Greenacres from her mother, so Amber pushed it into her pocket to read on the way.

'She says my uncle and Mrs Carter are gettin' wed the second week o' June,' she told Nancy as the coach rocked along the rutted lanes. 'But I don't see as I can go now. We'll have moved into the house by then an' I can hardly leave Mr Greenwood to take care o' Charlotte, can I?'

'So take her wi' you!' Nancy suggested. 'I dare say your family would love to see 'er an' a break after all the 'ard work you've done would do you the power o' good.'

'Hm, I'm not so sure the master would agree to it.' Amber chewed on her lip. 'Not after I took off wi' her before.'

'Well, you won't know if you don't ask him, will you?'

'I suppose I could but I'll have to choose me moment carefully,' Amber said thoughtfully.

They arrived at the house to find old Trampy Ned hovering by the back door and after Amber had given him some of the sandwiches she had brought for her and Nancy's lunch he tipped his hat to her and set off again as the two girls set to work.

The following week, Barnaby said a sad goodbye to the staff from Greenacres and sent them off with their wages and a bonus in their pockets – only Mrs Boswell would remain, a little like the captain of a sinking ship, until the auctioneers arrived to begin an inventory of the contents of the house. When they were done she would hand over the keys to the solicitor before beginning her journey to Nuneaton, a small market town in the Midlands where she was to stay with her daughter for a time before she looked for another post.

Then at last, he, Amber and Charlotte were ready to move in to their new home. As they stepped inside, Charlotte on Barnaby's hip, he smiled. 'Thank you for all the hard work you've put into this place, you've done a marvellous job,' he said appreciatively.

'I did it for Charlotte,' Amber said shortly, hurrying to the sink to fill the kettle and ignoring Barnaby's resigned sigh.

After he'd left to go the warehouse Amber unpacked their clothes in the bedrooms – Barnaby had decided that Amber and Charlotte should have the largest bedroom at the front of the house overlooking the sea, as there was plenty of room for Charlotte's cot in there, and Barnaby himself had chosen to sleep in the room at the back, which overlooked the rolling moors – then took Charlotte outside where she sat her on a blanket with her wooden bricks to play with, and made a start on digging the vegetable garden. Charlotte laughed and cooed as she tugged at the grass and tasted it and Amber couldn't help but smile to see the child looking so happy and content. After lunch the little girl went down for a nap so Amber set to making a meat and potato pie for their dinner. Thankfully Barnaby had ensured that the larder was full but she knew that soon she would have to venture into the village for shopping and she wasn't looking forward to it one little bit.

It was late afternoon when he returned and they were both ill at ease. 'Have you had a good day?' he asked as he lifted Charlotte to give her a kiss.

'Busy,' she answered without looking at him. 'And your dinner will be ready in about half an hour, but it's only a pie, mind. I'm not very good at fancy cooking.'

'I'm sure it will be delicious.' He eyed her quietly for a moment before saying tentatively, 'You know, if we're going to be living in the same house, we should at least make an effort to get along, for Charlotte's sake. Children can pick up on a bad atmosphere and I really want her to have a happy childhood.'

She paused before raising her eyes to his. She supposed he did have a point. 'All right, I'll try but don't expect me to ever like you.'

The meal was actually very tasty and Amber noticed how patient Barnaby was when he fed Charlotte. She was opening her mouth like a little bird for him and it was plain to see the bond between them.

'Perhaps I could help with the washing-up?' he suggested when the meal was over, but she shook her head.

'Thank you but I'll do it myself,' she said primly. And then deciding there was no time like the present she asked, 'Would it be possible for me to take Charlotte to Scarborough for a few days so I can attend me uncle's weddin'?'

She saw a brief flash of alarm in his eyes and he paused before saying, 'Yes, of course, if that's what you want. When is it?'

'In a couple o' weeks' time. I thought we could go on the coach from the market square.'

'There's no need for you to do that,' he said. 'I'd be happy to take you in the barouche.' He had chosen to keep his own stallion and the smallest of the carriages as well as the gentle nag that pulled it. Amber had told him that the barouche was rather a grand mode of transport to be taking to a sea captain's modest home but he had pointed out that it would be ideal for Amber to manage should she wish to shop in the village. Also, had he chosen to keep the larger carriage, he would have had to take at least one more horse to pull it and he didn't know if his father-in-law would stand for that. Amber had shrugged and said that she didn't mind walking and that she'd never driven a carriage in her life, but he'd assured her that he would teach her.

Now she stared at him thoughtfully. 'But ain't that a long way for you to go only to have to come all the way back again? We'll only be gone for a few days.'

'It'll be no trouble.' He smiled. 'Rather than come back I'll wait till you're ready to come home. I'm sure there'll be a hotel where I can stay and I can make it into a little holiday. To be honest, I feel rather in need of one at the minute after all that's happened.'

Amber shrugged. 'Fine, if that's what you want.' And for then the subject was dropped.

Once Charlotte was tucked up in bed Barnaby read the newspaper by the light of the oil lamp on the table while Amber stitched a dress for Charlotte. Eventually he rose from his seat and stretched and yawned.

'I'll go on up now, unless there's anything you need doing?'

She shook her head, keeping her eyes firmly fixed on what she was doing. 'No, nothin' . . . thanks.'

'Goodnight then.' She could feel his eyes burning into her as he stood over her.

'Goodnight.' Seconds later she heard his tread on the stairs and laying the dress aside, she sighed. Their first day of living together in the same house was over and it hadn't been so bad, so perhaps things wouldn't be as hard as she'd thought. She could only hope so because there could be no going back now.

Chapter Thirty-Eight

Over the next week, the little family started to get into a routine. Each morning before Barnaby left for work, he rode to the nearby farm to fetch them fresh milk, while Amber looked after Charlotte, kept the house clean and attempted to improve her cooking skills. She had been trying her hand at baking their bread and the first few attempts had bordered on disastrous. The first loaf was so firm she was sure one of them would break their teeth on it but Barnaby hadn't complained, in fact he'd made a joke of it. The second attempt had been slightly better but now she was quite proud of her efforts. The vegetable garden, with Barnaby's help, was now dug over and planted, but as it would be some weeks before it yielded any crops, she would have to rely on what she could buy in town. It was a task she was dreading but supplies were now running low and she knew she couldn't put it off any longer.

'I shall have to go food shoppin' today,' she informed him at breakfast.

He reached into his pocket and laid some money on the table asking, 'Will that be enough? I'm afraid Mrs Boswell saw to all the bills so I have no idea what you'll need. I shall have to make you a weekly allowance for that, and for anything you or Charlotte might need. Will you be taking the barouche?'

She shook her head. She'd had a couple of lessons that had gone quite well, but she didn't feel confident enough to take it out on her own as yet. 'Thanks, but no. It's a nice day so the walk will do us good. I thought I might take the little hand cart on wheels you found in the stables. I can drag that back wi' the shoppin' easier than carryin' it, an' Charlotte can sit in it an' all to save me havin' to carry her.'

'It'll be hard work dragging it up the hill,' he pointed out, but Amber sniffed.

'I ain't a weaklin', I'll be fine. An' as for the money, I won't need that much.'

'Please take it anyway,' he encouraged. 'Better to have too much than not enough. Get whatever you think we may need.'

Half an hour later, Amber dragged the little cart from the stables and after placing a blanket in it she gently sat Charlotte on it. The child thought it was great fun and giggled as her mother began to drag it along the cliff path. At the top of the steep hill Amber paused to catch her breath and looked down on her home town. It was a fine day and far out at sea beyond the harbour she could see the trawlers with their nets cast wide. It already seemed a lifetime since she had lived there; so much had happened in such a short space of time. After getting her breath back she moved on and soon came to the market square, which was teeming with housewives shopping.

There was a cluster of them standing outside Mr King's grocery store, and taking a deep breath and raising her chin, Amber moved towards them, painfully aware that they had all stopped talking to monitor her approach. Then Mrs Preston stepped from inside the shop, and Amber's heart sank.

'Well, well who do we 'ave 'ere then, ladies?' the old woman chortled, her lip raised into a sneer. 'If it ain't the little whore from up on the hill! How's your fancy man then, eh, lass?'

Amber felt colour flood into her cheeks but she kept walking towards her with her head held high. But Mrs Preston wasn't done with her yet, not by a long shot. 'So what's it like bein' a rich man's fancy, eh? It's 'is poor wife I feel sorry for,' she said with a shake of her head, addressing the women clustered around her. 'Not even cold in 'er grave she weren't afore you stepped into the poor lass's shoes. *Shame* on you.'

Amber's temper started to rise. 'I shouldn't call me too much if I were you, Mrs Preston,' she said in an icy voice. 'Not when your own family ain't blameless. Is it right what I hear? That your Bertie's on the run from the police for murder!'

'My son's *innocent!*' Mrs Preston spat as the women started to titter.

'And *so* am I,' Amber retorted. 'So, my advice to you would be don't make assumptions about things you know nothing about. I'm only there to care for this little one here an' there's nowt goin' on between me an' her father!'

'Huh, an' I'm a monkey's uncle! You don't fool us, Amber Ainsley. It's as clear as the nose on your face that the little 'un is yours! Just look at 'er! She's the bloody spit out o' your mouth an' it don't take much workin' out, does it? Afore she were born you worked up at Greenacres an' suddenly you up an' leave for months to "*care for your sick uncle?*" Why, you must think we're all dense. Next thing you know, when you come back he's sendin' you off to work for 'is posh friends afore settin' you up in the nursery up there to care for his children. Admit it, lass. That girl there is yours an' Greenwood's bastard!'

Amber had reached them by now and without another word she scooped Charlotte, who was sitting quietly sucking her thumb, into her arms and swept into the shop.

The shopkeeper's wife, Mrs King, had been a good friend of Amber's mother and she asked gently, 'What can I be gettin' for you, lass?'

Amber handed her the list she had made and as the woman busied herself piling everything onto the counter, Amber cradled Charlotte to her. The shouting outside had clearly unnerved the little girl.

'Right, that's flour, a twist o' tea, sugar . . .' Mrs Richards ticked everything off and once she had paid her Amber started to carry everything out to the cart. Some of the women had drifted away but Mrs Preston was still there and ready to do battle if the look on her face was anything to go by.

'It's all your fault my poor lad 'as gone off the rails,' she accused as Amber gently pressed Charlotte down amongst the groceries. 'It were when you dumped 'im for better prospects that 'e changed.'

'That's rubbish. I *never* dumped him,' Amber retaliated. 'We were never together to begin with.' With her nose in the air, she grasped the handle of the cart and turned it towards the butcher's, but she'd gone no more than a few yards when she felt something hit her squarely between the shoulder blades and reaching round to her back to feel what it was she felt raw egg dripping down her blouse.

'Go on, be off wi' you,' Mrs Preston shouted as she lifted another egg from her basket and aimed it at her target. 'We don't want scum like you comin' into town mixin' wi' decent bloody folk. You're nowt but a little whore!'

The second egg landed on Amber's arm and now Charlotte started to cry. Cheeks blazing, Amber moved on, painfully aware that everyone in the square was watching her closely. She had never felt so humiliated in her life but she was also aware that if she responded it could only make things worse and she didn't want to upset Charlotte any more than she already was. It was another half an hour by the time she'd bought everything on her list and was able to begin the hard trek back up the hill. It was only then that she allowed the tears of humiliation to fall, but strangely her anger was directed at Barnaby more than Mrs Preston. If he had kept his hands to himself none of this would ever have happened and once again her resentment of him flared. *But then*, a little voice whispered, '*It wasn't entirely his fault, you didn't exactly try to stop him – quite the opposite.*'

She had almost reached the top of the hill when she heard hoofbeats coming up behind her and turning about she saw Barnaby. She was red in the face and panting with the exertion of pulling the heavy load by then and without saying a word he leapt from the saddle, handed her the horse's reins and proceeded to pull the cart the rest of the way up the hill. With no other choice, she followed slowly behind him.

It was only when they reached the top that he noticed the stains on her blouse and her tear-stained face and his eyebrows creased into a frown as he asked, 'What's happened?'

'The townsfolk have put two an' two together an' realised that Charlotte is my girl,' she told him coldly. 'An' now they think I'm your fancy piece an' that you an' I are livin' in sin!'

'Oh, Amber . . . I'm *so* sorry.' He looked genuinely distressed but Amber was too angry to care how he felt.

'Well, it was only goin' to be a matter o' time afore the truth came out, weren't it?' She reached out to take the cart back again but he shook his head and before she could stop him, he lifted her as if she weighed no more than a feather and swung her up onto his saddle.

'You rest and walk alongside me. I'll take this the rest of the way.' And without giving her time to object he set off at a brisk trot as if the heavy cart weighed nothing.

The rest of the journey was made in silence and when they arrived back at The Crow's Nest, he gently took Charlotte into the house and laid her on the sofa before beginning to carry the shopping in.

'Why don't you go and get changed?' he suggested and for once Amber didn't argue with him. She'd had quite enough unpleasantness for one day and it had upset her deeply.

'Don't you have to get back to work?' she asked him when she came back downstairs.

'No, it won't hurt if I don't go back today. Jimmy can see to what we were doing and I'd rather hang about here in case there's any more unpleasantness. I'll make myself useful in the garden,' he said, leaving the room and going upstairs to change.

Amber stared after him thoughtfully. What had happened to her in the town seemed to have upset him almost as much as it had her and it surprised her. After all, she had never been anything more than a laundry maid he could toy with and then dump when he tired of her, had she?

Then, with a shrug she began to put the groceries away.

Early in the morning on the day before her uncle's wedding, Amber, wearing her best dress, carried the last of the luggage out to the barouche and Barnaby, looking very handsome in a smart pin-striped tail suit and a starched white shirt, loaded it onto the back.

Amber had written to her mother to tell her to expect them and her mother had written back to say that her uncle had bought her a new outfit for the wedding that he hoped would fit her and Amber could hardly wait to see it.

'Is that the lot?' Barnaby asked.

She nodded and clambered up onto the seat next to the driver's as Barnaby handed Charlotte up to her. The baby had started to jabber away in her own little language and if it was possible Barnaby seemed to be even more devoted to her.

'We should be there by early this afternoon if we make good time,' he told her as they set off, Charlotte giggling in delight.

As Barnaby had forecast, they drew up outside her uncle's home in Scarborough shortly after lunchtime and whilst Amber and Charlotte went to knock on the door, Barnaby began to unpack their luggage.

Her mother and Martha Carter answered the door and instantly started to coo over Charlotte.

'Oh, she's got so big,' her mother cried with delight. 'And she's so beautiful. The absolute double of you when you were her age.'

Her smile faded as she glanced towards Barnaby and she said politely, 'Thank you very much for bringin' them.'

'It was my pleasure, Mrs Ainsley.' He tipped his hat and gave a little bow and Alice couldn't help but notice how handsome he was. It was no wonder he had turned Amber's head.

'How shall we be able to let you know when she's coming home?'

'Oh, that won't be a problem,' he assured her. 'I'm just off to find a hotel to stay in, so I'll be close at hand.'

Alice looked slightly uncomfortable. He had put himself out to bring them after all, and it seemed churlish not to ask him to stay there.

'We, er . . . do have a spare room, if you'd like to stay here,' she said tentatively.

Barnaby frowned. 'I wouldn't wish to put you to any trouble.'

'It wouldn't be,' she assured him. 'And I'm sure you'd like to see Charlotte all dressed up tomorrow.'

He wavered. 'Well . . . yes, I would, actually, if you're quite sure. But what about my horse?'

'There's a farrier in the next road that would stable him for a small fee.'

'In that case, I'd be very grateful to accept your kind invitation.' He tipped his hat again and after hopping back into the driver's seat he set off to get the horse settled, leaving Alice to go back inside and tell Amber what she'd done.

'What did you have to go an' do that for?' Amber snapped.

'Because it would have been bad manners not to invite him to stay after he's brought you all this way!' Alice retorted. 'And he thinks the world o' Charlotte an' seems to me he's doin' his best to make up for the way he treated you.'

Amber scowled as she glanced across at her uncle and his wife-to-be who were making a great fuss of Charlotte. It was clear they were delighted to see her again. 'Then I dare say I'll have to make the best of it,' she said sulkily.

At dinner that evening Barnaby got on famously with her uncle as they discussed politics and world events in general, so after the meal, while the women saw to the washing-up, the men settled in Uncle Jeremiah's study with a glass of port and a cigar.

Once the washing-up was finished, Alice and Martha took Amber upstairs to see the outfit they had bought for her.

'Your mother chose it,' Martha said nervously as Amber stared at the beautiful pale-green taffeta gown hanging on the wardrobe in her room. 'I do hope you like it and that it fits because we won't have time to change it now.'

'It's stunnin',' Amber said and she meant it. The waist-line was fitted into a fashionable V at the front with a tight-fitting, low-cut top and puffed, elbow-length sleeves, and the skirt was full. It was trimmed at the neckline and the waist with white guipure lace and she knew the col-our would set off her strawberry-blonde hair and copper-coloured eyes to perfection. It was the sort of gown she had only ever dreamed of owning, although she recognised it was completely impractical for the life she led back at The Crow's Nest. 'But when will I ever get the chance to wear it again?'

'Don't worry about that,' Martha said with a wide smile when she saw how much Amber loved it. 'It's my wedding day and I want everyone to feel as special as I will.' She blushed like a girl and Amber and her mother exchanged a smile. Both Martha and her uncle seemed so happy that it was clear they were made for each other.

Next, Martha produced a dainty pair of satin slippers to complement the outfit and Amber giggled as she tried to picture herself wearing them when she was digging in the garden back at home or collecting the eggs from the chickens Barnaby had bought.

The next morning the house was in chaos as they all helped each other to get ready. Uncle Jeremiah looked very smart in his top hat and tails and gaily coloured waistcoat, and Martha looked beautiful in a lovely two-piece costume of pale lemon with a matching hat. She would carry a posy of sweet-smelling freesias, insisting that she was far too old to bother with a large fussy bouquet. Alice wore a gown in a fetching shade of blue and Biddy's outfit was in lilac, while Charlotte wore the pretty ivory coloured dress Amber had lovingly stitched for her, and everyone agreed she looked totally adorable.

Then, while the womenfolk kept a watchful eye on the baby, Amber dashed off to get ready herself. She had washed her hair the night before so before getting dressed she piled it high on the top of her head and teased it into ringlets that fell onto her slim shoulders. The gown fitted as if it had been made for her and when she appeared at the top of the stairs, she saw Barnaby in the hallway.

When he glanced up and saw her his eyes almost popped out of his head, and as she came slowly down the steps, he could scarcely take his eyes off her. This was Amber as he had never seen her before and he couldn't believe the transformation. He had always thought her pretty, although not in the ethereal way that his wife had been, but now he realised that she was quite beautiful.

'Why you look . . . just . . .' He was almost lost for words. 'Just *beautiful.*'

Amber felt beautiful in the wonderful gown and she blushed prettily and actually smiled at him.

Outside two carriages were waiting for them and they piled into them in high spirits. Her uncle, her mother and Martha went in the first carriage while Amber, Barnaby and Charlotte followed on in the next. The quaint little church where they had chosen to get wed was perched high above the town just below Scarborough Castle and when they entered, the scent of the flowers her uncle had thoughtfully ordered to be set on either side of the alter greeted them.

It was a very simple service but it was plain to see that the two people taking their vows as the sun shone down on them through the stained-glass windows were very much in love, and just for a moment Amber felt herself envying them. She would never know a love like that now, she thought, glancing at Barnaby. The happy couple left the church to a hail of rose petals and rice and then they all set off for a fine wedding breakfast at a smart hotel on the seafront.

In the early afternoon they returned to the house where the bride could change into her going-away outfit and soon after the carriage arrived to take them to the train station to begin their honeymoon.

'Eeh, it were a lovely service, weren't it?' Alice said dreamily as they sat enjoying a cup of tea after the couple had left. 'It'll no doubt be your turn next, lass!'

Amber scowled. 'I won't *ever* get married,' she said with conviction and a glare in Barnaby's direction, but Alice merely smiled.

'I wouldn't count on it. Never is a long time. But now, why don't you two take Fancy for a stroll along the front and enjoy the fresh air? You'll be back at home an' workin' again in the blink of an eye so make the most o' your break. Charlotte's fast asleep an' I'll keep me eye on her while you're gone.'

'Actually, that sounds like a very good idea,' Barnaby said with a grin at Amber and knowing that it would appear churlish to refuse she nodded.

'Very well, but then I really must get back an' pack if we're leavin' first thing tomorrow.'

And so they set off, Fancy frolicking on her lead ahead of them, and when Barnaby tucked her hand into the crook of his arm she didn't release it. In fact, she was surprised to find she quite liked it.

Chapter Thirty-Nine

The following morning, Amber and her mother said a tearful farewell, while Barnaby carried out their luggage to the barouche.

Charlotte was tearful too, although they guessed it was more because she couldn't take Fancy with her than because she was about to leave her doting grandmother. She and the little dog had taken a great shine to each other and had been inseparable during their time there and now Charlotte didn't want to be parted from her.

'We'll come and see Fancy again soon, sweet'eart,' Amber promised as she tried to prise the child away. Eventually, she somehow managed to get her outside into the carriage.

'Are you sure you'll be all right here all on your own?' Amber was concerned at the thought but Alice smiled.

'I won't be on me own,' she pointed out stoically. 'I've got little Fancy 'ere an' Biddy to keep me company. Now have a safe journey an' write to me often.'

Barnaby came to shake her hand. 'Thank you so much for having me, Mrs Ainsley, and for allowing me to attend your brother's wedding.'

Alice knew she should hate him after the way he'd treated her daughter and yet, after spending some time in his company, she'd actually grown to like him, especially when she saw how he doted on her granddaughter.

'You just take care o' my girls, now,' she told him sternly and he nodded before hopping onto the driver's seat and urging the horse on. Alice waved until they were out of sight before turning and going back into the house.

The mood on the journey home was much lighter than it had been on the way there and Amber felt as if she and Barnaby had reached some kind of a truce. She found that she could bring herself to at least be civil to him now and they chatted easily of this and that as the horse trotted along.

It was mid-afternoon when The Crow's Nest came into view and the good mood immediately disappeared as they saw that the front door was swinging open.

'Oh no, not again!' Amber breathed as she stared in distress at the flowers she had lovingly planted in the front garden. It had been a blaze of hollyhocks, lupins, lavender, roses and peonies when they left, but now they had all been trampled and she dreaded to imagine what they would find inside.

Barnaby's face set. 'But I locked the *damned* door!' he cursed as he led the horse round to the stable. 'Stay here while I go and check there's no one still inside.'

Charlotte was fast asleep in Amber's arms and she watched the door fearfully until he remerged some minutes later, his face grave. 'Whoever was here has made a right mess, so you'd best prepare yourself.'

He helped her down and took Charlotte from her, and steeling herself, Amber stepped through the back door and into the kitchen. Once again, the crockery from the dresser was smashed about the floor and the curtains had been ripped from the poles. But worst of all was the dreaded scrawling on the wall. This time someone had written *HARLOT* in huge letters and she cringed at the sight of it. Even so her face remained calm as she rolled her sleeves up and said quietly, 'Unfortunately it looks as if we're goin' to have to buy some new crockery.'

He was watching her intently and she could see how distressed he was. 'Never mind the crockery, it's your good name I'm worried about. Didn't I warn you this might happen?'

She shrugged. 'As me mam was fond o' sayin', while they're callin' me names, they're leavin' some other poor sod alone. Now, lay Charlotte on the sofa an' go an' get the horse settled, he'll be tired after the long journey. Then we'll put this place back to rights. I can't have Charlotte crawlin' through all this lot.'

'You don't think it could have been old Trampy Ned who did this do you?' He couldn't think of anyone else who came near the place.

Amber shook her head. 'No, I don't. Old Ned is a gentle soul, he'd never cause all this damage an' he wouldn't steal from us either.' Then she went to the cupboard to get the broom and started the long job of clearing up.

Barnaby took the horse to the stables, and after giving him a good rub down and filling his manger with food, he shook his head. His first feelings of anger had gone and now he just felt desolate. What a terrible ending this homecoming had been to their lovely time in Scarborough, but as Amber had pointed out, they would just have to get on with it, although he had come up with an idea that might make things easier for Amber. It was something he had been toying with for a while and now he decided to put it to her at the first opportunity he got.

It came later that evening as he and Amber were sitting in the kitchen after Charlotte was safely tucked up in bed. The house was now sparkling clean and tidy again. He'd noticed that she was actually a very good housewife and certainly not afraid of hard work. She was darning some socks by the light of the oil lamp when he said tentatively, 'Amber, I know things have been difficult for you so I thought . . .' He swallowed, setting his Adam's apple bobbing. 'I thought perhaps people might leave you alone if we were to get married.'

'*What?*' Her head snapped up as she stared at him in disbelief. '*Us* get married, you mean?'

'Why not? Think about it. I know I certainly shan't ever meet anyone I wish to get married to again and you've said that you've no wish to. It would be a marriage of convenience, obviously. We could still continue to have our own rooms and live as we are now. It would be a purely platonic arrangement, but it might stop tongues wagging. What do you think?'

'I-I don't know *what* to think!' He had taken her completely by surprise, but as she thought of his suggestion, she supposed it did make sense. At least if they were married Charlotte would have some security, and so would she if it came to that.

'Well, I . . .'

Sensing her hesitation and seeing the worried look on her face he hastened to assure her, 'As I said I would never lay a finger on you. I'm just trying to make things a little easier for both of us.'

She stared thoughtfully into space for a time before saying slowly, 'Then yes, I suppose it does make sense, for Charlotte's sake if nothing else. At least if we're wed then she won't be branded a bastard.'

'Is that a yes then?'

When she nodded, still looking nervous and uncertain, he stood up. 'Then I shall go and see the vicar of St Mary's tomorrow and arrange it for as soon as possible. Goodnight, Amber.'

He crossed to the door that led to the stairs and as she watched him go, she chewed on her lip and hoped she had done the right thing.

The following day Barnaby rode into Whitby to purchase new crockery and when he returned and carried it into the kitchen, Amber smiled at the sight of it. She'd expected him to buy plain white but this was patterned with little hand-painted poppies.

'This is so pretty but I'm afraid it must have been very expensive,' she commented as she examined it before arranging it carefully on the dresser. 'In actual fact, it's almost too nice to use for every day, but luckily I managed to salvage a few of the plainer pieces so we can still use those.'

He was ridiculously pleased to see her smiling and felt that the fancy crockery was worth the extra he had paid for it.

'I, er . . . I'm truly sorry for all the trouble and pain I've caused you in the past,' he said quietly, and she paused in what she was doing to stare across at him. 'And I've been to see the vicar. We can be married in three weeks' time once he has called the banns. I've also taken the time to ask Farmer Jennings and his wife if they will stand as our witnesses. Is that all right?'

During the time she had lived in The Crow's Nest, Amber had grown to like the Jennings. In fact, they and Trampy Ned, who came to the door often for food, were sometimes the only people she saw for days apart from Barnaby.

When she nodded, he lowered his head and repeated, 'Again, I'm so sorry for all the trouble I've caused you. I'm going to try and make it up to you, I promise.'

'It's all in the past now. What's done is done an' to keep sayin' sorry ain't goin' to change things, so can we just get on with things now?'

'Of course.' He made for the door to see what he could salvage of the flowers that had been trampled in the front garden and half an hour later he returned with a large bunch.

'It's not actually as bad as it looked but these had been knocked over and it seems a shame to throw them away. I thought you might like to put them in a vase?' He placed them awkwardly on the table to the side of her.

Amber was in the process of feeding Charlotte her lunch and she paused to stare at the blooms. No one had ever given her flowers before and even though they were only ones that had damaged stems she felt a blush burn into her cheeks, but she said nothing, as Barnaby turned and left the room. She had to admit that he'd worked beside her tirelessly since they'd returned to find the house in a mess again. He had insisted that he should be the one to scrub the graffiti from the wall and she'd been surprised to find that he'd done a remarkably good job of it. He had also fixed up the curtain poles for her and when she'd asked him early that morning if he shouldn't be going to the warehouse, he had told her that Jimmy would have to manage on his own until they had put everything back to rights. He was clearly trying his best to make things as comfortable as he could for her and Charlotte and so she decided that she would try harder from now on too.

Half an hour later, as Charlotte crawled about the flagstones, Amber stood back to admire the flowers she had arranged in a jug. They took pride of place in the centre of the table and as she leant towards them to sniff their perfume she smiled.

Later, as they ate lunch, Barnaby said tentatively, 'I was wondering if you might wish to invite your family to the wedding.'

Amber shook her head. 'No, I'll just write to me mother an' tell her about it after it's over. As you said, it's only a marriage of convenience so there's no need to make any fuss.'

'Very well, if that's what you wish.'

The rest of the meal was eaten in silence, and soon Barnaby went back to work in the garden, leaving Amber to wonder at why he'd looked slightly disappointed at her words.

Barnaby returned to work the next morning as he was expecting a delivery of wood that his ship would be transporting to France.

'If anything happens that worries you while I'm gone, lock yourself and Charlotte into the cellar until I get home; they won't be able to get to you in there if you put the wooden bar across the door,' he'd told her as he left and seeing the flicker of fear that shone in her eyes for a brief moment, he wished that he didn't have to leave her.

However, the day passed pleasantly and uneventfully and when Amber heard the sound of his horses' hooves late that afternoon, she began to butter some of the scones she had just baked. One thing she had learnt about Barnaby since being at the house with him was that he was always hungry.

When he entered the kitchen, he was carrying a box.

'I, er . . . I hope you don't mind but I bought Charlotte a present.' The guilty look on his face reminded her of the ones she had seen on her brothers' faces when they had done something naughty, and her heart ached as it hit her afresh that she would never see two of them again.

Charlotte was crawling towards him as fast as her little hands and knees would allow her to and when he placed the box down beside her and the child peeped inside it, she began to crow with delight. Curious, Amber inched closer and then she too smiled.

'Why, it's a *puppy!*'

He nodded as he lifted the tiny creature from the box to place it beside his daughter who was clapping her little hands excitedly. 'Yes, I got the idea when we were staying at your uncle's and I saw how taken Charlotte was with Fancy. Then today Jimmy told me that Farmer Jennings' dog had had a litter that he was getting rid of. They'd all been sold when I got there this afternoon, except this one who was the runt of the litter. Between you and me, I think he was intending to drown it, but he still charged me for her, not that I mind if it makes Charlotte happy. You don't mind, do you? I thought it might make you feel a little safer too, if you had a dog about the place when I was at work.'

'I don't mind at all!' Amber was almost as thrilled with the puppy as Charlotte was. 'But what breed is it?'

Barnaby grinned as he scratched his chin. 'Hm, now that's debatable. The mother is a Jack Russell. The farmers like them for rabbiting, but looking at her I have an idea this one might be a cross-breed.'

She was a tiny little thing; black and white with pointy ears, huge brown eyes and a very waggy tail and Amber instantly fell in love with her. 'But I thought Jack Russells didn't have tails?'

'No, I believe they usually have them docked when they're tiny but as I said, I think this one was destined for the bucket if I hadn't gone along when I did.'

Charlotte and the puppy were rolling around the floor together and it was already obvious that they were going to be the best of friends.

'I suppose we should think of a name for her,' Amber mused as she watched the antics and then with a grin she suggested, 'What about Socks? All her feet are black and look a bit like socks, don't they?'

'They do actually,' he agreed with a smile, and so the name was decided and once again Amber thought how considerate of him it had been to bring a little companion for their daughter; it was nice to think that they would grow up together.

The next visitor to The Crow's Nest was Nancy. She arrived the following Sunday afternoon and she came with gossip. 'There's been another two shops broken into in the market square,' she told Amber as she sipped at a glass of lemonade Amber had made that morning.

It was a glorious day with the sun shining high in a cloudless blue sky and they had carried the kitchen chairs out to the orchard where they could sit and watch Charlotte and Socks rolling about on the grass. 'Luckily there was no one 'urt this time.' She shook her head. 'Bertie Preston is still the prime suspect but no one 'as seen 'ide nor 'air of 'im for weeks, although he's got to be still hidin' out around 'ere somewhere. I tell you what, I wouldn't like to be in 'is shoes when they do catch 'im. I reckon he'll be for the noose if they can pin old Mrs Tilsley's murder on 'im. His mother's 'ouse 'as been robbed an' all an' she's furious. They took her rent money. I doubt they'd find much else in there.'

Amber shuddered and hoping to lighten the mood, she suggested, 'Do you fancy takin' Charlotte an' Socks down on the beach for a while? I could do with a paddle in the sea to cool me down.'

'Sounds good to me!' Nancy responded.

Amber had done her chores and, wishing to give them some privacy, Barnaby was busily digging the vegetable garden in readiness for the winter stock that he was going to plant. For Nancy it was a treat to be out in the fresh air after working in the smoky confines of the inn. Not that she was complaining. A job was a job at the end of the day and she considered herself lucky to have one, so with Amber carrying Charlotte they carefully made their way down to their own little private beach.

Within minutes Charlotte was happily crawling about picking up shells and tasting the sand as the seagulls wheeled and swooped in the sky above them.

'I noticed that you an' Mr Greenwood seem to be rubbin' along a bit better.' Nancy peeped at Amber out of the corner of her eye, a teasing smile playing at the corner of her lips.

'Well, I suppose I realised that it made sense to try an' get on at least. But don't get readin' anything more than that into it.'

'You could 'ave fooled me. Why, I couldn't miss the way he were watchin' you when we were sittin' outside.'

'Don't talk such rubbish,' Amber snapped more sharply than she had intended. She knew she should tell Nancy about the impending marriage. Word would spread through the town like wildfire once the banns had been read at St Mary's, and as Nancy was about the only friend she had left she supposed she should. 'I, er . . . have somethin' to tell you, as it happens . . . The thing is, Barnaby's asked me to marry him. It'll be a purely platonic marriage for Charlotte's sake, o' course. But we're sick of people callin' us names an' we thought it might shut 'em up.'

Nancy looked shocked then delighted and hoping to change the subject Amber asked, 'And what about you an' Jimmy?'

Nancy blushed prettily. 'Oh, we're gettin' on fine. In fact, to be honest . . . well, I reckon I'm a bit struck with him.'

'And does he feel the same about you?'

Nancy nodded. 'I reckon so, but we'll just 'ave to see 'ow things go.' She looked sad then as she said quietly, 'I were sorry to 'ear you 'ad another break-in while you were away at your uncle's weddin'. I don't know why folks can't just leave you in peace.'

Amber shrugged as she took the pins from her hair and shook it loose. 'I'm all right. And at least it wasn't so bad as the first time. I let Barnaby get most o' the shoppin' in now when he's in town an' I only go in when I have to, and when I do I only get called names – there's been no more egg-throwin'. That's part o' the reason we're gettin' wed.'

'Hm, well at least you ain't got Bertie Preston houndin' you anymore,' Nancy said. 'Most o' the police from the other counties they called in to look for him an' his cronies after the robberies 'ave left now, an' I doubt Bertie'll show his face round 'ere again.' She leant back on her hands and grinned with a mischievous twinkle in her eye. 'So when is the 'appy event to be? Can I be your bridesmaid?'

'No, you can't. Like I told you, it's goin' to be purely a marriage o' convenience. We'll just go to the church, come home an' things will go on as they are now. There'll be no guests or bridesmaids.'

'What? Ain't you even havin' a party to celebrate the day?' Nancy looked disappointed. 'Aw well, at least bein' Mrs Greenwood will give you some security, an' fancy the 'ouse 'aving its own little private beach, eh? It's lovely 'ere, ain't it?'

'I suppose it is.' Amber looked around as if she was seeing it through new eyes. 'We're certainly very comfortable.' Glancing up she saw Charlotte rubbing her eyes and told her friend, 'We'll have another ten minutes then I'd best get this little 'un back for her afternoon nap.'

Soon after they set off back up the side of the cliffside, but Amber was soon struggling as Charlotte, who seemed to get heavier every day, had fallen into a doze on her shoulder.

Then she saw Barnaby making his way down towards them. 'I thought this might happen,' he laughed. 'And she's quite a little heavyweight now so I thought I'd come and take her off you.' He took the child from her arms and surefootedly set off up the path again, as Amber glanced at Nancy who had a wide grin on her face.

'See what I mean?' she said cheekily and this time it was Amber's turn to blush. Now that she came to think about it, she and Barnaby had been getting on well lately and he was very kind. Every morning before going to work he would fetch fresh milk from the Jennings' farm, get the logs for the fire in and do any job he considered was too heavy for her to do. But then, she reasoned, he was only doing all that for Charlotte . . . wasn't he?

Ignoring Nancy's knowing stare she stuck her chin in the air, lifted her skirts and followed Barnaby.

Chapter Forty

It was the day before the wedding, early in July, and Amber was hanging washing on the line that Barnaby had strung up across the yard for her, when May Jennings appeared with a covered basket.

'How are you feelin', lass?' she chirped cheerfully. 'Are the pre-weddin' nerves settin' in yet?' Before Amber could answer, she went on, 'I brought you a cake for after the service. Every bride an' groom should 'ave a nice cake to cut. I gather you will be havin' a little do 'ere?'

Amber was acutely embarrassed as she stared into the kindly woman's face. 'Actually, we weren't planning on anything like that, Mrs Jennings. We were just going to go, get the service over with and come back here.'

May Jennings looked horrified. 'Well, that don't sound like much of a weddin' to me,' she said plaintively. 'An' what will you be wearin?'

Amber blushed. 'I, er . . . hadn't really given it much thought,' she admitted. 'It don't really matter, does it?'

'But *o' course* it matters. Now come on, if you ain't bought anythin' new we'll go in an' 'ave a look through your wardrobe.'

Amber reluctantly followed her into the house and minutes later they were staring into her wardrobe.

'Ah, now this would be *just* perfect.' May sighed with delight when her eyes lit on the beautiful green gown Amber had worn for her uncle's wedding.

'But don't you think it might be . . . a bit much for such a quiet weddin?'

'Too much, me foot!' May exclaimed indignantly. 'If a bride can't look beautiful on 'er weddin' day then when can she? You'll wear this, my girl or I'll 'ave somethin' to say about it, do you 'ear me?'

'Yes, Mrs Jennings,' Amber answered meekly. There didn't seem much point in arguing and she supposed it would be nice to wear it again, even if for only a short time.

'That's settled then. Me an' Bill will pick you up in the carriage at half ten, that'll give us plenty o' time to get you to the church for eleven.'

So saying she lifted the gown from the wardrobe, warning, 'An' just make sure you're wearin' this else I'll come in an' put it on you meself.'

When she had gone it hit Amber that this time tomorrow, she would be Mrs Barnaby Greenwood and the nerves really kicked in. *What if I'm makin' a terrible mistake?* she asked herself. Luckily common sense took over. She was doing this for Charlotte so that she could have respectability and that was reason enough for tying herself to a man she didn't love, or she hoped it would be. It was too late to back out now.

Amber and Barnaby were up early the next morning to get the chores done before they left for the church and despite the fact that they had been getting on better over the previous weeks, they were ill at ease with each other, so it was a relief when it was time to go inside and get ready. Amber had bathed in the large tin bath in the washroom and washed her hair the night before, so once inside she dressed Charlotte in a pretty little dress that she had lovingly hand-smocked then left her to play in the kitchen with Socks before going upstairs to get ready. Barnaby was already in his room getting dressed and as she passed his bedroom door, she wondered what he would choose to wear. These days she seldom saw him in the smart outfits he had once worn when he was the master of Greenacres, but she supposed it didn't really matter. Once the service was over, they would return home and get changed back into their work clothes and then everything would be just as it had been.

She quickly wriggled into the lovely silk underwear and petticoats her uncle had bought her to wear beneath her best gown before loosening her hair from its pins and brushing it until it shone and curled about her shoulders in gleaming golden waves. As she was getting herself into the dress she heard Farmer Jennings' carriage rattle into the yard and suddenly she was all fingers and thumbs and the tiny buttons up the back of her dress seemed impossible to fasten. Thankfully she heard footsteps outside on the landing moments later and after tapping on the door Mrs Jennings, all done up in her Sunday best bonnet and gown, stuck her head around it.

'Need any help, lass?'

'Yes, please,' Amber breathed. 'These damn buttons just won't do up.'

The woman chuckled as she hurried over to her and started to fasten them. 'I reckon this is a bad case o' pre-weddin' nerves. But there, you're all done, now turn around an' let's 'ave a good look at you.'

When Amber did as she was bid the old woman sighed with satisfaction as she swiped her work-worn hand across her eyes. 'I don't think I've *ever* seen a lovelier bride, lass. But there's just one thing missin'. Wait there a minute,' she urged as she quickly stepped out onto the landing. When she returned, Amber gasped at the sight of the beautiful posy she handed to her.

'I got me 'usband to pick 'em fresh from the garden before we come,' she told Amber. 'No bride should be wi'out a posy!'

It consisted of tiny white roses and the stems had been tied with a white ribbon that complemented the white guipure lace on the neck of her gown.

'It's beautiful, Mrs Jennings, thank you,' Amber said humbly. She hadn't even thought of carrying a posy.

'You're welcome, lass. Now let's go an' see what your husband-to-be thinks o' you. Be rights he should be at the church waitin' for you an' you shouldn't 'ave seen each other since last night. But then this is 'ardly a conventional weddin', is it? What wi' you both already livin' together, so we'll just make the best of it.' She grinned. 'Mind you, I don't reckon it's goin' to be as quiet at the church as you'd 'oped. Ever since the vicar read the banns out the whole town 'as been buzzin', which is why I wanted you to look your best. But come along now, we don't want you to be late for your own weddin'.'

She hurried off ahead of Amber and after taking a final glance in the mirror, Amber slowly followed her. As she carefully went down the stairs, clutching her posy of sweet-smelling roses, she saw Barnaby and Mr and Mrs Jennings waiting for her in the hallway. Barnaby was dressed in one of his smart pin-striped tail suits, and a white shirt with a gaily coloured cravat and matching waistcoat, and he looked so handsome that for a moment he took Amber's breath away. He was holding Charlotte but as he glanced up towards her his mouth gaped and she thought she detected the glint of a tear in his eye.

'Here, give the little 'un to me,' Mrs Jennings said bossily, wanting to give the couple a little time to themselves. 'We'll be out in the carriage waitin' for you both, but don't be late mind. The Reverend Rice don't like to be kept waitin'.'

Suddenly they were alone apart from Socks who was frolicking about their heels. Barnaby stared at Amber. 'You look *absolutely* beautiful, Amber. I can't think of one man who wouldn't like to be in my shoes today. But come along, we have a wedding to go to, I believe.'

Amber swallowed the lump that had risen in her throat as Barnaby tucked her hand into the crook of his arm and led her out into the sunshine.

Just as Mrs Jennings had predicted there were a number of people in the church but Amber knew they hadn't come to wish them well. They had just come to be nosy. Once or twice her voice faltered as she and Barnaby took their vows but at last it was over, and once they had signed the register, they were free to return to The Crow's Nest.

As they left the church, Mr and Mrs Jennings showered them in rice and rose petals and Amber couldn't help but think how wonderful this would have been had she been marrying a man she loved and who loved her. But then she glanced at Charlotte, who was clapping her little hands together in between picking the petals from the flowers in her posy, and she knew she had done the right thing.

Back at The Crow's Nest, Barnaby insisted that Mr and Mrs Jennings should join them for a celebratory glass of wine while he and Amber cut into the delicious fruit cake Mrs Jennings had made for them. But somehow one glass turned into two then three and by the time the kindly farmer and his wife took their leave in the early afternoon Amber felt quite merry.

'I'm afraid I ain't used to drinkin',' she told him, her eyes shining, and again he thought how very beautiful she was.

'Well, it is a very special day, Mrs Greenwood.'

She blinked to hear her new title used, wondering if she would ever get used to it. And then he did something very unexpected when he suddenly leant forward and asked softly , 'May I kiss you, Mrs Greenwood?' When she nodded he gently placed his lips on hers for the briefest of times. 'Just to seal our vows,' he said quietly, then he turned and left the room.

Amber stood frozen, her heart pounding. She was shocked to realise that she had felt herself responding to the kiss, which was quite ridiculous as she didn't even like him anymore, did she? But then she pulled herself together. *I'm just gettin' a bit carried away wi' the occasion*, she thought. But as she climbed the stairs to her room, she fingered her lips where he had kissed her.

Chapter Forty-One

'I'm afraid I may be quite late home this evening,' Barnaby told Amber one morning late in August. 'I have a cargo due in on the *Sea Serpent* today and we shall have to unload it all into the warehouse.'

'I shall keep something hot for you,' she promised as she finished feeding Charlotte, who usually managed to get more of her breakfast all over her hair than she did into her mouth.

'Dada . . .' The child held her arms out to him and he couldn't resist slipping over to her and giving her a kiss before leaving. She had only recently uttered her first word – dada – and had also taken her first faltering steps. Both Barnaby and Amber were totally smitten with her and she could wrap them both around her little fingers, not that it was a problem, because she was so happy and good-natured.

After Barnaby had left, Amber looked out of the open door onto the sunny garden and smiled at her daughter. 'I tell you what, if you're good for Mammy, I'll take you down to the beach today when I've done all my work,' she promised.

The past couple of months had passed pleasantly with no more acts of vandalism towards them or the house, although Amber still avoided going into town except when it was absolutely essential and so it could be lonely at times. About the only visitor she ever had apart from May Jennings and old Ned was Nancy who came as often as she could. However, Barnaby's new business venture handling cargo was doing well and so was his fishing trawler so all in all she supposed she had nothing to complain about. Even she and Barnaby were getting on much better now, and strangely that sometimes irked Amber. She still wanted to hate him but was finding it harder and harder. Only the day before, Charlotte had taken a tumble and they had both reached out automatically to catch her. As they did their hands had collided and Amber had snatched hers away as if she had been scalded. She instantly saw the look of hurt in his eyes as he mumbled an apology and she wondered why it had bothered her so much. She also wondered why his touch had sent little tingles up her spine!

Now she hoisted Charlotte from the chair and placed her on the floor and the infant immediately took two or three tentative steps before dropping to her knees and chasing Socks across the floor. She and the little dog were inseparable and Amber loved her almost as much as Charlotte did.

At eleven o'clock Charlotte went to bed for a short nap before lunch and Amber hastily did her outside work, feeding the chickens and collecting the eggs.

It was almost three o'clock that afternoon before all her chores were done and she took Charlotte and Socks down to the beach for an hour as she had promised. They were quite happy scampering about after each other, crawling into rock pools and generally getting into mischief, so Amber lay back on the sand, enjoying the feel of the warm sun on her face.

As she was lying there she happened to glance up towards the cliff top behind her and just for a moment she could have sworn she saw the outline of a man standing there, but by the time she blinked and sat up, shielding her eyes from the sun with her hand, he had gone. Even so, for no reason she could explain, she felt strangely unnerved so she quickly lifted a loudly protesting Charlotte, and with Socks trotting at her heels she climbed back up the steep path.

Once at the top she stopped to catch her breath, glancing first one way then another. There was no one in sight, so still being watchful she hurried back to the house.

The second she entered the kitchen she knew that some-one had been in there because the two freshly baked loaves she had left on racks to cool were missing. Her heart started to pound as she gently placed Charlotte on the floor and lifted the poker from the hearth.

'I-is anyone here?' she shouted nervously, but only silence greeted her.

Carefully she went from room to room wielding the poker in case she should come upon the intruder. Her search proved fruitless and she sighed with relief as she realised that whoever had been there had gone. Thankfully there was no damage done either so she supposed they had been lucky, although for the rest of the day her nerves were so taut that she jumped at every shadow.

It was almost seven o'clock that evening before Amber heard the welcome sound of Barnaby's horses' hooves in the stable yard and she was so relieved that he was home that she hovered in the kitchen doorway waiting for him to come across the stable yard.

'Oh, I don't usually get a greeting like this,' he said with a wide smile and a twinkle in his eye.

'Someone was in the house while I was down on the beach with Charlotte this afternoon,' she gushed. 'And whoever it was took the two loaves I'd baked this morning.'

'I see. And did they take anything else that you know of?'

She shook her head but he could see it had shaken her. 'No, I don't think so. I went from room to room to check there was no one still in there but they must have scarpered soon as they took the food.'

'In that case it was probably just a passing tramp who took advantage of the fact that you weren't about.'

Feeling calmer now that he was there and also slightly foolish, she nodded. 'Yes, you're probably right. And I suppose it was my fault for leaving the door open. But it was so stifling and we so rarely see anyone up here that I thought it would be safe to.'

He followed her inside asking, 'Has Charlotte gone to bed already?'

'I'm afraid so. She wore 'erself out down on the beach an' she was grumpy so I had to let her go early.'

'It's all right. But I am starving.'

She hurried to fetch him his meal, which she had been keeping warm over a pan of water on the top of the range, and they chatted about his day while he ate.

Just before they retired to bed, Amber said, 'If you don't mind listening for Charlotte, I think I'll just go for a short stroll before I turn in. It's been so hot today I've felt at times like I was goin' to melt.'

Amber slipped outside into the warm balmy evening. She was still feeling slightly nervous about the intruder who had entered the house earlier so decided not to venture too far and wandered across the grass to the top of the cliff and the path that led down to the beach where the cool sea breeze was like a balm on her hot skin. She was standing there staring out to sea and enjoying the peace and quiet when she suddenly sensed someone watching her and whirling about, she narrowed her eyes and gasped with fear as in the gloom she saw Bertie Preston standing behind her. The smell of stale sweat issuing from him was appalling and he now sported a straggly beard and his clothes were crumpled and stained.

'What's wrong? Ain't you pleased to see me?' he taunted her.

'I-I think you should leave, Bertie.' Her voice was more of a squeak. 'The police are out lookin' for you an' I wouldn't like to be in your shoes when they find you!' Her heart was thumping so loudly that she was sure he would hear it.

He grinned. 'Oh, I'm goin' never you fear,' he rasped. 'But not afore I take what's rightly mine!'

'What do you mean?'

'I mean you livin' wi' your fancy 'usband an' your bastard. It should 'ave been *me* that put a ring on yer finger an' a bairn in your stomach. I still might after what I 'ave in mind for you!'

Now she was really scared and took a tentative step back from him, very aware that they were perilously close to the edge of the cliff. 'Don't be so stupid, Bertie,' she snapped harshly. 'Just do yourself a favour an' get away before you land yourself in even *more* trouble an' I'll forget I ever saw you.'

He was coming closer and the ripe smell of him grew even stronger but she was too afraid to move any further back.

'I'm goin' to 'ave you right now an' then I'm goin' to leave your pretty face lookin' so ugly your old man won't want to come near you ever again,' he ground out and in that moment, as a weak moon sailed from behind a cloud, she saw the glint of a knife in his hand.

For a moment she stood rooted with fear but then she hastily stepped to one side hoping to be able to rush past him, but it was no good, because he grabbed her arm in a vice-like grip and threw her to the ground. For a second, she was so winded that she couldn't breathe, then with a superhuman effort she managed to roll away from him and crawl across the grass. She hadn't got far when she felt him tug on her skirt and before she knew it, he had flipped her over onto her back as if she weighed nothing, and as she stared up at him, she saw the hatred gleaming in his eyes. The knife slashed downwards, and though she turned her head, it wasn't quick enough and the blade slashed across her cheek and she felt something warm dripping down her face.

He was too heavy to push off but she began to kick and fight as best she could while he wrestled to lift her skirt. As she felt the cool air on her skin, she opened her mouth and let out a blood-curdling scream that made the birds in the nearby trees take flight. She felt him ripping her drawers aside as his other hand clamped across her mouth. She was crying so hard now that she was blinded by tears and despair tore through her as she felt him snatching at the buttons on his flies. Even before he had managed to undo them, she could feel his hardness and she knew that she was about to be raped. But suddenly he was hauled off her and as she rolled into a ball and began to sob, she heard Barnaby curse.

'Why, you *filthy* lousy bastard!' She had never heard Barnaby so angry as he threw a punch that sent Bertie skidding across the grass as the bloodstained knife flew out of his hand.

The next minute the men were rolling about in a tangle of arms and legs and she was suddenly aware that they were dangerously close to the edge of the cliff.

'Barnaby . . . be *careful*.' The words had scarcely left her mouth when they both disappeared and she let out another scream.

The seconds seemed like minutes but eventually she crawled to the edge and, looking down, she managed to just make out where they were. Barnaby had landed on a ledge halfway down but Bertie had fallen even further. She swiped the blood from her face and after tucking her skirt into her waistband she began to climb down to Barnaby, whose leg was twisted at an unnatural angle.

'Are you all reet? What can I do?' she sobbed when she finally reached him.

His hand rose to stroke her cheek. 'Y-you're hurt!'

'No, it's nothing.' She swiped at the blood flowing from her cheek again and glancing up the cliff she began to cry harder as she told him, 'I don't think I can manage to get you up there.'

Even in the gloom she could see that Barnaby's face was the colour of lint and he was clearly in a lot of pain.

'I-I think you'd better run to Jennings' farm and get help,' he said as his head lolled to the side and she knew that he had passed out.

She stared at him for a moment, torn between leaving him and doing as he said, but soon common sense took over and she scrambled up the cliff face and ran as if her very life depended on it. By the time she reached the farm her lungs felt as if they were on fire and the second she set foot in the yard the border collie ran from his kennel and began to bark furiously.

Somehow she managed to gabble out to the farmer and his wife what had happened as Mrs Jennings made her sit at the table.

'You'd best get the men together and take a door to carry them up,' she told her husband. 'Meanwhile I'll get Johnnie to ride into town for the police and the doctor. I'm afraid you're going to need stitches in this, my dear, it's very deep. You were lucky, another inch an' he'd 'ave had your eye out!'

She had fetched a bowl of water and a clean piece of huckaback to bathe the wound, but Amber pushed her hand away.

'No . . . you don't understand, I have to go back to make sure Barnaby's all reet an' my baby is all alone in the house.'

'In that case, I'll come back with you an' tend to you there,' May Jennings told her in a voice that brooked no argument. 'You're in no state to be left on your own, lass.'

Fifteen minutes later, with Farmer Jennings and three of his farmhands the solemn procession set off and Amber was able to show them exactly where the fight had taken place on the clifftop. 'Barnaby is about halfway down,' she told them, her voice quavering. 'He's stuck on a sort o' ledge an' Bertie's a little bit further down from him.'

'You just get yourself back to the 'ouse wi' my missus, lass. We'll find 'em an' when the police an' doctor arrive send 'em over 'ere to us.' Bill nodded at his wife and she took Amber's arm and led her away as, carrying the door, the farmer and his men began to descend the cliff.

Thankfully Amber found Charlotte was still sound asleep when they got back to the house, so finally she allowed May Jennings to press her into a chair while she bustled away to get some hot water. Up until that time, Amber had been almost numb with shock but as the woman tenderly cleaned her face and tried to stem the bleeding the tears came and Amber couldn't stop shaking.

'Have you a drop o' brandy in the place? It'll calm you down.'

'Y-yes, I think Barnaby has some in there.' When Amber nodded towards the cupboard beneath the dresser the woman fetched it and tipped a generous measure into the hot sweet tea she had just made for her, before adding some to her own for good measure.

'Now, get that down you,' she ordered. 'It's good for shock.'

Minutes later two policemen from the town arrived along with the doctor and Mrs Jennings directed them to where the rescuers were battling to bring the two men up the cliff face. Barnaby was the first to be carried into the kitchen on the door and when Amber saw his leg bent halfway between his knee and his ankle, she gasped with horror and leaning over the arm of the chair she promptly vomited all over the floor.

'We'd best get it in position while he's unconscious because this is going to hurt like hell,' the doctor said. 'I'll need some nice straight pieces of wood as well to use as splints.' He glanced up at Amber. 'And once I've seen to him, I'll see to you, young lady.'

Amber nodded numbly; she could hardly take in what had happened but she knew that it was all her fault. If she hadn't gone out to get some air . . . The voices around her became fainter and thankfully she knew no more.

'That's it, lass. Come on 'ave a sip o' this.'

Amber blearily opened her eyes to find herself lying on the settle looking up into Mrs Jennings' concerned face.

'B-Barnaby . . .'

'It's all right, lass, they've set his leg,' the woman told her.

'An' Bertie?'

May Jennings glanced towards the doctor before slowly shaking her head. 'I'm afraid there was nowt could be done for Bertie Preston.'

'*What?* You mean the fall killed him?' Amber gasped, her eyes wide open now.

May shook her head. 'No, lass, it were the knife your 'usband stuck in 'is chest that done for 'im.'

'But Barnaby *didn't.*' Amber struggled to sit up. 'I was there, they went over the cliff edge but Barnaby didn't stab him! Bertie dropped the knife when Barnaby dragged him off me. And where *is* Barnaby?' She looked around wildly for a sight of him but apart from one of the policemen and Farmer Jennings the room was empty.

'They've 'ad to arrest 'im. He's been taken to the cells.'

'But they *can't* do that! He was only protecting me and he's injured! His leg . . .'

'Don't worry, the doctor can look out for him just as well there as he could if he were 'ere,' Mrs Jennings told her with a sad shake of her head.

'Are you ready to tell me exactly what happened now, Mrs Greenwood?' the police constable asked as he stepped forward with his notebook and pen to the ready, and slowly, with tears streaming down her face, Amber told him all she could, although she could see by the look on his face that he didn't believe a word she was saying. 'But I'm telling you, Barnaby *didn't* stab him!' she ended with a sob as May Jennings put her arm about her.

The policeman nodded as he shut his notebook and put it away in his pocket. 'Thank you, Mrs Greenwood, we may wish to speak to you again to make a formal statement but for now I'll say goodnight.' And with a solemn nod, he quietly let himself out.

'I reckon it'd be better if I stayed 'ere tonight, Bill,' Amber heard Mrs Jennings say. 'This poor lass is in shock an' she's a little 'un to care for. Can you manage on your own?'

Feeling like she was in the grip of a nightmare, Amber barely noticed him leave. 'But why have they taken Barnaby to the station?' Amber cried in anguish.

Mrs Jennings cleared her throat. 'He's been charged wi' murder, lass. May God 'elp 'im!'

And on that solemn note the doctor stepped forward to stitch the gash in Amber's face.

Chapter Forty-Two

All through the night Amber lay staring at the shadows as they danced across the ceiling, but no matter how hard she tried, sleep evaded her so eventually she got up, crept downstairs and lit the oil lamp. Mrs Jennings was fast asleep in Barnaby's room and luckily Charlotte hadn't stirred so after making herself a strong cup of tea, Amber carried it to the back door and with a shawl about her shoulders she sat in her long cotton nightgown and watched the sun rise. A thick mist lay across the grass and as she stared sightlessly out to sea, she felt sick with fear. What would happen if the police didn't believe what she had told them? She knew that Barnaby hadn't stabbed Bertie but who would believe her? They clearly wanted to believe the worst of him and if she couldn't prove that he was innocent she was all too aware of what would happen. He would hang. She shuddered at the thought and a tear slid down her cheek making the newly stitched wound smart.

She was still sitting there when Mrs Jennings joined her shortly after six o'clock and she sniffed her disapproval. 'Whatever are you doin' sittin' there, lass?' she scolded. 'You'll catch your death o' cold. You've had a nasty shock and you should be abed.' She bustled over to fill the kettle and once she had set it on the range to boil, she threw some logs onto the fire and poked the ashes to get it going.

Amber just stared at her dully. She felt as if all the fight had been sucked out of her, and now she was afraid for Barnaby. Mr Jennings arrived soon after with a large jug of fresh milk and as he glanced at Amber, not quite sure what he should say to her, his wife told him, 'That were good timin'. The kettle's just about to boil. Sit yourself down an' have a cup o' tea then you'd best get along to milk the cows.'

As they all sat at the table together, Mr Jennings commented, 'You've got a right shiner on you there, lass. It were a good job Barnaby came along when he did, eh?'

'Is it?' she answered quietly. 'It might have been better if he hadn't heard me scream. He wouldn't be sittin' in a cell charged wi' murder then. But *I swear* to you both on Charlotte's life that he didn't do it! He *didn't* stab Bertie!'

'It ain't me as you 'ave to convince,' Mr Jennings said gently, feeling sorry for the girl. 'Is there anythin' more we can do for you?'

'Yes, there is as it happens. I'd be grateful if Mrs Jennings could stay to keep her eye on Charlotte just long enough for me to get into town an' back so I can see how Barnaby is. I don't really want to take the baby to a jail.'

'Of course I will, but would you just 'ave somethin' to eat afore you go?' Mrs Jennings leant across the table and gently squeezed her hand. Poor lass, it seemed that trouble followed her about.

Amber shook her head as she stood up and walked unsteadily towards the door leading into the hall. 'Thanks, but I couldn't eat a thing at the minute an' the sooner I get off the sooner I'll be back.' So after hastily dashing upstairs to throw on some clothes she practically ran out of the door.

Mr and Mrs Jennings looked at each other and sadly shook their heads. It looked like Amber would have yet another battle on her hands if she was going to try and clear Barnaby's name, because at the moment it did look suspiciously like he had stabbed Bertie, despite what she said.

The walk into town seemed to take twice as long as it normally did and Amber had to frequently stop to rest against the trees. She was covered in bruises from Bertie's violent treatment of her and added to this her face was hideously swollen and throbbing, but still she pushed on – nothing could have stopped her. By the time the police station came into view she felt close to collapse but forcing herself to stand upright she marched inside and up to the desk where a young policeman was doodling on the blotter.

'I've come to see Barna— my husband, Mr Greenwood,' she informed him and he swallowed.

'Right . . . I'll, er . . . just go an' get the sergeant. Luckily, he's just come in,' he said and scuttled through the door behind him.

He returned with the same policeman who had come to the house the night before.

'I've come to see how Barnaby is,' she told him without giving him a chance to speak.

'Well, the doctor's in with him at the moment,' he explained. 'I'm afraid he has a fever this mornin' an what with that an' his leg . . .' He shook his head and Amber's stomach did a somersault. Was the sergeant trying to tell her that Barnaby wasn't going to make it?

'I *still* want to see him,' she said stubbornly and after hesitating for a moment he sighed and lifted a large key that was hanging with some others on a nail behind the desk. The girl certainly had spirit, he had to give her that. Most young women would still be in bed recovering after what she had been through the night before.

'Just for a few minutes then.' He lifted the flap in the counter and led her to the door that would take them down to the cells. 'By rights I shouldn't be allowing anyone to see him until he's seen the solicitor,' he told her. 'But there's not much chance of that happening yet. He's well and truly out of it.'

The sergeant could hardly take in what had happened the night before – and it wasn't just the incident on the cliffs. He had been called in early when one of the neighbours in Argument's Yard had noticed that Mrs Preston's door was flapping open in the breeze, and when they'd gone in to check on her, they'd found a bloodbath. The woman was covered in bruises and the house looked as if a hurricane had gone through it, but worse than that was the fact that she was quite dead with a knife on the floor beside her and her wrists slashed. Whitby was usually such a quiet place and now here he was with two deaths to deal with in one night!

He unlocked the door and Amber followed him down some steep stone steps that had been worn in the centre from the numerous feet that had trampled up and down them over so many years. It felt damp, certainly not the sort of place for an invalid to be, she thought, but she was afraid that the sergeant might change his mind about allowing her to see Barnaby so she held her peace until they reached the bottom where she saw three cells all in a row along one wall.

The doctor was bending over a low bed in one of them, but at the sound of their footsteps, he straightened and Amber got her first glimpse of Barnaby. His face was flushed and wet with sweat but as she involuntarily called his name, he turned his head and gave her a weak smile.

The cell was unlocked, and rushing into it, Amber dropped to her knees and took his hot hand in hers, whispering, 'How is he, Doctor?'

'Not good I'm afraid.' Turning to the sergeant, he asked, 'Could I have a word please . . . outside?'

The two men left to stand in the far corner where they couldn't be overheard as Amber turned her full attention back to Barnaby whose grip on her hand was surprisingly strong.

'Ah . . . your face,' he groaned as he tried to focus his eyes on the livid wound on her cheek.

'It's nothing, it'll soon heal.' Without thinking she raised his hand to her lips and gently kissed his fingers and to her surprise she saw tears on Barnaby's cheeks.

'I-I'm so sorry for everything I've put you through,' he said in a trembling voice.

She shook her head. 'This wasn't your fault,' she insisted. 'If you hadn't come along when you did . . . Well, I dread to think what he might have done.'

'A-and Charlotte . . . is she all right?'

'Absolutely fine,' she assured him but her temper was rising by the minute. Barnaby was clearly very ill, far too ill to be locked up in a police cell and she determined to say

414

as much when the doctor and sergeant came back. Luckily, though, she didn't have to.

'Mrs Greenwood.'

'Yes.' Her head snapped round at the sound of the sergeant's voice.

'It's highly unorthodox but the doctor has recommended that your husband should go home to be nursed. The magistrates are not due into town until early next month and hopefully he'll be on the mend by that time. But I should warn you, he will have to return to jail and go before them. I imagine he will be sent to court to stand trial and be sentenced at that point.'

That was all in the future but for now Amber was just grateful that Barnaby could come home where she could make sure that he received proper care.

'I shall drive you both back to The Crow's Nest in my carriage,' the kindly doctor informed her. 'As I've pointed out, Mr Greenwood is hardly in any condition to try to escape and he needs more care than I'm able to give him while he's locked up in here.'

It took almost half an hour for the doctor and the sergeant to manhandle Barnaby up the stairs and into the doctor's carriage, and by then the colour had drained from his face and his lips had turned a frightening shade of pale blue.

'I was hoping you'd make an official statement before you left,' the sergeant grumbled once they'd managed to get him as comfortable as possible in the carriage. 'And I will of course hold you personally responsible if he does try to run away. And myself or one of my officers will be visiting every day to check on his progress.'

Amber stared at him in disgust. 'Come as often as you please and does he *really* look capable of running anywhere?' she spat sarcastically. 'And as for the statement, I've already told you what happened. My story will be no different this mornin' to what it was last night! I ain't in the habit o' tellin' lies an' I'm tellin' you, Barnaby *did not* stab Bertie. The knife that Bertie cut my face with was sent flyin' when the two of 'em were fightin' afore they went over the edge o' the cliff. So can I *please* take him home now?'

'Er, yes, yes of course.' The sergeant stood to one side as the doctor climbed into the driver's seat and Amber scrambled into the back to cradle her husband's head in her lap.

As it rattled away the sergeant offered up a silent prayer that he had done the right thing. There was one thing for sure – his head would be on the block if he hadn't, but there was nothing he could do about it now, so with a sigh he turned and went back into the small police station.

Once they arrived back at the house, Mrs Jennings, Amber and the doctor somehow managed to get Barnaby inside and into bed although the journey had clearly taken its toll on him and he looked ghastly. His face was the colour of putty, with sweat running down his cheeks.

'Get that window open an' get some air to him,' Mrs Jennings said bossily. 'Then he'll need bathin' with cool water. Do you think you can manage?'

Amber nodded wearily, although she felt dreadful herself. 'Of course.'

'Right lass, well as much as I'd love to stay an' help I need to get back to me chores but I'll tell you what, I'll take little Charlotte wi' me for a couple o' days. She'll love it up at the

416

farm an' it will give you more time to concentrate on Barnaby if you ain't got to worry about her. What do you say?'

Amber chewed on her lip. She had never been parted from Charlotte since they had been reunited but she knew it made sense. Barnaby needed her far more than Charlotte did at the present time and so she finally nodded and hurried away to pack a little bag of clothes and Charlotte's favourite rag doll.

'I'll send the mister over wi' more milk an' a steak pie later on,' Mrs Jennings promised as she set off with Charlotte excitedly clutching her hand a short time later.

'Thank you.' Amber watched the child toddle away with a lump in her throat before hurrying back inside where she fetched a tin bowl full of cool water and a clean piece of huckaback to bathe Barnaby's face.

By the time the doctor reappeared late that afternoon, Barnaby was incoherent and rolling about the bed, although after checking his leg the doctor was pleased to find there was no sign of an infection.

'It's a bad break and he'll probably always have a limp, but it's the fever that worries me more at present,' he informed her.

'Is there any more I can do?'

'No, my dear. You are doing all you can.' He fished in his bag and produced a small glass phial telling her, 'Put a few drops of this into some water and try to get him to drink it. It will probably knock him out in his weakened state but that won't be a bad thing. I don't want him thrashing about so much that he disturbs the splints on his leg.'

'He *will* get better, won't he, doctor?'

As the man stared into her anxious eyes, he wished that he could give her better news but he was painfully aware that Barnaby's condition could go either way at the moment.

'If we can just get this fever to break there's every chance that he'll make a full recovery,' he said sympathetically. 'Just carry on as you are, you're doing a good job. Keep him cool and get lots of liquid into him.'

After he'd left, Amber continued her vigil at Barnaby's side. By bedtime she was so exhausted that she could barely keep her eyes open and eventually she lay her head on the side of the bed and dropped into a doze.

The sound of the cock crowing made her blink wearily and almost instantly she felt a change in the room. She could no longer hear Barnaby's laboured breathing and with a frightened start she sat up and stared down at him only to find him watching her intently.

'Oh . . . you're awake.' She was so happy that tears sprang to her eyes.

He gave her a weak smile. 'It'll take more than a fall down a cliff to keep me down,' he said weakly.

She was thrilled and confused all at the same time. After all, theirs was a marriage in name only and she didn't even like him . . . *did she*?

She thought back over the last months, of all his attempts to make amends for what he'd done. He'd taken in Charlotte, found her work, then, against all odds, found a way that she could care for her own baby. And despite his love for his daughter, he'd not once reprimanded her for taking her away from him. It had been within his power to have her arrested and ensure she never saw Charlotte again, but instead, when she'd returned, he'd apologised to *her*. Even as his life was falling apart around him, he continued to care for both of them, doing everything he could to ensure their safety. And when Bertie had attacked her, he'd put his own life at risk to save her.

And then it hit her like a ton of bricks – she *did* still care for him, very much in fact, although she had no idea when her feelings towards him had started to change. Perhaps it had been when she had seen him being such a loving father to Charlotte? Or was it when she had seen his broken body being carried up the side of the cliff? Or perhaps it had been a slow softening – one she'd refused to acknowledge – as day by day he showed her how sorry he was. Whenever it was though, she would have been heartbroken to lose him and she didn't quite know how to deal with the tender feelings that were flowing through her.

Suddenly flustered she pulled her hand from his and stood up, aware that she must look terrible. 'I-I'll go and get you some tea,' she said and she flew from the room as if old Nick himself was snapping at her heels.

Chapter Forty-Three

Over the following week, Barnaby continued to make good progress, although he was still in a lot of pain with his leg and the many cuts and bruises he had sustained from his fall down the cliff. Amber continued to nurse him devotedly and every day it became harder to hide the tender feelings she had developed for him.

Charlotte had come home and she spent hours in Barnaby's room listening to him read from the storybooks he had bought for her. And then one day the doctor arrived with the sergeant in tow.

'I'm so sorry, but we shall have to take him back to the cells now, Mrs Greenwood. The doctor informs me that he is well enough to be moved and the magistrates will want him to appear in front of them when they arrive.'

Amber bristled. 'But *why*? He still can't go anywhere with his leg in splints and we could always bring him into town when he's due to appear!'

But despite her protestations Barnaby was loaded onto the back of the police wagon and taken away. Both Charlotte and Amber were devastated, although the sergeant had promised faithfully that they would make him as comfortable as was humanly possible.

'It's so unfair,' Amber told Mrs Jennings with tears in her eyes when her kindly neighbour walked over later that day with fresh milk and an apple pie. She had been wonderful to them and Amber didn't know how she would have managed without her.

'It is that, lass, but life is often unfair.' She had grown to be very fond of Amber and utterly doted on little Charlotte.

And now Amber forced herself to ask the question that had been keeping her awake at night. 'What do you think will happen to him, Mrs Jennings?'

The old woman swallowed nervously. The whole town was buzzing over Barnaby's fate and the common opinion was that if he couldn't prove that he hadn't stabbed Bertie Preston he would be hanged. But as well as what had happened to Bertie, the town was also buzzing about the death of Mrs Preston. It appeared that someone had seen Bertie there late on the evening she had been killed and they had been quarrelling. Most people surmised that he had gone to his mother for money yet again, and when she had none to give him, he had killed her in a fit of rage, but now that Bertie too was dead it was doubtful if they would ever know what had really happened.

'I don't rightly know, lass,' she answered tactfully, avoiding Amber's eyes. 'The offence is too serious for the magistrates to deal with here so I reckon they'll send him to crown court to be tried and then it'll be up to the judge.'

'He's going to hang, isn't he?' Amber suddenly burst into tears and in a second, Mrs Jennings had her wrapped tight in her arms.

'Best try not to think about it.' She felt angry that the police hadn't taken into account what Amber had told them and yet she also understood that the evidence against Barnaby was very incriminating. 'You'll just have to let things take their course.'

Amber nodded, her gaze fixed on Charlotte who was happily rolling about the floor with Socks, oblivious to what was happening. Thank goodness for that at least, Amber thought, and wiping her eyes and nose she went to put the kettle on.

Minutes later a familiar face appeared at the door. It was Trampy Ned and she suddenly realised that she hadn't seen him since before the night of Bertie's attack.

'Mornin' missus.' He nodded towards Mrs Jennings.

'Mornin', Ned.'

Amber cut him a large slice of apple pie and wrapped it in a piece of muslin. When she handed it to him, he looked at her with a worried frown as he saw her eyes, which were red and swollen from weeping. 'Would you like a cup o' tea? I was just about to make one,' she asked him.

He swept the old hat off to reveal sparse grey hair that stood about his head like a halo, but he backed away. 'No, thanks, missus. I'll be on me way now. Ta-ra.' And with that he took flight.

Mrs Jennings smiled. 'Poor old thing. He ain't had much of a life, as he? Still, he seems content in 'is own way an' at least lots o' the townsfolk look out for 'im.' She herself was often supplying him with food when he visited the farm and she knew that, like Amber, she was just one of many.

The next few days passed in a blur of misery for Amber. Every day she walked down to the police station whilst Mrs

Jennings watched Charlotte and the sergeant allowed her to have a few minutes with Barnaby, who was trying his best to keep his spirits up. Finally news came that the magistrates were due the following day and a cold hand gripped Amber's heart.

'Listen, I want you to know that if anything should happen to me, you and Charlotte will be secure,' Barnaby told her soberly when she visited him that evening. The sergeant had informed her that he was due to be taken before the magistrates at eleven o'clock the following morning and she intended to be there to hear their decision.

'Don't talk like that,' she said, shaking her head.

He caught her hands and made her look at him. 'I have to,' he said quietly. 'I'm innocent but it's no good burying our heads in the sand. We both know what might happen with no witnesses to prove that I didn't do it. That's why the sergeant allowed my solicitor to come and see me to put everything in order. I want you to know that everything I have will be yours should the worst come to the worst. Jimmy is doing a splendid job of keeping the warehouse and the boats running smoothly and that should give you a decent income for the future, plus The Crow's Nest will be yours so you and Charlotte will always have somewhere to call your own. Here's the solicitor's name, his rooms are in the market square.'

Despite promising herself that she wouldn't, Amber started to cry and he lifted his hand to gently stroke her hair while his other arm slid around her shoulders. It was the first sign of affection they had openly shown to each other since the night his fever had broken, and placing her small hand over his large one Amber started to cry harder.

'Lastly . . . I want you to know that although I did you wrong, I wouldn't have missed having this time with you.' His voice was little more than a whisper now as she stared up at him through a veil of tears. 'I thought my first wife was beautiful when I first met her, but I soon discovered that her beauty was merely skin deep. Since getting to know you I've seen that you are truly beautiful both inside and out. I know that when we wed it was supposed to be purely for Charlotte's sake but somewhere along the line I've come to care for you deeply, so do you think you could at least tell me that you've forgiven me . . . just in case . . .'

'Oh Barnaby, I've come to care for you too,' Amber told him chokily, just as the sergeant appeared at the bottom of the stairs that led to the cell. He had come to tell her that their time was up but seeing their closeness he decided to give them a little longer and tiptoed away back upstairs.

'And as for forgiving you . . .' She sighed. 'I've had a lot of time to think and I realise now that what happened wasn't all your fault. I knew when I lay with you that you were a married man and so I was as much to blame as you were – it wasn't as if you forced me into our relationship. I also understand now why you sent me away when you found that I was having Charlotte. You were in an impossible position, so of course you had no choice when you discovered that Louisa was having a child too. As things have turned out you gave me the greatest gift of all when you got me with child so yes, I forgive you.'

'Then knowing that I shall die a happy man.' Barnaby wrapped his arms about her and she rested her head against his chest, listening to his heartbeat and feeling as if her own heart was breaking.

As she made her way home that night, she shivered in the mist that had floated in from the sea. Autumn was fast approaching and already the leaves on the trees were losing their colour and the evenings were cooler.

Back at The Crow's Nest she found Mrs Jennings dozing in the chair at the side of the fire with Charlotte curled up asleep on her lap and her heart broke afresh as she looked down at her daughter. Charlotte adored her father; how would she cope if he never came home again? Socks scampered over to meet her and she bent to stroke his silky ears, pushing the thought away. Tomorrow would be soon enough to think about that, for now she just had to try and get through the night.

Once Mrs Jennings had gone after promising to be back bright and early in the morning, Amber got Charlotte settled in bed and sat downstairs thinking back over her visit to Barnaby. It was funny, now that she came to think of it, how determined she had been after having Charlotte that she would never get wed, and yet here she was, not only married but married to the child's father, who had turned out to be the man she had grown to love. It was like something out of one of the penny romance novels her mother had liked to read when she could afford to, only in those they always had a happy ending, whereas her ending looked set to be far from it. It would be too cruel if she were to lose Barnaby now when she had only just realised how much he meant to her.

The minutes ticked by, each one feeling like an hour, and all was silent save for the clock on the mantelpiece and the sound of Socks softly snoring in his basket. As dawn broke, Amber filled the tin bath with hot water from the copper and washed herself from head to toe before washing her hair. She then sat wrapped in a towel by the fire and brushed her hair until it gleamed. She was painfully aware that this might be the very last time she would see Barnaby if the magistrates chose to send him to be tried and she was determined to look as nice as she could for him.

By the time Mrs Jennings arrived, Amber had fed and changed Charlotte, released the chickens from their coops and was dressed in her Sunday best blouse and skirt.

'You look bonny, lass,' the kindly woman told her. 'All that's missin' is a smile.'

'I'm so afraid of what might happen to him, Mrs Jennings,' Amber confided in a shaky voice as she put her best bonnet on and a warm shawl about her shoulders.

'I'm sure you are.' Mrs Jennings put her arm about her and gave her a gentle squeeze. 'But worryin' yourself into the grave ain't goin' to change nothin' so go an' smile an' be brave for 'im! I've no doubt he's just as scared as you are.'

The visiting magistrates always heard the cases in a room above the inn in the market square and although it was early, Amber was shocked to see a crowd already forming outside when she arrived. She expected to be met with the usual hostility so she was surprised when the crowd parted to allow her to be first in the queue.

'Come on, lass,' one of the women encouraged. 'It's your husband up afore the magistrates so it's only right you should get the best seat. Good luck – 'e's a good man is Mr Greenwood.'

'Th-thank you.' Amber stumbled past her and soon the door opened and the crowd climbed the stairs to the room where the magistrates were seated in a row behind a table. In their black clothes they reminded Amber of a row of crows.

The only other case to be heard that day was a man who was up for being drunk and disorderly, so it had been decided that, as his case was not so serious, he would go first. After a short hearing, the drunk was given a fine and told that if he reoffended, he would be sent to court, and he went off with a spring in his step.

By then, though, Amber was so wound up that she barely heard a word the stern-faced magistrates said and her eyes stayed fixed on the door for a sign of her husband, oblivious of the crowd chattering around her.

Suddenly there was a hush and, turning, Amber saw Barnaby being led into the room. He was leaning heavily on a crutch and two police officers stood on either side of him, as if they were expecting him to try and escape. His eyes immediately scanned the room and when they found her, he gave her a smile. He looked tired and was still far from well but as he was led to stand before the magistrates, he kept his head high and she was proud of him.

It took only a matter of minutes for the magistrates to read what he was charged with, and, after conferring in hushed voices, the most senior of the magistrates stood up and said solemnly, 'Barnaby Josiah Greenwood, you stand before us charged with the murder of Albert Preston, the most heinous of crimes, and so we recommend that you shall be transported at the earliest opportunity to the cells below Pickering High Court where you will be kept until you stand before Judge Alberton who will decide your fate.'

A gasp of dismay went up around the room and Amber's hand flew to her throat. Judge Alberton was commonly known as 'the hanging judge', and for a moment, she felt the floor rush up to meet her and had to grip the back of the chair in front of her to stop herself from falling.

'*NO!*' her tortured voice echoed about the room. 'This isn't *fair*! He was only protecting me and he *didn't* murder Bertie!'

'Be silent, young woman, otherwise you will find yourself on a charge of breaching the peace,' the magistrate snapped.

Barnaby, his head lowered, was being led away and Amber began to elbow her way through the crowd to get to him, but it was no use, for by the time she had managed to get to the door Barnaby had already been pushed onto the prison cart outside. Lifting her skirts Amber raced to the other side of the market square and when the cart pulled up, she gripped the sergeant's arm.

'*Please*, Sergeant Mellor, may I see him, just for a few minutes?'

He looked over his shoulder before taking her elbow and whisking her into the police station as the two young constables outside helped Barnaby down from the cart.

'Just let us get him back into the cells and I'll give you ten minutes,' he told her in a low voice. 'But don't get telling anyone I allowed it or it will be my head on the block!'

Ten minutes later she again descended the steep stone steps to find Barnaby sitting on his bed with his head in his hands, but he was calm. Most men would have been shaking at the fate that was soon to befall them and she couldn't help but think how brave he was being.

'Oh, Barnaby, what are we goin' to do? This is all my fault,' she cried as she held his hand through the metal bars of the cage. 'If I hadn't gone out that night an' you hadn't heard me scream . . .'

'Stop it.' He gave her hand a little shake. 'It wasn't your fault that Preston attacked you, and you have tried to help me.'

'But they won't believe me,' she whimpered.

He sighed before saying, 'Listen, I want you to go home and forget all about me. I've brought you nothing but trouble, but at least you and Charlotte will be set up financially for life. You'll never know how relieved that makes me feel. And don't be frightened, Preston can't hurt you anymore and you have the Jennings and Jimmy to help you.' His face softened then as he told her gently, 'But before you do go, there's one more thing I need to tell you. I love you, Amber. I didn't know what true love was when I was with Louisa so I want you to know that I'd rather have had the short time I've spent with you and our daughter than a lifetime with anyone else.'

'Oh!' Her eyes were so full of tears that his face was swimming in front of her. 'I love you too . . . so much. I don't know how I can go on without you.' And it shocked her afresh to realise that she meant every word she said. Somehow this man, who she had once thought she hated, had crept into her heart again and now she couldn't envisage life without him.

'Go now,' he said in a shaky voice. 'And promise me that you won't try to come when they . . . you know? I want you to remember me as I am now. Will you do that last thing for me, my love?'

She nodded numbly, unable to speak, then turned and stumbled blindly back up the steps.

Chapter Forty-Four

Two days later, Mrs Jennings informed her tentatively, 'I heard that they're movin' Barnaby to Pickering tomorrow, lass, an' that he's before the judge the followin' day . . . I thought I should tell you.'

Amber clutched the edge of the sink where she was peeling potatoes and nodded. Through the window she could see Charlotte and Socks playing amongst the trees in the orchard and everything was just going on as any other day, and yet nothing was the same. The house felt empty without Barnaby's presence and she missed having him to talk to. Time and again she had been tempted to go into town and beg the sergeant to let her see him just one more time, but she didn't want to break the promise she had made to him and so, somehow, she had managed to stop herself.

'That's it then,' she said brokenly. 'I think we both know what the outcome will be! I've been prayin' that somethin' would happen to show that me an' Barnaby were tellin' the truth. He's told them that he's innocent but they won't believe him and now . . .'

As her voice trailed away and Mrs Jennings rushed forward to envelope her in her arms, the tears came so fast that she could hardly breathe and all the older woman could do was hold her tight. Seeing her mother cry, little Charlotte, who had entered the room and was pottering about the floor with Socks, began to cry too and the mood was gloomy.

Long after Mrs Jennings had left, Amber sat staring into space. She could only imagine how awful and frightened Barnaby must be feeling and the worst of it was she could do nothing to comfort him. Somehow, she managed to get through the day and after Charlotte was tucked up in bed, she went to stand on the cliff overlooking their little cove and sent up a silent prayer for mercy, although she had little hope of it being heard. Judge Alberton wasn't known as 'the hanging judge' for nothing and with no witnesses to back their story all the odds were stacked against Barnaby being believed.

In the early hours of the morning, she finally went to bed but sleep eluded her and she lay listening to the distant sound of the waves breaking on the shore, her thoughts tortured. It seemed so unfair that just when she and Barnaby had come to realise how much they meant to each other that he should be snatched away and there was not a thing she could do about it.

She rose early and after making herself a pot of tea and forcing herself to drink a cup, she busied herself collecting the eggs and letting the chickens out of their coop to peck about the yard. There was a thick sea mist floating across the land and the silence was so eerie that she could almost have believed she was the only person left on earth. She certainly felt that way because now that Barnaby was about to be snatched away from her the future looked bleak.

Her thoughts were so far away that it was some time before she became aware of the sound of a horse climbing the hill towards the house and after glancing towards it, she was shocked to see that it was the doctor in his carriage. There was someone on the seat beside him, but because of the mist she couldn't make out who it was until they drew closer and then the breath caught in her throat.

'*Barnaby!*' The basket flew from her hand, but she barely noticed the eggs smashing around her as she ran towards him, her skirts flying. 'B-but I don't understand!' Her voice came out as a squeak. 'I-I thought they were taking you to Pickering today.'

Barnaby was grinning like the cat who'd got the cream and so was the doctor as he drew the horse to a halt.

'And so they were, my dear,' the doctor answered for him. 'But fortunately, a witness who saw what happened on the night of the attack came forward at the eleventh hour, as it were, in the early hours of this morning, and because of his statement, which backed the story you and Barnaby gave to the police, Barnaby is now a free man, so I thought I'd bring him home to you.'

Amber felt the floor shift as shock coursed through her and she gripped the side of the coach to steady herself.

'*What*? You . . . you mean that you are *free*?'

Barnaby chuckled. 'Free as the wind,' he said happily. 'Although my leg still isn't healed so I would appreciate some help in getting down so that I can give my wife a kiss.'

Both the doctor and Amber hurried forward to assist him and once he was on the ground, he caught Amber to him and gave her a resounding smack of a kiss on the lips which made her feel even dizzier than she already did.

'But who was it who helped you?' she asked breathlessly when he finally let her go.

'It was old Trampy Ned,' the doctor informed her. 'Turns out that he was in the town the night that Mrs Preston was beaten. Bertie had already stolen her rent money and it seems that he went back for more, but she refused him and so he beat her up quite badly. Something in her must have snapped because when Bertie left, his mother followed him to the top of the cove. Ned saw Bertie attack you and he saw Barnaby rush to defend you and then he saw both men go over the edge of the cliff. It was when you ran for help that Mrs Preston climbed down to Bertie and stuck the knife in him before going home and doing away with herself. Poor woman, she probably couldn't live with what she had done, although I believe Bertie got everything that was due to him and she did the world a favour by ridding it of him. And so, thanks to Ned, this is the end of it. Now all you two have to do is put this whole sorry incident behind you and live happily ever after, as they do in all the best stories.'

With their eyes fixed on each other Barnaby took his wife in his arms again, gazing at her adoringly. 'Oh, I think we can manage that, Doctor,' he said softly.

Suddenly feeling in the way, the doctor climbed back up onto his carriage and left with a broad smile on his face, but neither Barnaby nor Amber noticed as Barnaby led his starry-eyed wife back into their home to join their little daughter.

Acknowledgements

A massive thank you to my editor, Sarah Bauer, and the amazing 'Rosie Team' at Bonnier, who somehow managed to keep publications running smoothly all throughout lockdown even though they had to work from home. I really don't know how you managed to do it but I'm very glad you did!

Also special thanks to my brilliant agent, Sheila Crowley, and Sabhbh Curran, her assistant, who are always at the end of the phone with support, advice and encouragement. Not forgetting the brilliant Gillian Holmes, my copyeditor, who helps to make the books as good as they can be, and Kati Nicholls, my proofreader. I should also thank my long-suffering husband and family, who are used to me disappearing off to my office at the unlikeliest of times and to all my wonderful readers who make my day with their lovely reviews and messages.

Thank you all.

Welcome to the world of Rosie Goodwin!

Keep reading for more from Rosie Goodwin, to discover a recipe that features in this novel and to find out more about Rosie Goodwin's next book . . .

We'd also like to welcome you to Memory Lane, a place to discuss the very best saga stories from authors you know and love with other readers, plus get recommendations for new books we think you'll enjoy. Read on and join our club!

www.MemoryLane.Club

 www.facebook.com/groups/memorylanebookgroup

Hello everyone,

I do hope this finds you all well and looking forward to the spring and being able to get out into your gardens again! It doesn't seem long since I was writing to you all for the release of the hardback and wishing you all a Merry Christmas and now, here we are already with Christmas just a distant memory. All that shopping, wrapping and preparation and it's over in the blink of an eye. Still now we can all hopefully look forward to a brand-new year and visits to the garden centres to see what plants they have to tempt us with and some sunshine after the long cold days!

It's been a very busy year for us and it's hard to believe that we've now had a whole year in our new house.

I know many of you have been looking forward to the release of *The Season for Hope* in paperback and here it is! I'd like to say a big thank you to all that have already read the hardback and for all your lovely messages and reviews. They really do mean the world to me and make all the time I spend locked away in my office with my imaginary characters worthwhile.

Pre-Christmas wasn't a good time for me as we lost two of our fur babies within weeks of each other. First

Honey and then Sassy, two of our little Shih Tzus, and as any of you dog owners will know they left a huge hole in our lives and in our hearts. Thankfully, we still have our other four dogs to keep us on our toes and they love nothing more than pottering about in the garden with us. Funnily enough, it's where I get most of my ideas for my stories from!

I also had my writing to escape into and so soon we'll see the release of *A Lesson Learned*. In this one we'll meet Sapphire and it is the last of my Precious Stone series. In this story we get to tour the canals of Warwickshire and I loved researching how the 'boat people' lived. I absolutely loved writing this series and am sad to see it end but don't worry, I already have lots of other stories in line for you!

Things still haven't got quite back to normal as far book signings and events are concerned as people are still being cautious with Covid still rearing it's ugly head but let's hope that they will this year.

Don't forget for those of you who haven't joined already, to become members of The Memory Lane Book Club on Facebook where you'll be kept informed of what myself and the other Memory Lane authors are up to and have the chance to win some lovely prizes.

And so now I suppose all that remains for me is to wish you all a very happy spring! Hopefully you'll all be planning your summer holidays and enjoying spending time in your gardens in the sunshine.

Stay safe everyone and I'll look forward to writing to you all again very soon,

With love
Rosie xx

If you enjoyed *A Season for Hope*, you'll love the
next book in the Precious Stones series . . .

A Lesson Learned

Nuneaton, 1869

When young Saffie's parents fell in love, her mother
was cast out by her well-to-do family. Choosing love
over money, they eloped, deciding to raise
their daughter on the canals.

For as long as she can remember, Saffie has loved
learning and it is her dream to become a teacher,
but what use is an education to a canal girl?

Will Saffie step out of the shadow of the past
into the light of her dreams?

Coming soon.

Read on for a sneak peek . . .

Prologue

November, 1851

'Come on now, one more good push should do it. An 'ere, bite on this els'n you'll be wakin' the dead wi' yer screamin', wench.' The old woman unceremoniously pushed a piece of wood between Olivia's teeth as tears streamed down the girl's pale cheeks. She felt as if she was being ripped in two and desperately wanted Reuben by her side, but the men had taken him off to the inn, leaving the women to deal with the birth.

'That's a good little wench,' Old Mother Adams told her as she narrowed her eyes and peered between the girl's slim legs. 'I can see the 'ead now. Another good couple o' pushes an' yer should be a mother. Come on, gel.'

With the last of her strength, Olivia pushed with all her might and seconds later the stifling cabin echoed with the sounds of a baby's cry.

The old woman, who was clad in a shawl and the customary black bonnet, common to the boatwomen, held aloft a small bloodied body triumphantly. 'It's a little wench,' she told Olivia as she quickly cut the cord that bound the child to its mother then deftly placed the shiny penny that she had ready over the child's belly

button and tied it securely. Then she wrapped the wailing baby in a towel and handed her to her mother. 'An' a bonny little wench at that.'

Olivia stared at her daughter in awe, oblivious to the sound of footsteps pounding along the towpath outside.

Suddenly the cabin door burst open and Reuben Doyle rushed in, his face pale. 'Is it all over?'

'Aye, lad, nearly,' the old woman responded. 'Have a peep at yer new daughter then make yerself scarce till I bid yer to come back in.'

Cap in hand, Reuben quietly approached the bed and at the sight of the new mother snuggling the newborn he smiled.

'She's just perfect, Reuben.' Olivia smiled up at him, her face glowing.

A glimpse at the child confirmed what she was saying: the little one had a thatch of thick black hair as dark as the night, just like her mother's, and her eyes were a beautiful bright blue, nothing like the pale blue so common in most new babies.

'Ah, Livvy, me love.' Reuben was so emotional that he was almost lost for words and, as always, Olivia's heart swelled with love at the sight of him. With his shoulder-length curly brown hair and brown eyes, he was a very handsome young man.

'What do you think we should call her?' Olivia asked and his face broke into a broad grin.

'Why, it's got to be Sapphire, ain't it? Our boat's called *The Blue Sapphire* an' wi' eyes that colour what other name could we find that'd suit her as well?'

Olivia nodded in agreement. 'And we'll call her Saffie for short, eh?'

He smiled, but then Mrs Adams shooed him away so he went to rejoin his friends in the inn where he would stand them all a jug of ale to wet the baby's head.

Once she was finally alone, Olivia stared at her brand-new daughter. In some ways it seemed much longer than a year since she had left her mother and father, and it hadn't been easy. Reuben Doyle had lived on the canals all his life and soon after Olivia had joined him, he had bought *The Blue Sapphire*, a seventy-two-foot wooden-hulled narrow-boat, for them to live and work on. It had a long hold at the front for ferrying the cargo and the living quarters was a small cabin at the back of the boat. It was so small they had to make every inch count and for some time Olivia had felt claustrophobic, but she had grown used to it and now took great pride in their home. There was a tiny black-leaded range that served for cooking and heating the room and it gleamed, as did the large copper kettle that stood on top of it. A cupboard housed their bed, which folded away neatly during the day giving them more living space, and next to it a bench seat also pulled out to make yet another bed. Shelves ran along the top of the cupboard on which stood pretty plates and pieces of ornamental brass, again

polished to a high shine. Flowered curtains hung at the tiny windows and rag rugs, which Olivia had painstakingly made on dark winter evenings when Reuben was at the inn, were thrown across the planked floor. She had strongly objected to him going off and leaving her alone of an evening when she had first joined him, but she was used to that now, too.

The outside of the cabin was painted red and blue with castles and roses, and on the cabin roof were a number of buckets and watering cans that Reuben had also painted in bright coloured patterns. At the moment the hold was full of coal that gleamed in the cold moonlight and Olivia was aware that whether she had just given birth or not, tomorrow they would have to continue their journey to deliver it to a factory in Coventry. Neither births nor deaths stopped the boatmen from doing their job and, as Olivia had soon learned, they worked hard for every penny they made.

But for now she snuggled down onto the thin mattress and sighed with contentment as she placed baby Saffie to her breast for the first time. As the baby suckled, just for an instant she thought of the grandparents who would never get to know the child and she felt sad. But her parents had made their feelings clear on the night she had walked out to join Reuben and she knew there could be no changing their minds, and so she would just to have to make the best of things.

Meat and Potato Pie

A firm favourite of the servants of Greenwood House. Warm and filling, this meat and potato pie is a perfectly wholesome dish for a long winter's evening.

Serves 4

Ingredients

For the pie filling

- 350g stewing beef, chopped into chunks
- 125g onion, diced
- 50g carrot, diced
- 25g celery, diced
- 1 bay leaf
- 50ml Worcesertshire sauce
- 1 tbsp oil
- 250g potatoes, peeled, cut into chunks
- Salt and pepper to taste

For the pastry
- 300g flour
- 75g lard
- 75g butter
- 4–6 tbsp water
- Pinch of salt
- 1 egg

Recipe

1. For the pie filling, put the beef and diced onions into a large, lidded saucepan. Season with salt and pepper. Cover the contents of the pan with water and bring to boil. Cover the pan with a lid, reduce the heat and simmer gently for two and a half hours, or until the meat is tender.

2. Once the meat is tender, add the carrot and celery and cook for 20 minutes. Add the bay leaf and Worcesertshire sauce and continue to cook for a further 10 minutes or until the sauce has reduced by half.

3. Preheat the oven to 200°C/400°F/Gas 6.

4. For the pastry, tip the flour and salt into a bowl, and add the cubes of butter and lard. Using your fingertips, rub the fat into the flour until the mixture has a breadcrumb texture. Add the water and mix until the pastry begins to come together. Knead the dough lightly, shape into a ball, wrap in cling film and chill in the fridge for 30 minutes, or until the beef mixture is cooked.

5. Boil the potatoes in salted water until tender. Drain and set aside.

6. Remove the pastry from the fridge. Cut a small amount of pastry and roll it out on a lightly floured work surface to a 3mm thickness. Cut the pastry

into thin strips. Dampen the rim of a pie dish with water, and line the rim with the thin strips of pastry.

7. Strain the meat and vegetables, reserving the sauce. Spread the filling in an even layer in the base of the dish. Layer the potatoes on top of the filling. Pour the reserved sauce over the filling, until just below the top of the potatoes.

8. Roll the remaining pastry out on a floured work surface to a 3mm thickness, and cut to the size of the pie dish. Brush the strips of pastry on the rim of the dish with beaten egg, and place the pastry lid on top. Press the edges to seal, and brush the lid of the pie with the remaining beaten egg. Cut a few slits in the lid of the pie to allow steam to escape.

9. Cook in the preheated oven for 50–60 minutes, or until the pastry is golden-brown and the filling is bubbling inside.

10. Serve the hot pie with a side of green vegetables.

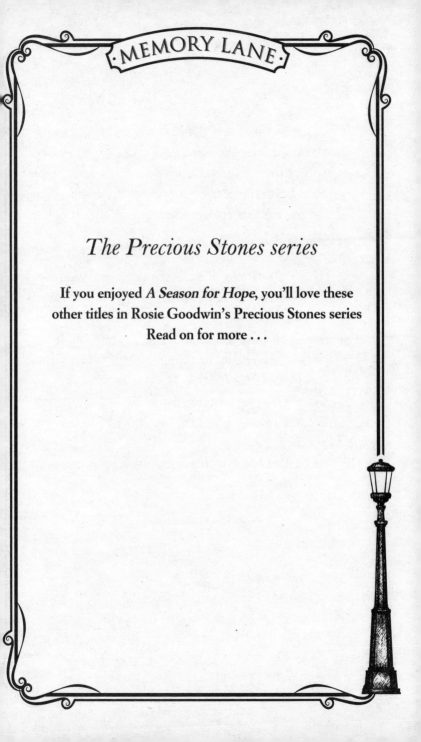

The Precious Stones series

**If you enjoyed *A Season for Hope*, you'll love these
other titles in Rosie Goodwin's Precious Stones series
Read on for more . . .**

The Winter Promise

1850.

When Opal Sharp finds herself and her younger siblings suddenly orphaned and destitute, she thinks things can get no worse. But soon three of them – including Opal – are struck down with the illness that took their father, and her brother Charlie is forced to make an impossible decision. Unable to afford a doctor, he knows the younger children will not survive. So, unbeknownst to Opal, Charlie takes their younger siblings to the workhouse. When she finds out, Opal is heartbroken.

Charlie starts taking risks to try to support what's left of the Sharp family and earn Opal's forgiveness, but he takes it too far and finds himself in trouble with the law.
Soon, he is sent on a convict ship to Australia.

As poor Opal is forced to say goodbye to the final member of her family, she makes a promise to reunite them all one day.

Will she ever see her family again?

An Orphan's Journey

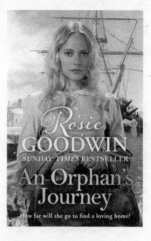

1874.

Growing up in extreme poverty in London, Pearl thinks life can get no worse. But when her parents discover there's yet another baby on the way, they have to tighten the belt even further. Pearl's mother decides to send her and her younger sister Eliza to the workhouse, where they are forced into a new life of hardship and struggle.

Pearl's hopes are raised when the workhouse offers the sisters a new life in Canada and they board an orphan ship transporting unwanted children across the seas. Pearl hopes their luck has finally changed when she and Eliza are hired by the kindly Mrs Forbes to work in her grand house together. But when Pearl meets their mistress's bullying son Monty he reveals he will stop at nothing to make her life a misery.

Will Pearl ever find the home she so craves?

A Simple Wish

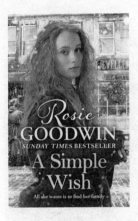

1885.

Life is hard for Ruby Carter. Working at her parents' bakery, her gentle mother protects young Ruby from her cruel father and loves her unconditionally. That is until her mother is stricken with a fatal illness and, from her deathbed, reveals that Ruby was adopted.

Overcome by grief and alone with the violent man she once called her father, Ruby has no choice but to flee. At just fifteen, homeless and alone, she is relieved when a kindly stranger named Mrs Bamber takes pity on her and welcomes poor Ruby into her home.

But soon, Ruby learns Mrs Bamber is not as generous as she first seemed – she forces Ruby into a life of crime as a jewel thief in Birmingham's jewellery quarter. With nothing to her name and nowhere to go, Ruby has no choice but to steal. But Ruby is determined that she will atone for what she's done and be reunited with her birth parents.

Ruby's only wish is to find her family.

A Daughter's Destiny

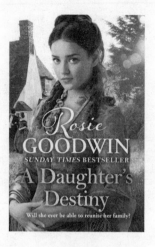

1875.

Emerald Winter has lived a privileged life with her parents and her younger sister Abigail in the stately Astley House. But all that suddenly changes when her father disappears, leaving the family in enormous debt.

They are forced to throw themselves at the mercy of Emerald's uncle who begrudgingly allows them on his farm.

Desperate to find work, Emerald must leave her family and travel to London to become the companion of a distant aunt she's never met.

Rebellious Abigail is unwilling to lower herself to menial farm chores and instead runs away, finding work as a hostess in a Soho club where she soon attracts trouble.

Will Emerald ever be able to find happiness and reunite her family again?

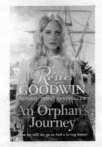
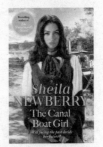